A to Z of

Foreclosures

Real Estate Worth Millions Acquired with $101

Harsimran Singh, Ph.D.

ੴ

TABLE OF CONTENTS

Dedication

I dedicate this book to my darling wife,
Dr. Satnam "Baby" K. Sabharwal.
Her Baby-like smiles and positive attitude
have been the greatest asset
to our real estate assets.
And, now you're holding this asset,
in the form of knowledge,
in your hand.

Preface

My inspiration to write this book came from seeing a real estate book I saw at the bookstore. This book claimed that individuals could make up to $60,000/year following the steps the author had provided. Having over 25 years of real estate experience, I felt that I could offer guidance that would yield much greater results. I contemplated the book's boast and remained restless until I picked up a pen and wrote the first chapter of this book.

I hope that my knowledge of real estate will help you gain a better understanding of this lucrative business. This book offers guidance that will strengthen your financial stability and allow you to spend more time with your family. I pray that every reader of this book is able to experience the joys and happiness that I've been able to achieve through gaining financial independence.

I remember my two sons Gunit and Pavit, as I brought them along to closings and meetings even when they were very young. Those little hands have become great helping hands in our successful real estate business today. Similarly, I extend to you the same knowledge and experiences that I've shared with my sons, as I would feel selfish if I confined this knowledge to only my immediate family. It is necessary for us to share our knowledge and strengths to help others.

I hope this book will allow you to recognize and take advantage of the potential for success that I've been fortunate to find in this great country.

Acknowledgements

I am always grateful to my brother, Dr. Pritipal Singh Sabharwal, who gave me the first lesson in real estate.

I am extremely thankful to Mr. Francis J. Burgweger, Jr., Attorney at Law, for his contributions in helping me write this book. Mr. Burgweger, Jr. is admitted to practice law in the State of Connecticut. It may have been extremely difficult to present this book in this form without his help. I feel fortunate to have met both Mr. And Mrs. Burgweger who dedicated their lives in offering volunteer services to so many organizations..

I am also thankful to Mr. Daniel Padernacht, Attorney at Law, who reviewed this book to its entirety. Daniel is admitted to practice law in the State of New York. He graduated from The John Marshall Law School (Chicago) and has an undergraduate degree in Economics from Fairfield University. I am extremely impressed by his knowledge and experience. His father, the late Mr. Howard Padernacht, a long time investor in real estate, did a great job training Daniel in real estate investment. Howard Padernacht took his son Daniel with him, at a young age, to closings, meetings and property inspections. He did exactly what I did by taking my sons to the closings, meetings and property inspections when they were very young.

I am grateful for Mr. Paul Elliot to have contributed the following Foreword.

Foreword

As a veteran real estate developer, landlord and broker, I must say that this book is apropos of what knowledge needs to be brought forward in this recession. Dr. Singh speaks from his vast experience in both residential and commercial real estate and brings wisdom for everybody and anybody interested in today's real estate market.

In my personal experience as a real estate investor and developer, I have seen foreclosure markets in the past, similar to the current condition of the United States real estate market. This book shows and teaches all that is needed to gain success, such as mine, in this type and other types of markets. I highly recommend this book as required reading for anybody even remotely interested in real estate foreclosures, financing, and purchasing at any level they currently find themselves.

Paul Elliott has over 30 years of real estate experience and is the President & CEO of Soundview Realty Group, with office locations in Manhattan and Medford, New York. He owns 650,000 sq. ft. of built out commercial space including office, industrial, and retail, as well as over 300 acres of development projects between New York, Vermont, and Florida. Additionally, he is the owner of a 218 unit apartment complex in Savannah, Georgia and a 140 acre golf course, including a steakhouse and clubhouse, in Wading River, New York.

PART I - INTRODUCTION TO THE FORECLOSURE PROCESS

Opportunity:

In this time of economic uncertainty, when the country is facing a credit meltdown, investors in real estate are asking themselves whether any realistic opportunities remain available to them. The answer is a resounding "Yes." Uncertainty always provides opportunity.

Urban legend tells us of an old Chinese curse: "May you live in interesting times." Of course, we all know that curses can be inverted blessings. These are interesting times, and they open doors to opportunistic investors.

Where does an opportunistic investor look to find these opening doors? Although there is any number of areas an investor could look into, acquiring properties through the foreclosure process offers multiple opportunities. Examples of investors doing just this abound.

One prime example is the opportunities presented by the collapse of the savings and loan association industry in the late 1980's. That crisis arose out of extensive speculation in real estate by savings and loan associations. In that crisis, many savings and loan associations became insolvent and were taken over by the Office of Thrift Supervision. Congress passed a law entitled the Financial Institutions Reform Recovery and Enforcement Act, commonly known as FIRREA (pronounced Fie-Ree-Ah). FIRREA created the Resolution Trust Company, commonly referred to as the RTC. Savings and loan associations had acquired many real estate assets in the course of the crisis. The RTC was charged with the task of disposing of those assets. Under then existing market conditions, investors were able to purchase properties at substantially discounted prices. A number of real estate investors made fortunes in the aftermath of the savings and loan association collapse.

1

Similar opportunities exist in the economic conditions arising out of the recession of 2008. However, the traditional methods of investing in real estate through foreclosure may not apply in this new era. The customary practice of foreclosure investing was to acquire a home from an economically distressed homeowner, finance the purchase through customary lending sources, rehabilitate the home as needed and sell it to a new purchaser. Because of the economic pressures on homeowners, investors could acquire properties at discounts to their values. Rising home prices assured returns on investments. Some fortunate investors could flip a house without even putting any money down. Now, with home prices falling, in some cases by as much as forty to fifty percent from their highs of just a year or two ago, quick sales are difficult, credit is tight and investors have to take risk into account. This does not mean that foreclosure investing is no longer viable. It means that investors need to broaden their horizons and make informed decisions. This book will help investors achieve both of these objectives. To make informed decisions, an investor needs to understand how the foreclosure process works. Therefore, we begin with an introduction to basic foreclosure.

CHAPTER I-1 BASICS

A. A Brief History of Real Property Secured Lending; Mortgages and Foreclosures

Foreclosures arise out of the real property secured lending process. In this process, a lender (a person or entity with money) loans money to a borrower (a person or entity that wants to use the money for a specified period of time) that owns real property. The borrower promises to repay the loan, usually with interest, within a certain period of time. The borrower may make other promises, such as agreeing to pay taxes on the real property. The borrower agrees that if he fails to repay the loan or fails to perform any other promise he has made, the lender can take the real property and either sell it or keep it, depending on local law. This scenario developed in medieval England and traveled to the United States along with the English colonists who settled in America.

To fully understand the foreclosure process, it is helpful to have an understanding of the process's history and underpinnings. The foreclosure process in effect in the United States derived from English common law. The English legal system was comprised of different courts. For our purposes, we will discuss the court of law and the court of equity.

Under the English common law, a borrower would give his lender a deed to the borrower's land to secure the debt. In these transactions, the borrower was referred to as the "mortgagor," the lender was referred to as the "mortgagee," and the deed was the "mortgage." For the sake of clarity, we will continue to refer to the parties as the borrower and the lender. This deed appeared to give the lender absolute title to the land, and the English courts of law treated the lender as the owner, even to the extent of allowing the lender to take possession of the land and evict the borrower before any default occurred (unless the parties had agreed otherwise). The borrower was absolutely obligated to pay the debt on the date agreed upon. If the borrower made timely payment, the deed to the lender was supposed to become void, and title to the land would revert to the borrower. Title did not change automatically; the lender had to issue a deed back to the borrower. However, if the borrower was even one day late in making payment, the lender retained title to the land, and the borrower lost his title to the land. These strict rules had the potential for unfair results, and as you might expect, unfair cases arose. The English law courts were not sympathetic, so aggrieved parties turned to the English courts of equity.

The courts of equity determined that a defaulting borrower continued to have rights in the land which was referred to as an equity. By paying his debt, the borrower could "redeem" his equity, so this was referred to as the "equity of redemption." In the example of the borrower who was late making one payment, and the lender taking the land, the English equity courts permitted the borrower to redeem his land by paying the debt. However, it was unfair to the lender to give the borrower an unlimited amount of time to redeem the land. To deal with this, the courts allowed the lender to cut off the rights of redemption. This act of cutting off the redemption rights was referred to as "foreclosing." The lender had to commence an action in the

3

equity courts to accomplish the foreclosure. The lender could also cut off the right of redemption by purchasing the right from the borrower. Conversely, the borrower could sell or give the equity of redemption to a purchaser or other person.

These ancient concepts have influenced the modern day foreclosure process which we will now examine in some detail.

B.   Definition of Real Property – a.k.a. Real Estate

The term foreclosure as used in this book always involves real property, or real estate. What is real property? Real property is: (1) land; (2) the things that are constructed on land – referred to as "improvements," such as buildings, roadways, bridges, tunnels, telephone poles, wells and towers; (3) things that were moveable at one time but are now attached to and have become an integral part of improvements – referred to as "fixtures," such as chandeliers and other light fixtures, furnaces, heating and air conditioning ducts, fences, septic tanks, elevators and garage doors; (4) minerals while they remain in the ground, such as gravel, oil or iron ore; and (5) trees and plants while affixed to the land. As used in this book, the terms "real property" and "real estate" are used interchangeably.

The ownership interests in cooperative apartments are represented by proprietary leases and shares of stock in the cooperative that owns the building. Although the shares of stock are technically personal property, we will consider them to be a part of the realty for the purposes of this book.

An investor needs to know the meaning of the term "real property" so that when he is negotiating the purchase of a property, he has an understanding of exactly what is included (or not included) in the transaction. For example, if an investor contracts with a homeowner to purchase a furnished house, and the investor intends to include the furniture in the deal, then the investor must be sure to list the furniture as a part of the contract. Otherwise, the seller will have the right to remove the furniture. Similarly, if the homeowner contracts to sell a house but carves out the fixtures, when the investor enters the house

4

after the closing, the investor may find that the chandeliers have been removed - legally.

Real property also includes the interests that a person can have in the real property. Ownership interests can vary. The most complete ownership interest is called "fee simple absolute," which is frequently referred to as "fee simple." This means that any and all ownership rights and interests in or associated with the real property are owned by the owner. There are lesser ownership interests. An owner may have an estate for years, which means that the rights of ownership will terminate after a pre-determined period of time. An owner may have a fee simple title subject to a condition. The owner will have absolute ownership until a specified event occurs, at which point ownership will go to another person or entity. The transfer can be automatic or it can require that the new owner take some action. An automatic transfer is called a "fee simple determinable", and a transfer that is triggered by some act of another person is called a "fee simple subject to a condition subsequent." If an investor is acquiring property through a foreclosure and finds that the title is something less than fee simple, there could be a limitation on the investor's rights. Once raised, the issue will need to be resolved.

Interests in real property extend beyond ownership. The most common interest other than ownership is a leasehold interest. In a lease, the real property is owned by the landlord and leased to the tenant. A lease gives the tenant the exclusive right to occupy the real property for a specified term. Normally, occupancy is not completely exclusive because knowledgeable landlords reserve the right to enter the leased premises in order to inspect, perform maintenance and to take other appropriate actions. Typically, the tenant pays rent to the landlord for the right to occupy the premises. Additionally, the landlord and tenant will agree to perform certain promises, which vary depending on the kind of property and the type of lease. For example, in a typical office building, a tenant occupies only part of the property and does not have access to the utility areas or the building's exterior. In these cases, the landlord agrees to maintain the building. Also, the taxes on the building are not assessed upon individual tenants but are levied against the entire building. Therefore, the landlord pays the taxes, and any recover is included in the rent. In the case of a big box retailer, the tenant occupies and has access to the entire building. Such a tenant might agree to perform the maintenance in exchange for a reduction in the rent. Some single-tenant buildings are leased pursuant to what are called "triple net leases." In these leases, the tenant pays taxes, insurance and repair and maintenance.

An investor who is prepared to expand his horizons beyond homes can find opportunities in the market for rental properties. Of necessity, the investor needs an understanding of leasing issues. These will be addressed in another chapter.

C.   Structure of a Typical Deal

As noted above, foreclosures arise out of real estate secured transactions. The typical transaction is a loan from a lender to a borrower secured by the borrower's real property through a mortgage or deed of trust.

The first essential element is the loan (although technically, a mortgage can be given to secure the performance of a non-monetary promise). The loan can be a purchase money loan made to finance the purchase of a home or other real property. It can be a home equity loan given to a homeowner whose home's value exceeds the amount of debt secured by the home. It can be a business loan made to finance the purchase of restaurant equipment or drill presses or tool and die machinery. It can be a loan given for virtually any purpose.

The parties to a real estate secured transaction will normally be the lender and the borrower. There are many different types of lenders. First, there are the banks. Banks are institutions that, among other things, take deposits and use the deposits to make loans. Banks are subject to governmental regulation. National banks are regulated by the Federal Government, and state banks are regulated by state officials. Certain banks have access to the Federal Reserve System where they can borrow money on an overnight basis. Deposits are insured by the Federal Deposit Insurance Corporation.

Second, there are the savings and loans associations, credit unions and mortgage companies. Savings and loans associations take deposits and make mortgage loans to finance various aspects of home ownership, such as construction, purchase, refinance and repair. Credit unions are financial institutions owned cooperatively by their members that take deposits from the members and make mortgage loans to their members. Credit unions can be chartered by the Federal Government or a state government. Deposits in federal and state credit unions are insured by the Federal Government's National Credit Union Share Insurance Fund.

Third, there are investment banks. During previous real estate collapses, investment banks were sources of funds for investors acquiring properties from the Resolution Trust Company and other sellers. With the current credit crunch, a number of investment banks have either disappeared or been acquired by commercial banks. However, if an investor is a client of an investment bank or stock brokerage firm with a substantial account, that investment bank or firm may be in a position to make mortgage loans.

There are also federal programs that affect and can facilitate mortgage loans. These will be discussed in greater detail below.

As varied as the types of lenders may be, they do not compare in variety to the kinds of borrowers an investor may encounter in the foreclosure process. One unfortunate aspect of any economic crisis is the severe impact on homeowners. Many of the borrowers caught up in foreclosure are homeowners. Closely related to homeowners are homebuilders and developers. These are the borrowers who have either (i)completed the construction of a home or other building and now cannot sell it or find tenants to occupy it or (ii)have exhausted their funds in the course of construction and cannot complete the home or other building. Others affected by a widespread recession include real estate investors who may have overextended themselves or retailers and other merchants whose customers have lost the incentive to patronize their businesses. Additionally, manufacturers whose sales have plummeted may be unable to make the payments coming due on the mortgages on their factories. These are just a sample of the types of borrowers an investor might encounter while pursuing opportunities in foreclosures.

7

Naturally, in any real property secured loan, there will be real property. In many recessions, the largest number of properties foreclosed upon is residential. Residential properties can encompass single family homes, duplexes, multi-unit apartment buildings, condominiums, cooperatives and mobile homes. However, in a severe economic squeeze, commercial properties are also likely to be impacted. Commercial properties range from a stand-alone hot dog stand to a store on Main Street to a restaurant in midtown Manhattan; they include a neighborhood shopping center or a regional shopping center or an office building or a department store or a movie theater. The types of commercial properties are limited only by the region's economy. The same can be said of industrial properties that may be securing a mortgage loan.

D.   More Detailed Description of Documentation

The documentation of a mortgage loan can be important to an investor. If the investor finds a deal where it makes sense to take over the loan in some way, the investor needs to know and understand what the documents provide and how they will affect the transaction. Mortgage loan documentation will always include a promissory note and a mortgage or deed of trust, and a commercial or industrial loan will also feature a loan agreement, an assignment of rents and leases and a personal property security agreement.

A loan agreement entered into between the borrower and the lender will contain the borrower's promises to repay the loan and other relevant covenants, such as promises to keep the building in good repair and to keep property taxes current and to pay all insurance premiums in a timely manner. The loan agreement may contain monetary agreements by the borrower, such as a promise to maintain certain debt to equity ratios. The loan agreement may also contain representations and warranties made by the borrower. The covenants, representations and warranties in the loan agreement will be secured by the mortgage or deed of trust. Accordingly, it is incumbent on the investor who acquires real property subject to a mortgage securing a loan agreement to be sure the investor will be able to perform the covenants and maintain the representations and warranties contained in the loan agreement.

All mortgages that securitize a loan will be coupled with a promissory note. The promissory note represents the borrower's debt obligation. If the debt is discharged, the mortgage is of no further force even if it remains of record on the borrower's title. A mortgage cannot stand alone; it must have an obligation that it secures. Banks and other lenders sell their loans to generate funds to make more loans. This is described in more detail in the section on securitization below. However, in the purchase of a loan, the buyer must verify that the seller of the loan transfers the promissory note to the purchaser; it is the note that represents the loan obligation.

The promissory note contains the borrower's promise to pay the debt and interest on the debt. Other promises and provisions likely to be found in the promissory note include the due date for payment, the place where payment is to be made, a grace period for payment, a provision for late charges, a description of the mortgage or deed of trust securing the promissory note, and a provision regarding the borrower's right to prepay the note or restrictions on the borrower's right to prepay the note. Borrowers have no absolute right to prepay a promissory note. That right must be negotiated. Hence, some notes have a provision for a prepayment penalty. That is, if the borrower pays the loan off prior to its maturity date, the lender can charge a penalty to the borrower. Additionally, one of the most important provisions in the note is the acceleration clause. Invariably, the promissory note will contain an acceleration clause. This provision allows the lender to declare the entire amount of the loan due and payable in the event of a default, including the borrower's insolvency or bankruptcy.

The reason for an acceleration clause is that each installment of a mortgage loan is only a small amount of the principal plus interest. If a borrower defaults in making one or two payments and there is no acceleration clause, the lender can collect only the small amount in default upon foreclosure. Any other proceeds from the sale at foreclosure would go to the holders of any junior liens and then to the borrower. The large balance of the loan would remain unpaid and the real property collateral would have been sold so there is no longer any security for the balance of the loan. By declaring the entire balance

9

due and payable, the lender can collect the entire unpaid balance from the proceeds of the foreclosure sale.

In order to secure the debt evidenced by the promissory note, there must be a mortgage or a deed of trust. First, we will describe the mortgage.

The mortgage is an instrument given by the borrower to the lender to secure the borrower's obligations to the lender. Originally, the mortgage took the form of a conveyance of title to the mortgaged property. Today, there are a number of states that still recognize this form; they are called title theory states. In a title theory state, the borrower receives equitable title to the real property but the actual title is placed in the name of the lender. When the loan is paid in full, the title is deeded back to the borrower. The borrower's equitable title ensures the borrower's rights of ownership and use of the property.

In most states, however, the mortgage transformed into an instrument that created a lien on the real property. These states are called lien theory states. In a lien theory state, the borrower has actual and equitable title to the real property.

Some states are hybrid or intermediate theory states. These states blend qualities of title theory and lien theory states.

The mortgage is recorded in the land records of the county (or in some states, the city or town) where the real property is located. Recording is intended to give notice of the existence of the mortgage to anyone interested in the property. Foreclosure investors need to be familiar with the recording system.

The recording system takes advantage of the fact that real property is immobile. Real property is sometimes referred to as a bundle of rights. Many different parties can have different rights in the same parcel of land. For example, assume Party A owns a plot of land improved by a building. Party A leases this land to Party B; this gives Party B a possessory right or leasehold interest in the land.. Party B may or may not record a notice or short form of the lease in the local land records. Party B subsequently subleases space in the building to

10

Party C. Party A also granted his neighbor, Party D, an easement to run a driveway over the land, creating a non-possessory right of way over the land. Party D recorded the easement in the local land records. In addition, Party A financed the development of the land by granting a mortgage or deed of trust on the land and building to Party E, creating a security interest in the realty. Party E recorded the mortgage or deed of trust. Assume now that Party F desires to purchase the land, demolish the building and construct a new building covering the entire property. If Party F simply buys the land and building without doing anything more, Party F cannot carry out his plan to demolish the building because (1) Party B has a leasehold estate which gives Party B a right to exclusive possession of the land and building for the term of the lease; (2) Party C has a sublease for similar rights in a part of the building; and (3) the new building will interfere with Party D's easement, also allowing Party D to prevent the construction. In addition, the real property is subject to the mortgage, and Party F will need to make payments on the debt to prevent a foreclosure. Party F will be charged with notice of all of these interests, and Party F's title will be subject to all of these matters.

Why will Party F's interest be subject to these matters? Because land is physical and immovable, a plot of land can always be located and inspected. A foreclosure investor who acquires an interest in land and improvements will take subject to everything of which the investor had actual notice and everything of which the investor had constructive notice. Actual notice is anything that the foreclosure investor actually knew about. Constructive notice is (1) anything that an inspection of the property and inquiry regarding the things found would have revealed, such as the presence of tenants or the existence of oil wells on the land or roads running across the land, and (2) anything that has been recorded in the appropriate land records.

How does a foreclosure investor protect himself or herself against these problems? The answer is by an inspection of the real property and a review of the public land records.

In the hypothetical example, an inspection of the property would reveal the presence of Party C in the building, and an inquiry of Party C would have revealed the leasehold interest of Party B. An

11

inspection would also reveal Party D's driveway through evidence of its construction or by tire tracks running across the land. The inspection would give the foreclosure investor actual notice of the interests of Parties B, C and D (assuming there were physical signs of the driveway right-of-way). The foreclosure investor cannot refuse to inspect the real property and then claim lack of notice because the law deems the foreclosure investor to have constructive notice of everything that an inspection and inquiry would have revealed.

The mortgage or deed of trust could not have been found by a physical inspection. However, the foreclosure investor is charged with constructive notice of everything that could have been discovered by a search of the appropriate land records.

A search of the land records would reveal the existence of Party D's easement and Party E's mortgage or deed of trust. The foreclosure investor would also learn about the existence of the lease to Party B if it was recorded. The lease itself would not necessarily be recorded but a short form stating its existence would be found in the records. For these reasons, foreclosure investors must both inspect the real property, making an inquiry of anything found during the inspection, and they must search the land records before making any final decisions to take action regarding the real property.

The mortgage contains a description of the land and its improvements and any other collateral that has been mortgaged to secure the debt. The mortgage also contains promises by the borrower to perform its obligations under the promissory note and the loan agreement (if any) as well as the mortgage itself. Obligations under the mortgage can include promises to pay taxes and insurance, to maintain the property in good condition and repair, to pay any prior mortgages, to keep the real property free and clear of any liens and to pay the lender's attorney fees. The mortgage describes how to handle the proceeds in the event of condemnation of the real property. The mortgage also contains an acceleration clause effective upon a default, including the borrower's insolvency or bankruptcy. The mortgage, or a separate agreement, describes the borrower's obligations in the event of an environmental issue, such as a leaking underground storage tank. Many mortgages contain a due on sale clause that permits the lender to declare a default and accelerate the loan in the event the borrower sells the real property or otherwise transfers it. A transfer could include a transfer of the ownership interest in the owner, such as a transfer of all of the stock of a corporate borrower.

The mortgage contains a description of the steps that the lender must go through in order to foreclose the mortgage. In lien theory states, this typically involves the commencement of a law suit to foreclose the mortgage.

Deeds of trust are typically used in title theory states. In those states, the borrower executes and records a deed of trust to secure the promissory note. The borrower is the grantor and he conveys the property to a trustee who holds title to the property for the benefit of the lender which is referred to as the beneficiary. Although the deed of trust takes the form of a transfer of title, the borrower continues to own the real property. The trustee becomes involved only if there is a default. Following a default, the lender records a notice of default and instructs the trustee to sell the property to satisfy the debt. The trustee gives a notice of sale, and the property is sold at a public auction. The courts are not involved, so the process is referred to as a non-judicial foreclosure. The trustee is typically a title insurance company or an attorney.

In states that utilize a deed of trust, the borrower deeds the property to a third party, or trustee, naming the lender as the beneficiary if the borrower defaults. Conversely, when the borrower pays the entire amount of the loan, the trustee deeds the property back to the borrower

The terms of a deed to trust are similar to those of a mortgage except as to the nature of remedies and the exercise of those remedies.

E.   Default by Borrower & Foreclosure by Lender

If the borrower defaults, the lender has the right to declare a default, accelerate the loan and foreclose the mortgage or deed of trust. In lien theory states, the foreclosure process includes the commencement of a judicial proceeding in the appropriate court. When a lender files a lawsuit, the borrower has the right to file an answer with the court. The answer can admit or deny the lender's allegations, raise defenses to the lender's claims or make claims against the lender. Some borrowers who are clearly in default do not even answer the lawsuit. In those cases, the court enters a default judgment against the borrower. After the borrower files his answer, the borrower has a certain amount of time, prescribed by state law, in which to cure the default and bring the loan current. If the borrower fails to cure the loan and has not raised any defenses to the lenders' claims, the court conducts a hearing to confirm the existence of a loan default. However, in some cases, the failures of mortgage servicers to do a thorough job of administering loans have given borrowers defenses against foreclosure actions. For example, in some publicized cases, the borrower claimed to have made payments that the lender did not record in its statements. In other cases, the borrower claimed that the loan servicer had miscalculated late charges and interest and that the demand was incorrect. These issues are addressed in the foreclosure law suit. In most states, if the court finds in favor of the lender, the court orders that the property be sold at a public auction.

In title theory states, the trustee records a notice of default. If the borrower has a defense against the claim of default, the borrower must go to court to stop the sale. The borrower will have a certain amount of time, prescribed by state law, in which to cure the default and bring the loan current. If the borrower fails to cure the loan, the trustee records and publishes a notice of sale and then proceeds to sell the property at public auction.

At the public auction, the lender has the right to bid. Prior to the auction, the lender usually calculates the amount that it intends to bid at the auction. The lender, assuming it has accelerated its loan, could bid the amount of the debt, the accrued interest, all late fees and charges, attorney fees and any other costs that the mortgage authorizes the lender to incur. If the value of the property is considerably less than the amount of the debt, the lender is likely to be the only bidder. However, if there is equity in the property, holders of junior liens and foreclosure investors are likely to participate in the bidding. The highest bidder will become the owner of the property. Sale proceeds go first to the lender until he is paid in full. Any remaining proceeds go to the holders of junior liens and then to the borrower.

CHAPTER I-2 THE MORTGAGE MELTDOWN
OF 2008 AND FOLLOWING

Near the end of 2008, the National Bureau of Economic Research announced that the economy had been in recession since the beginning of the year. Experts and talking heads have identified several causes for the recession. Some of the causes of the recession have limited the strategies that foreclosure investors were able to use in more prosperous times, and therefore these causes are relevant to foreclosure investors. If an investor elects to participate in the foreclosure process, it is important to understand what these causes are and how they could affect the investor.

A.   Subprime Mortgages

One cause of particular relevance is the effect of the subprime mortgage collapse. What is a subprime mortgage loan?

A subprime mortgage is a mortgage loan given to a subprime borrower.   A subprime borrower was defined by an Expanded Guidance for Subprime Lending Programs, issued by the Office of the Comptroller of the Currency, the Federal Reserve Board, the Federal Deposit Insurance Corporation and the Office of Thrift Supervision in 2001. Under this document, a subprime borrower is a borrower with a troubled credit history. Such a borrower may have gone through a bankruptcy, or had judgments lodged against him, or may have been delinquent in paying his debts, or may have a low credit score. The Guidance cautioned lenders that loans to subprime borrowers carried a higher risk of default. Notwithstanding this caution, many lenders made loans to subprime borrowers.

In addition to subprime borrowers, some lenders gave loans to borrowers with a diminished ability to repay the loan. It has been reported that loans were made to borrowers whose income was far below the amount required to repay the loan. It has also been reported that adjustable rate mortgage loans (ARMs) were made to people who could pay the initial interest rate but could not afford subsequent adjustments in the rate. These loans were used to purchase homes.

Loans made to people who could not afford to repay them eventually went into default and foreclosure. Loans made to subprime borrowers did not immediately go into default, but as the economy entered a recessionary stage, economic pressures became too great for many subprime borrowers and they too defaulted on their mortgages.

As these properties went to foreclosure, the economy began to contract. Home prices began to decline. In addition to the decline in home values, some mortgage loans had been made on the assumption that prices would continue to increase. In these cases, the debt to value ratio would not have supported the loan had the property been correctly valued. As a consequence, the amount of the mortgage debt exceeded the value of these properties. Some homeowners did not see any reason to continue to pay a price for their homes that was significantly greater than the home's value, and they walked away from the property.

The contraction of the economy, combined with a growing number of foreclosures, accelerated the decline in home values. In some parts of the country, property values declined forty to fifty percent. As prices declined, potential buyers were reluctant to purchase homes because they did not know how low prices would drop, and they did not want to overpay for their homes. Accordingly, foreclosure investors who bought at auction with the intent of flipping the property ran the risk that there would not be a market for the property.

Declining home values would not necessarily impact foreclosure investors if they accurately calculated the value of the property they were considering. However, the subprime crisis combined with the securitization debacle acted to confound the real estate market.

B.   Effects of Securitization on Lending

Mortgage lenders use money to make mortgage loans. That money is repaid in installments, typically over thirty years. In order to obtain more funds to make more mortgage loans, lenders sell their mortgage loans. One manner of selling loans is securitization.

Securitization is the process of gathering mortgage loans together into a pool and selling investment instruments such as bonds to investors. The interest and principal on the investment instrument are paid by the income from the underlying mortgages. Although we are describing the securitization of mortgage loans, various other types of loans, such as car loans, can also be securitized. Many pools contained various types of mortgages, some prime, some subprime. The concept was that even if a few mortgages went into default, there would be an income stream from the other mortgages. These investment instruments were rated by rating agencies. Some were rated AAA.

Once foreclosures began occurring in major parts of the country, defaults began occurring under the investment instruments. Many banks had invested in these instruments, and the value of the instruments either evaporated or became questionable. This impacted many banks' capital, resulting in a credit crunch and making it more difficult to procure financing. For example, it has been reported that homebuilders, who were not in default under their loans, had their loans called by their banks resulting in default and abandoned subdivision developments.

CHAPTER I-3   DEFAULTS BY BORROWERS

The recession has impacted a large number of borrowers. In evaluating a foreclosure prospect, it would be helpful to understand the different reasons why a default may occur.

A.   Typical Reasons for Default

Even without a recession, there are a variety of reasons why a borrower may be in default under a mortgage loan. The manner in which a foreclosure investor approaches a borrower can vary depending on the reason(s) for the default.

One common reason for default is the borrower's loss of a job. Many articles have been written about the tendency of Americans to live beyond their means, affecting the amount of one's savings. When a job is lost, there may not be savings available to help sustain the borrower. There are many causes for job loss. In a recession, many employers cut back on their work forces to preserve cash flow. The job loss is aggravated in a recession because the borrower may not be able to find another job. Unemployment benefits may not be sufficient to make the mortgage payments. In this case, the borrower does not seem to have many options and may be willing to negotiate a deal in order to preserve his or her credit rating. Such a borrower can be a prospect for negotiation before a default occurs. However, identifying these individuals can be difficult, and contacting them would be a very delicate matter.

Overextension of credit is another reason for default. In recent years, thanks to relaxed mortgage underwriting standards, banks allowed borrowers to overextend themselves in the real estate market. Some investors acquired houses at the height of the market with the expectation that they could quickly flip them at a profit. When values began to fall, the profit disappeared. If the investor paid more for the house than he could afford, the investor's overextension is likely to lead to foreclosure or bankruptcy.

Another common reason for default is the death of the bread winner. Income may stop or be seriously interrupted, especially if the deceased did not carry life insurance. This can be a particularly trying time for the survivor who must deal with the loss of a loved one and the family's source of income. Persons in such a situation may be gratified to receive an offer that will alleviate, if not solve, their financial problems.

Divorce is a reason for default. A divorce can disrupt a family's mortgage payments. In many homes today, a second income is required to make the mortgage payments. A divorce deprives each spouse of the other's assistance, leading to the potential for default. Another situation is in a hostile divorce where one or both spouses try to inflict damage and pain on the other. In cases like this, the couple may be focused more on their disputes than on their credit standing. One or both may be willing to allow the mortgage to go into default.

Illness or disability can be as devastating as the loss of a job. Indeed, in the case of a job loss, there is always the possibility that the individual will find another job. Disability could be permanent, and illness can be quite debilitating. Additionally, illness or disability affects the ability of other family members to work, or seek employment, if they must care for the person suffering from the illness or disability. Moreover, the cost of medical treatment of the illness or disability can impinge on a family's ability to make mortgage payments to the point where a default arises. This may be a situation where the homeowners would welcome a proposal that relieves them of their mortgage obligations.

Bankruptcy of the wage earner can arise in a healthy economy as easily as in a recession, but the existence of a recession increases the likelihood of bankruptcy. Bankruptcy can arise for any of the reasons given for default, such as loss of a job, illness or disability. However, in a recessionary environment, other reasons can apply, such as failure of the family business due to economic conditions. Investors in real property face these consequences when properties cannot be sold at a price at least equal to debt. Bankruptcy is a common event of default under a mortgage. Even if the borrower has kept the loan current, if a petition in bankruptcy is filed by or against the borrower, the lender can declare a default. Although the Federal Bankruptcy Code prohibits the enforcement in bankruptcy of clauses that terminate a contract solely upon the commencement of a bankruptcy proceeding (such clauses are called "ipso facto" clauses), the prohibition applies only to contracts in which the parties still have obligations to perform, such as a lease (such contracts are called "executory contracts"). Courts have held that the prohibition does not apply to a mortgage.

The condition of the economy can impact a property owner's ability to keep its mortgage payments current. For instance, the bankruptcy and collapse of a major company may result in defaults under that company's leases, leaving landlords with empty premises. The loss of a major tenant can lead to a default if the space cannot be re-let or must be re-let at a lower amount. The subject of depressed rents is discussed in more detail below. However, the loss of a major tenant and the concomitant loss of rental income may lead to a default.

Depressed rents are another aspect of a contracting economy that can lead to a borrower's default. A number of tenant-occupied buildings that were purchased in the years preceding the 2008 recession were acquired under the assumption that rents would continue at the current level or would increase. As major tenants fail and go into bankruptcy, more and more space becomes available on the market. Even if the landlord needs to keep its rents high to support his mortgage payments, he cannot do so because the market rental values have fallen. Further, they are competing with other landlords that will make their space available at reduced rents in order to fill their space to generate an income stream. This is particularly true for those landlords who acquired their buildings at the lower end of the market and do not have as much difficulty making mortgage payments in a depressed economy.

A property going underwater is another reason for default. "Underwater" means that the amount of debt on the property exceeds the property's value. This can be the result of a contracting economy. Sometimes a property that is underwater is described as being upside down. A property can be slightly underwater, in which case the owner may continue to make mortgage payments on the assumption that the economy will improve. However, a property severely underwater may prove too daunting for the borrower. The borrower can view his mortgage payments as pouring good money down a sink hole, never to be recovered. When a borrower reaches that conclusion, it is more likely than not that the borrower will abandon the property. The difficulty that this kind of situation poses for the foreclosure investor is that the investor cannot come in and take over the loan payments. The investor would be pouring its money down the same sink hole. These kinds of situations require creative thinking on the foreclosure investor's part.

B.   Owner's Delinquency

In addition to the array of reasons why a borrower might default on a mortgage loan, there are various types of defaults. A foreclosure investor needs to understand each kind of default before committing to the property or offering to address the default.

Certainly the most common default is a monetary default. This kind of default can include a failure to pay principal or interest on the loan or failure to pay a late charge or fee. Upon the occurrence of a monetary default, the lender has the right to declare a default. Following the declaration of default, the borrower has a period of time within which to cure the default. For properties that are not underwater, this can be a good time for the foreclosure investor to intervene. The cost of cure is less than other situations and the property is likely to be in good condition because the default is recent and there has not been a lengthy period of time in which the property could deteriorate.

The other kind of default – a non-monetary default – arises when the borrower fails to perform a covenant in the mortgage or other loan documents. This kind of default is less common than a monetary default for a number of reasons. First, if the default is the failure to pay taxes or insurance premiums, it is likely that the borrower would be unable to pay the debt service on the loan, so there would probably also be a monetary default. Second, a non-monetary default could be difficult to prove because failure of performance can be a subjective matter. For example, if the borrower has agreed to maintain the property in good condition, and the lender believes that the property has not been well maintained, the lender can find himself in an argument with the borrower as to whether or not the maintenance has been satisfactory. This dispute is subjective by its very nature and may be difficult to prove. The lender would need to produce experts who could testify as to the quality of the maintenance and the borrower would respond in the same way, resulting in a battle of experts. Such battles can be costly, time consuming and have no assurance of success. Third, if the debt service is being paid and the value of the property continues to exceed the amount of the debt, the lender does not have a strong incentive to declare a default. On the other hand, if the collateral value has declined significantly, banks have reportedly accelerated the debt and foreclosed even if the debt service has been paid.

In any case, if the default is a non-monetary default, the foreclosure investor must investigate whether the investor has the capability of curing the default. Some covenants are unique to the borrower, and an intervening third party may not be able to perform the covenant. One example of this situation is a set of financial covenants. In some cases, these types of covenants are crafted to reflect the borrower and its business and would not apply to a foreclosure investor in a different line of business. If the default cannot be cured by the foreclosure investor, then there is little reason to attempt to negotiate a purchase prior to the auction sale.

A very important covenant that foreclosure investors need to look for and deal with is the "due-on-sale" clause. This clause applies to investors in at least two ways. The first way arises if the borrower sells the real property to the investor. That sale would trigger the clause and give the lender the right to exercise its rights under the clause. The second way is if the borrower through his own actions, has triggered the clause and the lender has declared a default. In either case, the lender's exercise of the clause can disrupt a foreclosure investor's plans, so it pays to understand the clause.

The typical due-on-sale clause gives the lender the right to declare a default and accelerate the debt upon the happening of any of these events without the lender's prior written consent: a transfer of title by the borrower to all or part of the real property collateral; a transfer of any interest in the real property; or a transfer of any interest in the borrower. For example, if the borrower is a partnership comprised of two partners, and one partner sells his partnership interest, that sale would be a transfer of an interest in the borrower and would trigger the due-on-sale clause. Carefully drafted due-on-sale clauses are triggered if one of the partners is a corporation and a shareholder of the corporation sold his shares. This would be an indirect transfer of an interest in the borrower. Another example could be the creation of a long term lease with an option to purchase. A lease is an interest in the real property, and the creation of the lease would be the transfer of an interest in the real property. Such leases can be structured to be the economic equivalent of a purchase and sale and could trigger the due-on-sale clause.

Due-on-sale clauses came into prominence during the period of sky high inflation in the late 1970's. Prior to that period, interest rates and inflation did not diverge dramatically. However, in the late 1970's, interest rates reached the mid-teens or higher. Lenders who were borrowing money to finance their lending activities were being charged high interest rates. These lenders expected to charge their borrowers correspondingly high interest rates. However, the debts secured by many mortgages bore interest at considerably lower rates. Consequently, purchasers of real property would negotiate to acquire the property by either assuming the mortgage or by taking title subject to the existing mortgage or deed of trust. This enabled the purchaser to finance the purchase at interest rates that were well below the market rates. In order to stop this practice, lenders enforced their due-on-sale clauses. There was considerable controversy as states reacted differently to the lenders' practices. Eventually, the Federal Government enacted legislation called the Federal Depository Regulations Institutions Act of 1982, commonly known as the Garn-St. Germain Act. Pursuant to this legislation, real property lenders were authorized to utilize and enforce due-on-sale clauses notwithstanding any state laws to the contrary. Although the underlying legislation has been subsequently amended, the authorization of due-on-sale clauses continues in effect. There are certain exceptions to enforcement. These exceptions include transfers due to the death of the owner, a transfer to the borrower's spouse or children, a transfer in connection with a divorce or separation and a transfer into a trust in which the borrower is a beneficiary that does not transfer rights of occupancy in the property. Additionally, the due-on-sale clause is not triggered by the creation of a lease for three years or less without an option to purchase. A foreclosure investor interested in acquiring a property either needs to assure that the investor's proposed transaction falls within the exceptions or he must obtain the lender's consent.

Whether a lender will enforce its due-on-sale clause depends on the circumstances. During a recession, the Federal Reserve may set the federal discount rate low to stimulate a recovery. This often results in lower interest rates for borrowers. A foreclosure investor who is willing to acquire a property subject to a mortgage with an interest rate at or above current rates may be able to convince the lender to consent to the transfer. Similarly, a lender may be willing to consent to a transfer to a solvent purchaser rather than incur the costs of foreclosure and of having a non-performing asset on its books. It has also been reported that some lenders simply ignore transfers. If a lender becomes aware of a transfer and takes no action, a foreclosure investor can argue that by its inaction, the lender has waived its rights to trigger the due-on-sale clause. However, if the lender is not aware of the transfer, that argument is not available and the investor remains at risk of the lender declaring a default. This risk could impact the foreclosure investor's willingness to invest funds in the rehabilitation of the property.

CHAPTER I-4   FORECLOSURE PROCEEDINGS

A.   Two Foreclosure Regimes

There are two different foreclosure regimes in effect in the United States, and the one in effect in a given state depends on that state's laws. The two regimes are judicial foreclosure and non-judicial foreclosure. Judicial foreclosure involves the local court having jurisdiction over the real property. There are two types of judicial foreclosure. One requires the court to conduct a foreclosure sale to satisfy the secured debt, and the other, called "strict foreclosure," requires the court to deed the property directly to the lender without a sale. Non-judicial foreclosure is commenced privately without involving the court system.

Some states recognize only mortgages and require lenders to foreclose under a judicial proceeding. Other states recognize only deeds of trust and require lenders to foreclose by non-judicial power of sale. Still other states recognize both mortgages and deeds of trust and allow a lender to elect to proceed under either a judicial proceeding or a non-judicial private foreclosure, depending on the type of property involved and the kind of instrument securing the loan.

For example, California permits lenders to use mortgages without power of sale, mortgages with power of sale and deeds of trust with power of sale. Mortgages without power of sale are foreclosed judicially, mortgages with power of sale can be foreclosed non-judicially and deeds of trust are foreclosed non-judicially. However, in California, mortgages are rarely used. In Vermont, lenders use mortgages, but a mortgage can be foreclosed judicially using strict foreclosure (if the court finds the borrower in default under the loan, the lender is allowed to take possession of the property), or judicially by a foreclosure sale. or non-judicially by private sale, depending on the type of property being foreclosed.

Investors that wish to learn which procedure their states utilize can find this information on the Internet. Tables describing the procedures used in different states can be found on various web sites on the Internet. For example, the RealtyTrac.com site displays a table that will show the foreclosure investor information on these topics: the state, whether the procedure is judicial or non-judicial, the process period, the number of days in the sale publication period, the number of days in the redemption period and the official who conducts the foreclosure sale. American Foreclosure Specialists' website gives a brief overview of each state's foreclosure proceedings. Other sites can be found using your web browser.

B.   Judicial Foreclosure – Court Proceedings

In a judicial proceeding, after issuing the notice of default and following the expiration of the reinstatement period, the lender under a mortgage can commence foreclosure proceedings. After the expiration of such period of time as required as may be required by state law, the lender in a lien theory state will contact its attorneys and instruct them to commence a foreclosure action. This involves filing a lawsuit in the appropriate court. Typically, the appropriate court will be a trial court located in the same county as the real property. The law suit will name the borrower as a defendant. It will also name any other person or entity that has an interest in the real property such as junior lienors or ground lessees. The purpose is to dispose of all interests in the real property that are subordinate to the mortgage and interest of the lender. That way, the lender can take clear title to the real property. If the law suit fails to name someone with an interest in the real property, then the lender's title will be subject to that interest.

Some states will require the lender to send a special notice to borrowers who are homeowners. For example, the New York Real Property Actions and Proceedings Law Section 1320 requires that owners of residences with not more than three units be given this notice printed in boldface type:

> NOTICE YOU ARE IN DANGER OF LOSING YOUR HOME
> If you do not respond to this summons and complaint by serving a copy of the answer on the attorney for the mortgage company who filed this   foreclosure proceeding against you and filing the answer with the court, a default judgment may be entered and you can lose your home.
> Speak to an attorney or go to the court where your case is pending for further information on how to answer the summons and protect your property.
> Sending a payment to your mortgage company will not stop this   foreclosure action.
> YOU MUST RESPOND BY SERVING A COPY OF THE ANSWER ON THE ATTORNEY FOR THE PLAINTIFF (MORTGAGE COMPANY) AND FILING THE ANSWER WITH THE COURT.

At the time the lawsuit is filed, the lender will record a *lis pendens* in the local real estate records. The term *lis pendens* means "suit pending." A *lis pendens* is a notice to the world that a lawsuit has been filed against the real property. By recording in the public land records, the lender gives "constructive notice" that the lawsuit has been filed. "Constructive notice" means that everyone in the world is deemed to know the contents of the notice and will be aware of the lawsuit. The notice will describe the real property, the court and the parties. Anyone who acquires any interest in the real property will be subject to any results that flow from the lawsuit. The recording of a *lis pendens* provides a means for foreclosure investors to identify potential acquisitions. This topic will be discussed below.

The contents of a *lis pendens* are prescribed by state law. Typically, a *lis pendens* will contain the following information: the names of the parties to the lawsuit, the fact that a mortgage is being foreclosed, a legal description of the real property, the date of the mortgage, the names of the mortgagor and the mortgagee and the mortgagee's recording information.

Where the real property is commercial or industrial property occupied by one or more tenants, the lender will normally seek the appointment of a receiver to take possession of the property and collect the rents during the foreclosure proceedings. This is done so that the borrower cannot pocket the rents or commit a default under the leases that would allow the tenants to abandon their premises, thus causing the value of the collateral to deteriorate. The authority to appoint a receiver arises out of the assignment of rents and leases that a commercial borrower executes at the same time as the mortgage. Also, the mortgage itself will contain an assignment of rents and leases.

A foreclosure investor who seeks to acquire a distressed property needs to know whether or not the rents have been assigned and are being collected. This could affect the price a lender is willing to accept.

C.   Non-judicial Foreclosure – Trustee's Sale

In a non-judicial proceeding, the security instrument most commonly used is a deed of trust. The parties to a deed of trust are the borrower, referred to as the grantor or trustor, the trustee and the lender, referred to as the beneficiary. The trustee is ordinarily a title insurance company or an attorney. The deed of trust will contain a provision whereby the borrower grants to the trustee the power to sell the real property in the event of a default. This provision is known as the "power of sale." Because the trustee has a private power to sell the real property, the trustee need not go to court to effect a sale. The proceedings are conducted outside of the court system and are therefore non-judicial. Hence, this type of foreclosure is referred to as a non-judicial proceeding.

Following the expiration of the reinstatement period, the lender can commence foreclosure proceedings. After the expiration of such period of time as required by state law, the lender in a title theory state contacts the trustee and demands that the trustee issue a notice of sale.

The notice of sale specifies the date, time and place of the sale. The trustee sends copies of the notice of sale to the borrower, any other persons or entities with an interest in the real property, such as junior lienors, and in some states, to any person who has recorded a request for any notices of default or sale. The trustee also records the notice of sale.

D.   Judicial Foreclosure Trial

At the foreclosure trial, the lender must prove the existence of the debt and the fact of default. The borrower raises any defenses that he may have against the claim of default. The court conducts a trial, and if the lender is successful in proving its case, the court issues a judgment of foreclosure, ordering a sale of the real property by auction. In some states, the court appoints a referee to calculate the amounts owed to the lender and to any other holders of liens on the real property. In some cases, if the borrower has no defenses, or if the real property is seriously underwater, the borrower may simply walk away from the real property, not appear for the trial, and allow the court to enter a default judgment in favor of the lender. In either case, the parties incur the costs of attorney fees, court filing fees and other miscellaneous fees. Plainly, the judicial process can be costly and time consuming. Many established lenders utilize lawyers that specialize in foreclosure that are able to prepare and file the necessary papers with a minimum of time and expense. However, while these lenders can minimize the expense of a foreclosure case, there is still a cost that a lender is happy to avoid.

A non-judicial foreclosure proceeding does not involve the courts unless the borrower has defenses to the foreclosure and elects to file a lawsuit against the lender to enjoin the foreclosure. In such a case, the borrower names the lender as a defendant and seeks to prove that the lender acted improperly by declaring a default.

E.   Deficiency Judgments

In depressed markets, the amount of the debt is likely to exceed the value of the real property. Accordingly, when the foreclosure sale has been completed, and the bid price has been paid to the lender, there will be some amount of the debt remaining unpaid. For example, assume the borrower took a loan of $250,000 to purchase a $275,000 home. The borrower has paid the loan down to $240,000 but the value of the home has declined to $200,000, and the borrower has abandoned the home. The lender commences a judicial foreclosure action that incurs court and foreclosure costs of $15,000. The borrower owes the lender $255,000 (the loan balance of $240,000 + foreclosure costs of $15,000 = $255,000). At the foreclosure sale, the highest bid is $200,000 which is applied to pay part of the debt. The unpaid balance is $55,000.

Depending on state law, and the foreclosure procedure that was employed, the lender may have the right to sue the borrower for the unpaid balance. The unpaid balance is called a "deficiency." In our example, the $55,000 amount represents the deficiency. The lender may sue to obtain a judgment requiring the borrower to pay the deficiency – hence, a "deficiency judgment."

The lender must decide before commencing its foreclosure proceeding whether or not to pursue a deficiency judgment. If the lender chooses to pursue a deficiency judgment, the lender has to follow a certain set of procedures. If the lender elects to forego a deficiency judgment, the lender may be able to follow a different set of procedures. Often, the procedures that prevent a deficiency judgment are cheaper and more efficient than the procedures under which a deficiency judgment is permitted. The tradeoff therefore is the possibility of recovering a deficiency judgment versus the probability of a quicker and cheaper foreclosure. The procedure chosen by the lender can affect the options available to the foreclosure investor. Moreover, a borrower may feel differently about agreeing to do a deal with a foreclosure investor if the borrower knows that he can walk away from the foreclosure without further liability than he would if the borrower is concerned that the lender will be pursuing a deficiency judgment. For example, if the lender is not able to pursue a deficiency judgment, the borrower might be willing to sell its equity of redemption for a nominal amount. For these reasons, the availability of a deficiency judgment can become relevant to the foreclosure investor.

Deficiency judgments are frequently not available to lenders who elect to proceed by private sale, such as by a foreclosure under the power of sale contained in a deed of trust. One reason is that the amount of a deficiency is measured by the amount of proceeds generated at a foreclosure sale. Even if the sale is by public auction, which ordinarily tends to set a fair price for the real property, the sale is conducted privately without court supervision. The courts do not want to award deficiency judgments based on sales that were conducted without court supervision because of the potential for abuse or misconduct. Also, remember that it is usually the lender that is the high bidder at a foreclosure sale, especially if the real property has lost significant value. If there are no other bidders, the lender can bid a low amount to preserve its right to sue for a deficiency judgment. This gives the lender control over whether there will be a deficiency and the amount of the deficiency. Legislatures have been reluctant to give lenders so much discretion in foreclosures.

In times of constricted markets, the notion that deficiency judgments have value can be chimerical. The borrower must have assets to make it worth a lender's while to pursue a deficiency judgment. However, if the borrower had assets, the borrower probably would not have defaulted on the loan. Even if the borrower has some assets, the lender would incur court costs and attorney's fees to pursue a judgment. It is true that all promissory notes will contain a promise by the borrower to pay the lender's attorney fees, but that promise is only worth something if the borrower has the money to pay the fees. Further, the lender may be caught up in a lawsuit for an extended period of time. If the borrower resists, the lender's business can be disrupted by depositions of the lender's employees and appearances as witnesses. A suit for a deficiency judgment can cost the lender time and money with, in many cases, little likelihood of recovery. Therefore, there tend to be fewer deficiency judgment actions in recessions. Lenders are more likely to put the money that could be spent on an action to recover a deficiency judgment to more productive use by making new loans or otherwise gainfully employing their capital. However, one possibility is that groups of lenders that have incurred deficiencies may sell those loans to collection agencies or other investors. The collection agencies may find it worth their while to pursue deficiency judgments where banks might not. Therefore, the foreclosure investor should not rule out the possibility of such an action.

Two other sets of borrowers that might be exposed to deficiency judgments are second home owners and real estate investors. The second home or the realty investments constitute assets that a lender with a deficiency judgment can attempt to seize. These borrowers are more likely to need to work out a deal with their lenders in lieu of foreclosure

An action to obtain a deficiency judgment is a judicial action. It is a lawsuit brought by the lender in a court to recover a judgment for the amount of the deficiency. New York State provides an example of the procedure for obtaining a deficiency judgment. Although New York allows non-judicial foreclosure, the procedure is seldom used. One reason is that it is difficult to obtain title insurance following a non-judicial foreclosure sale. After the real property has been sold at auction and the lender has commenced its action to recover a deficiency, the court determines, in the words of the relevant statute "the fair and reasonable market value of the mortgaged premises as of the date such premises were bid in at auction or such nearest earlier date as there shall have been any market value thereof . . . ."[1] The court then enters a judgment for an amount equal to the difference between the amount owed to the lender and the greater of the market value as determined by the court and the foreclosure bid price.

New York is an example of a state that has a fair value requirement. California is another example. California permits both judicial and non-judicial foreclosures, although, in California, almost all lenders use deeds of trust with power of sale and pursue non-judicial foreclosure. However, for the lender that wants to pursue a deficiency judgment, the lender commences a judicial foreclosure and then obtains a deficiency judgment for the difference between the property's fair market and the amount of the debt. If the property's value exceeded the amount of the debt, the lender cannot obtain a deficiency judgment. Florida has similar fair value protection for the borrower. In Florida, the lender must establish that the value of the real property was less than the debt. The borrower can present evidence that the value of the property exceeded the amount of the

---

[1] New York Real Property Actions And Proceedings Law Section 1371.

debt. If the borrower can make that case, the Florida court will deny the lender a deficiency judgment.

A brief summary of each state's foreclosure procedures can be found at a web site maintained by Default Research Inc. at http://www.defaultresearch.com/laws .

CHAPTER I-5 DISPOSITION OF PROPERTY

In most states, if the court finds that the borrower is in default of the loan, the court will order a foreclosure sale by auction. In some states, under certain circumstances, a court will order a strict foreclosure without any auction. In a title theory state, the lender instructs the trustee to record a notice of sale. After the lapse of the required amount of time, the property is sold at an auction. In some cases, the borrower negotiates with the lender for the right to dispose of the real property by a deed in lieu of foreclosure. This chapter will describe these different means of disposing of the real property.

A.   Foreclosure Sale

Foreclosure sales are utilized in both judicial and non-judicial foreclosures. In either case, a sale by auction is conducted. At the auction, the lender has the right to submit a credit bid in an amount up to the amount owed to the lender. The amount owed to the lender can include the accelerated principal amount, the accrued interest, late fees and charges, penalties, attorney fees, the costs of a title search and appraisal, court costs and the costs of the sale, including advertising, marshal fees and trustee or auctioneer fees.

The lender ordinarily calculates the amount it intends to bid prior to the auction. If the borrower is solvent and has assets that can be applied to the debt, then there is a possibility of recovering partial or full payment. In this scenario, the lender will bid less than the amount of the debt. If the lender bids the entire amount owed, some states hold that the lender's purchase at that amount satisfies the debt. That is because it is assumed that the lender would not bid more than the property is worth, and if it is worth the amount owed, then the lender's debt has been repaid. Accordingly, if local law permits deficiency judgments, and the property is underwater, the lender will want to bid below the amount of the debt and then seek a deficiency judgment.

Other potential bidders at the sale include holders of junior liens, who will be wiped out by the sale, prospective homeowners and foreclosure investors.

The auction is conducted by an auctioneer, a court official, the trustee under the deed of trust or, in some states like Colorado, a public trustee.

In order to participate as a bidder, a foreclosure investor must demonstrate to the auctioneer that he has available the funds necessary to close a purchase of the real property. In some states, a bidder will have to show the auctioneer a cashier's check, a bank check, or cash for a specified percentage of the highest bid to use as a deposit. In other states, such as California, the bidder must demonstrate to the trustee the ability to pay the entire sum of the highest bid at the close of the auction. In other states, there is a bidder's fee that must be paid in order to participate. In those states in which a bidder needs a percentage of the highest bid, the successful bidder has a small amount of time to pay the balance of the bid price. The period of time can be as soon as the end of the business day on which the auction occurred or it may be thirty days after the auction. If the successful bidder does not come up with the additional cash, he loses the property and the deposit. In some communities, a prospective bidder must register with the county clerk's office. Some localities charge the highest bidder a premium of a specified percentage of the bid in addition to the real property's bid price. In short, procedures differ from state to state and county to county within each state. Accordingly, it is incumbent upon the foreclosure investor to become thoroughly familiar with the procedures that apply to any property the investor is considering.

The property is deeded to the highest bidder. The lender is entitled to make a credit bid in an amount up to the full extent of the debt. As noted above, the lender may elect not to bid the full amount of the debt if the property is underwater and there are no other bidders.

The foreclosure investor that participates in a foreclosure auction sale may find himself competing with holders of junior liens. If there is substantial equity in the real property, and the junior lienor has a significant investment in the real property, there may be incentive for the junior lienor to bid at the foreclosure sale. The junior lienor would have to pay the amount of the mortgage but he could make a credit bid for the amount of the junior lien.

Proceeds from the auction first go to pay costs incurred by the court in conducting the sale and then to the foreclosing lender. Any remaining monies will be paid to junior lien holders and then to the borrower.

If there are insufficient funds to pay the foreclosing lender in full, the foreclosing lender may seek to recover a deficiency judgment against the borrower. Normally, if a lender conducts the foreclosure by private sale, the lender cannot recover a deficiency judgment. However, if the sale is through a judicial proceeding, many states permit the lender to pursue a judgment for the unpaid balance. To effect this deficiency judgment, the court is charged with a fair value procedure to ascertain whether the sale was concluded at a fair price. The court then enters a judgment against the borrower for an amount equal to (1) the amount owed by the borrower with interest, plus the amount of any prior liens with interest, plus the costs and disbursements of the foreclosure proceeding, including the referee's fee and disbursements, minus (2) the higher of the bid price or the fair market value as determined by the court. Depending on the state, deficiency judgments can also be obtained in a strict foreclosure.

When developing a strategy for approaching and negotiating with a defaulting borrower, it aids the foreclosure investor to know whether the borrower is subject to a deficiency judgment and the amount of that judgment. This information is useful in determining how willing the borrower will be to negotiate a pre-foreclosure sale and the purchase price that the borrower might be willing to accept.

The foreclosure investor's strategy can also be affected when there are excess proceeds sufficient to pay the lender but not the junior lien holders. That will be addressed in the discussion of redemption below.

34

B.   Strict Foreclosure

In medieval England, if a borrower was a day late in making a payment, the mortgage holder could immediately take title under the procedures endorsed by the courts of law. In some states, that procedure is still available where the equity is insufficient to return any benefit to the borrower. The lender files a judicial proceeding and in a strict foreclosure can take title to the real property without an auction sale. For example, in Connecticut, the proceedings are judicial, but if there is no equity in excess of the lender's debt, the court will forego a sale and order the real property deeded to the lender. In Vermont, lenders commence judicial proceedings that can lead either to strict foreclosure or to judicial foreclosure by power of sale.

C.   Deed in Lieu of Foreclosure

One alternative to a foreclosure is for the borrower to negotiate with a lender to deed to the real property to the lender without going through a foreclosure proceeding. This concept is called a "deed in lieu of foreclosure."

The transaction includes an agreement between the borrower and the lender. The lender agrees that the debt is paid in full and agrees to either inscribe on the borrower's promissory note that the debt has been paid or surrenders the note to the borrower. Moreover, the lender agrees that he will not pursue a deficiency judgment against the borrower. The borrower agrees to deed the real property to the lender. Under a deed in lieu, the borrower gives the lender a deed that conveys all of the borrower's right, title and interest in the real property to the lender.

Why would a borrower agree to deliver a deed in lieu of foreclosure? If the borrower is in default and has no realistic prospects of bringing the debt current, a deed in lieu can be the most efficient and least expensive route to take. It saves the costs of responding to a lawsuit. It also helps the borrower's credit rating because there is no record of a foreclosure judgment entered against the borrower. Finally, and significantly, it relieves the borrower of any obligation to repay the debt. However, in some instances, rather than releasing the debt, the lender retains the right to foreclose its mortgage or deed of trust and covenants not to sue the borrower for a deficiency judgment. Depending on the circumstances, the lender may agree to retain the borrower as a manager of a rental property such as a shopping center.

What advantages does a deed in lieu of foreclosure give to a lender? First, if the lender and borrower reach an early agreement, the proceedings are more efficient because they are completed much quicker than a foreclosure. The sooner the lender can take possession of the real property, the sooner it can sell the property, remove a non-performing asset from its books and employ the sale proceeds in a useful enterprise. A deed in lieu will also avoid any redemption period. Additionally, if the property is a rental property, there is a risk that tenants will claim defaults by the landlord under their leases. Under a deed in lieu, the lender can take control of the real property quickly, receive the rents and cure any leasehold defaults to prevent tenants from vacating the property.

There can be difficulties for a borrower negotiating a deed in lieu of foreclosure. If the real property is encumbered with a home equity loan, the lender's decision to accept a deed in lieu may depend on applicable state law. Unless state law provides otherwise, the lender would be taking title subject to a second lien. Upon the recording of the deed, the second lien becomes a first lien, and the lender is then obligated to pay the debt service on the home equity mortgage. Thus, the lender is assuming a debt. The lender must keep the debt current to avoid foreclosure of the home equity mortgage and it would be difficult for the lender to sell the property unless the lender paid off the home equity mortgage. Of course, these concerns apply whether the mortgage is a home equity mortgage or any other type of junior lien. Hence, any junior lien on the real property may prevent the borrower from convincing the lender to accept a deed in lieu of foreclosure. This would be a situation where the lender retains the right to foreclose the mortgage while agreeing not to sue the borrower for a deficiency judgment. The effect of state law is addressed below.

There can also be tax disadvantages to a borrower from use of a deed in lieu of foreclosure. When the lender accepts the deed, the lender forgives the unpaid amount of the debt. Monies received by a borrower are not taxed as income because they must be repaid. In contrast, if those moneys are forgiven and need not be repaid, the borrower has received income that may be taxable. However, this result may be changed by the Mortgage Forgiveness Debt Relief Act of 2007. According to Internal Revenue Service advice posted on the IRS website, debt up to $2,000,000 forgiven during the tax years from 2007 through 2012 will not be taxed as income if the debt was secured by the taxpayer's principal residence. The forgiven or cancelled debt must have been used to buy or construct one's principal residence or to refinance such debt. A borrower needs to confer with his or her accountant or tax attorney to determine if and how this exclusion applies, however, it may facilitate deed in lieu transactions.

There can also be difficulties for a lender arising from the use of a deed in lieu of foreclosure. First, a foreclosure eliminates all interests in the real property that are subordinate to the lender's mortgage. Thus, any second mortgages or mechanic's liens or judgment liens are expunged upon the completion of a foreclosure. A deed in lieu of foreclosure is outside of the foreclosure process and there is no effect on subordinate liens. In order to retain the ability to deal with unknown second mortgages, the mortgage or deed of trust must contain a provision to the effect that the mortgage does not merge into the deed, and the deed in lieu agreement and other documents must be consistent with this anti-merger provision. If there is an anti-merger provision, some states will keep the mortgage alive and allow the lender to foreclose the mortgage after acceptance of the deed. In other states, the result can be different, especially if the lender is aware of the junior lien. The lender may need to create a separate entity to take title. Second, the lender agrees to give up all rights to sue the borrower for a deficiency judgment. This may not be a concern if the borrower is insolvent or judgment proof. However, if the borrower has assets and has just decided to walk away from a property that is underwater, the lender may decide to seek a deficiency judgment. In that case, the lender is unlikely to accept a deed in lieu of foreclosure. Third, there may be potential liabilities that a lender is not willing to risk. These include possible environmental liabilities, significant deterioration of the asset requiring major repairs and defaults by the borrower under leases on the real property for which the lender as a new owner may become liable. Further, the costs of the transaction, such as environmental inspection and title insurance are likely to be borne by the lender since the borrower has little in the way of funds.

Having a lender that is willing to accept a deed in lieu of foreclosure can benefit a foreclosure investor. The lender presumably will have incurred fewer costs in connection with the foreclosure. This reduces the amount of cash that the lender will be seeking when it sells the real property. If the foreclosure investor can identify a prospective property before the lender has commenced a foreclosure proceeding, there will not be a public notice of the default, and the investor can work with the borrower and lender without competition from other investors.

D.   Redemption by Owner or Junior Lienor

Under the law of many states, the borrower has a statutory right of redemption following a foreclosure sale. Those states may also grant a right of redemption to junior lienors.

The statutory right of redemption is the right of a borrower, after conclusion of the foreclosure sale, to pay the redemption amount and redeem the property. You will recall that the notion of foreclosure originated with lenders in England suing to foreclose the borrower's equitable right of redemption. Not all states permit redemption, and some states permit redemption in only certain types of foreclosure proceedings. In some states, such as New Jersey, the right of redemption is not found in the statutes but is a matter of equity created by the courts. Also, property sold under a federal income tax lien can be redeemed within 180 days after the sale by paying the delinquent tax plus interest at twenty percent. The notion of redemption is another reason for investors to be thoroughly familiar with applicable foreclosure procedures.

The redemption amount can be the entire debt and all foreclosure costs where the lender has bid in the entire debt. In some states, it is the amount bid at the foreclosure sale plus interest, all taxes, assessments, costs and certain other expenses. This is because the amount is paid to the foreclosure purchaser, and that amount would be the purchase price paid at the foreclosure sale.

A borrower might have an incentive to go into foreclosure and then redeem the property. For example, assume that the borrower took out a first mortgage on a home twenty years ago. Since that time, the amount of the debt has been reduced significantly, the value of the home has appreciated and considerable equity has been built up. Then, the borrower took out a home equity loan in an amount greater than the amount of the first mortgage. If the borrower gets into financial difficulty, he might allow the foreclosure to go forward to wipe out the home equity loan and then redeem the first mortgage. This seems an unlikely scenario, but this or other circumstances could arise. Foreclosure investors need to be aware of such possibilities.

CHAPTER I-6 STAGES OF FORECLOSURE

Now that we have reviewed the basics of the foreclosure process, we can turn to the various stages that arise during a foreclosure. The opportunities available to a foreclosure investor differ depending on the stage of the foreclosure.

Foreclosures can go through up to four stages. The four stages are:

(1) the period of time during which the borrower begins to miss payments but the lender has not yet formally declared an event of default. This stage is called the "pre-foreclosure stage."

(2) the period of time that begins with the lender formally declaring the borrower to be in default and ending with the foreclosure sale. This stage is called the "default and sale stage."

(3) the period of time that begins after the completion of the foreclosure sale and ends with the expiration of the borrower's redemption period. This stage is called the "redemption period."

(4) the period of time following the expiration of the borrower's redemption period (or following the completion of the foreclosure sale in those situations where there is no right of redemption) during which the lender owns the real property. This stage is called the "REO stage."

Each of these stages offers different opportunities and presents different challenges to the foreclosure investor. The motivations affecting the borrower and the lender can change from one stage to the next. Accordingly, the foreclosure investor needs to be cognizant of the forces impacting each stage. The techniques, advantages and disadvantages of investing at each stage are addressed in Part IV.

A.   Pre-Foreclosure Stage

Because the foreclosure investor should be open to every type of investing opportunity, the investor should be prepared to look at residential, commercial and industrial properties. Each type of deal can involve very different parties and interests. It is therefore difficult to describe a typical situation because there can be so many variations. However, because the beginner foreclosure investor is more likely to focus on owner-occupied residences, we will start with that scenario.

Ordinarily, the borrower is the owner of a single family residence or house. Nevertheless, it is not unusual to find that the borrower resides in a condominium or a duplex. The borrower may even own two houses, and the property in trouble is a vacation home. The foreclosure investor needs to ascertain the nature of the property involved.

In most cases, the borrower has missed a payment of principal and interest (or just interest under an interest-only loan). If the default continues beyond the late payment date, the lender will assess a late payment fee. When a borrower misses a payment, the lender will contact the borrower, often by a letter noting that a payment was late or delinquent. The lender may include a description of the steps the borrower must take to bring the loan current. After the loan has been in default for about a month, the lender may send notice to credit rating agencies. This provides an incentive to the borrower to resolve the matter quickly which is a factor that a foreclosure investor should bear in mind. If the default continues, more and more payments are missed and the amount in default continues to mount. The practice of lenders at this point varies from lender to lender. Some may allow partial payment to correct the default, and others may require payment in full. Some lenders of commercial developers have called the entire loan due, even if no payments were in default, based on other covenants in the mortgage loan documentation.

Some lenders make telephone calls to the borrower urging payment. Other lenders turn the loan over to a collection agency. The costs of collection are then added to the amount due. The actions that a lender or collection agency is allowed to take may be circumscribed by state law. For example, in California before a lender can even declare a default, the lender must give the borrower the following counseling:

> A mortgagee, beneficiary, or authorized agent shall contact the borrower in person or by telephone in order to assess the borrower's financial situation and explore options for the borrower to avoid foreclosure. During the initial contact, the mortgagee, beneficiary, or authorized agent shall advise the borrower that he or she has the right to request a subsequent meeting and, if requested, the mortgagee, beneficiary, or authorized agent shall schedule the meeting to occur within 14 days. The assessment of the borrower's financial situation and discussion of options may occur during the first contact, or at the subsequent meeting scheduled for that purpose. In either case, the borrower shall be provided the toll-free telephone number made available by the United States Department of Housing and Urban Development (HUD) to find a HUD-certified housing counseling agency. Any meeting may occur telephonically. California Civil Code Section 2923.5(a)(2).

Pennsylvania is another state that provides counseling to delinquent borrowers under the Pennsylvania Homeowner's Emergency Mortgage Assistance Program. Under this measure, the lender's notice of default must advise the borrower as follows:

If you comply with the provisions of the Homeowner's Emergency Mortgage Assistance Act of 1983 (the "Act"), you may be eligible for emergency mortgage assistance:
If your default has been caused by circumstances beyond your control,
If you have a reasonable prospect of being able to pay your mortgage payments, and
If you meet other eligibility requirements established by the Pennsylvania Housing Finance Agency.
<u>Temporary Stay Of Foreclosure</u> -- Under the Act, you are entitled to a temporary stay of foreclosure on your mortgage for thirty (30) days from the date of this Notice (plus three (3) days for mailing). During that time you must arrange and attend a "face-to-face" meeting with one of the consumer credit counseling agencies listed at the end of this Notice. This meeting must occur within thirty-three (33) days of the date of this notice. If you do not apply for emergency mortgage assistance, you must bring your mortgage up to date. The part of this notice called "how to cure your mortgage default," explains how to bring your mortgage up to date.
CONSUMER CREDIT COUNSELING AGENCIES -- If you meet with one of the consumer credit counseling agency listed at the end of this notice, the lender may NOT take action against you for thirty (30) days after the date of this meeting.

A borrower who pursues one of these counseling options may be open to negotiating a transaction with a foreclosure investor.

Mortgage consultants recommend that the borrower discuss the situation with the lender. Even if the borrower has no chance of paying off the loan or curing the default, talking to the lender might produce a solution. The foreclosure investor certainly wants to talk to the lender because that may be the best way to close a successful investment.

The foreclosure investor should note that many banks have sold their loans as a part of a securitization package, and the loan may now be administered by a loan servicer acting on behalf of either the lender or

42

the holders of the bonds or other instruments issued pursuant to the securitization.

At some point in the process, usually somewhere between sixty and ninety days after the first default, the lender takes the first steps toward foreclosure. The loan may be transferred from the lender's loan servicing department to its foreclosure department. The name that such a department goes by depends on the lender, but the most common name is the "loss mitigation department." Persons working on delinquent loans in that department are called "loss mitigators." It is their job to minimize losses on a delinquent loan. A foreclosure investor can help them perform that job by negotiating a transfer of the property at a mutual satisfactory price or terms.

The lender sends a formal notice of default to the borrower. The lender is usually required to notify the borrower by certified mail. This notice states the names of the parties, the recording information for the mortgage or deed of trust, a description of the real property, that a default has occurred, the nature of the default and it states that if the default is not cured by a certain date, the lender will accelerate the entire loan. In states that utilize private sale, the notice of default is recorded in the land records. This is the first public notice of the default and it is a source of information for foreclosure investors.

B.   Default & Auction Stage

Regardless of the nature of the default, once a borrower has defaulted, the lender has the right to declare a default and pursue its remedy of foreclosure. There are some critical steps that occur during the period of time between the declaration of default and the commencement of the foreclosure. The borrower's rights change as this period of time passes. The foreclosure investor should understand how these rights change in order to deal effectively with them.

Ordinarily, a borrower has a grace period in which to make a payment after the specified due date. Some promissory notes provide that the grace period is without additional cost, while under other promissory notes, late payment results in the borrower incurring late payment fees. In some commercial loans, the interest will step up to a default rate.

43

However, the borrower has the right to make the defaulted payment and pay the additional charges. Once the grace period has passed, late fees and other charges will accrue. The lender may or may not contact the borrower to inquire about the delinquent debt. At some point, depending on the practices of the lender's loan servicer and the terms of the promissory note, the lender will become entitled to declare a default.

The first step in the lender's enforcement of its mortgage or deed of trust is to send to the borrower a notice of default. The timing of the notice of default, the contents of the notice of default and the means by which it is delivered (say by registered or certified mail) are controlled by state law and therefore will differ from state to state. The foreclosure investor should study the requirements of the state in which the investor is operating and familiarize himself with these procedures. However, typically a notice of default will identify the real property, the borrower, the lender, the trustee (in the case of a deed of trust), the amount of the loan and the balance due, the date and recording information of the mortgage or deed of trust and it will identify the right of a lender for an election to sell the real property. Any right to reinstate the loan should be described. Additionally, the notice of default may warn the borrower that if the loan is not reinstated within a specified period of time, the borrower will have to pay the entire accelerated debt to prevent a foreclosure.

The notice of default must precisely describe the nature of the default. The description of the default should include the amount of principal and interest past due, any interest and taxes past due and any other aspects of the default. The purpose is to give the borrower adequate notice of the nature of the default and give the borrower or any junior lienors or foreclosure investors an opportunity to cure the default. Most state laws give the borrower the right to cure the default and reinstate the loan. The borrower has the right during the reinstatement period to pay the past due principal, interest, late fees, penalties and other charges. If the borrower makes that payment, the default is cured and the foreclosure process comes to an end.

Each state has its own requirements for notice. For example, New York State requires that borrowers be given notice of ways they can obtain assistance regarding their foreclosure. The notice prescribed by Section 1303 of the New York Real Property Actions and Proceedings Law provides that the notice must contain a page in a separate color in large font stating the following:

Help for Homeowners in Foreclosure
New York State Law requires that we send you this notice about the   foreclosure process. Please read it carefully.
Summons and Complaint
You are in danger of losing your home. If you fail to respond to the summons and complaint in this foreclosure action, you may lose your home. Please read the summons and complaint carefully. You should immediately contact an attorney or your local legal aid office to obtain advice on how to protect yourself.
Sources of Information and Assistance
The State encourages you to become informed about your options in foreclosure. In addition to seeking assistance from an attorney or legal aid office, there are government agencies and non-profit organizations that you may contact for information about possible options, including trying to work with your lender during this process.
To locate an entity near you, you may call the toll-free helpline
maintained by the New York State Banking Department at
_____ (enter number) or visit the Department's website at _____ (enter web address).
Foreclosure rescue scams
Be careful of people who approach you with offers to "save" your home. There are individuals who watch for notices of foreclosure actions in order to unfairly profit from a homeowner's distress. You should be extremely careful about any such promises and any suggestions that you pay them a fee or sign over your deed. State law requires anyone offering such services for profit to enter into a contract which fully describes the services they will perform and fees they will charge, and which prohibits them from taking any money from you until they have completed all such promised services.

During an event of default, the lender can accelerate the loan and declare the entire amount of principal due and payable. After the lender has sent a notice of default, the borrower and all persons or entities with interests in the real property, such as holders of junior liens on the real property, have a right to cure the default by paying all amounts due within a specified period of time. This right is called the right of reinstatement. Even if the lender has accelerated the entire debt, the borrower has the right during the reinstatement period to reinstate the loan without paying the accelerated amount. In some states, the lender is not permitted to accelerate the loan until the expiration of the reinstatement period. However, when the right of reinstatement expires, the borrower or third parties must pay the entire accelerated debt in order to preserve title to the real property. Notably, a lender still has the right to accept past due payments and waive the acceleration. A foreclosure investor should keep this in mind when negotiating with a lender. The lender may be willing to waive the acceleration to have a solvent investor owning the property and making timely payments.

Following the expiration of the period within which the borrower may reinstate the loan, the lender may proceed to foreclosure.

In judicial foreclosure states, the lender commences a lawsuit to foreclose the mortgage. In connection with the filing of the lawsuit, the lender records a *lis pendens* in the land records. The *lis pendens* gives all the world notice that a lawsuit affecting the real property has been commenced. Anyone who takes any interest in the property will have that interest subject to the results of the lawsuit. The recording of the *lis pendens* provides a source of information about the default. Foreclosure investors use the recording of a *lis pendens* to identify potential investment properties.

In non-judicial foreclosure states, the trustee under the deed of trust records a notice of default. The recording of the notice of default has the same effect as the recording of a *lis pendens*. Notice is given to the entire world, including interested foreclosure investors.

These *lis pendens* and notices of default can be obtained from county recorders' offices, some of which have posted their records online.

For example, the Miami-Dade County Clerk of the Courts offers online record searching. To conduct a search, a foreclosure investor needs certain information such as the names of the parties to the document. The foreclosure investor can search for *lis pendens* filings in the Miami-Dade County records on a specific date or over a range of dates and can obtain the mortgages involved. The Miami-Dade County Clerk's office has prepared a set of instructions that can be seen at http://www2.miami-dadeclerk.com/MFS/Help.aspx.

This information can also be obtained from websites for a fee. This is addressed in greater detail in Chapter III-1 below.

After the reinstatement period expires, the lender can conduct the foreclosure. In judicial foreclosure states, foreclosure is accomplished by the lawsuit filed by the lender against the borrower. The lender presents its case against the borrower, and the borrower presents any defenses. The judge then rules on the matter. If the judge finds the borrower to be in default, the judge will order the real property sold to satisfy the debt.

In non-judicial foreclosure states, the trustee records or files a notice of sale fixing the date on which the real property will be sold. On that date, the trustee conducts the auction.

In strict foreclosure states, there is no auction. If the court finds that the borrower is in default, the court orders the real property deeded to the lender in whole or partial payment of the debt.

In either type of foreclosure, the lender is allowed to make a credit bid in an amount up to the total amount of the debt. Consequently, the lender need not make any payments at the sale. All other bidders must establish their qualifications to bid and demonstrate their ability to pay the bid price. The highest bidder must pay a deposit upon the fall of the auctioneer's hammer and pay the balance within the time set by state law, which can be as short as the day of the sale and as long as 30 days after the completion of the sale.

The court or trustee issues a deed to the highest bidder after full payment is made. In situations where the borrower does not have a right of redemption, the delivery of the deed is final and cuts off all rights of the borrower in the real property. In situations where the borrower has a right of redemption, the title does not vest in the highest bidder until the period of redemption has expired. Depending on the state and the type of procedure employed, the period of redemption can run for as long as a year.

In some strict foreclosure states, the foreclosure commences with the filing of the lender's lawsuit against the borrower. The borrower must file an answer within a specific period of time. Failure to answer will result in the court entering a default judgment against the borrower. If the borrower answers, the matter is set for trial. If the real property is underwater, the court enters a judgment of strict foreclosure conveying the property to the lender. After the judgment of strict foreclosure is issued, the court determines the period of time in which the borrower and any other persons with an interest in the real property have the right to redeem the property by paying the debt. If the debt is not paid, the title vests in the lender.

C.   Redemption Stage

As discussed in Chapter I-5, in many states, the borrower has a right of redemption following a foreclosure sale. Briefly, this is the right of a borrower, after conclusion of the foreclosure sale, to pay the redemption amount and redeem the property.

In some states, the high bidder at the foreclosure sale does not purchase the real property at the closing of the sale but rather the right to own the property after expiration of the redemption period. Accordingly, in those states, the borrower can continue to occupy the property or collect the rents if it is an investment building.

One disadvantage to foreclosure investors is that the acquisition of a property at a foreclosure sale is not final at the closing of the sale. If the borrower redeems the property during the redemption period, the investor loses the property. Therefore, the investor must wait for the expiration of the redemption period. If the debt is not paid by a specific date, then title in the foreclosure purchaser becomes vested. Some states allow holders of junior liens to redeem the real property.

In some cases, the redemption period for junior lienors follows the borrower's period, extending the time of the redemption period. The period of redemption can run up to one year in some states.

A foreclosure investor that is the successful bidder at a foreclosure sale may need to invest substantial sums rehabilitating the property or advertising for tenants or paying broker commissions to find tenants. While it may be a shock if the borrower or a junior lienor comes up with the cash needed to redeem the property, it is a possibility. In many states, the investor loses the investments made in the property. However, in some states, the cost of improvements made during the redemption period is added to the redemption amount. Foreclosure investors need to know what costs are included in the redemption amount before making any investments during the redemption period.

Foreclosure investors can address the potential problems caused by redemption rights by purchasing the rights from the borrower or junior lienors. These rights can be purchased before or after the investor closes the acquisition of the real property. Purchasing redemption rights may also be a means of acquiring the real property at a price below its fair value. The amount of the first mortgage may be less than the fair value of the property, but the second and other liens may have pushed the debt to an amount in excess of the property's value. After the junior liens have been eliminated, the foreclosure investor could acquire the property at a price below the market value.

If the lender bids less than the amount of the debt, to preserve the ability to sue the borrower for a deficiency judgment, the cost of redeeming the property could be even less. The redemption price may be less than the market value and, therefore, it can be acquired at a price through redemption that is less than the price a lender would charge after it took title to the property. The redemption period could be used by the foreclosure investor to conduct its due diligence on the real property.

In states where junior lienors have redemption rights, foreclosure investors may consider purchasing the junior lien at a discount and then redeeming the property, especially where there is equity.

D.   Post-Foreclosure Stage – REO's

The final stage of foreclosure occurs after the expiration of the redemption period when title to the real property is finally and irrevocably vested in the lender. However, if the lender is not the high bidder at the foreclosure sale, this final stage never occurs because the person who made the successful bid becomes the owner of the property. If that occurs, the property is removed from the market and the foreclosure investor ordinarily has no further interest in the property unless the investor contacts the high bidder to enter into some kind of partnership or other deal. Hence, the post-foreclosure stage only arises where the lender becomes the owner of the property.

Real property taken by banks and other institutional lenders as a result of foreclosure is referred to as "Real Estate Owned" or "REO." Real Estate Owned does not benefit a lender. Unlike the buildings which the lender utilizes for its business, REOs have been acquired as collateral. To realize any benefit from REOs, the lenders must dispose of the REO. This presents the foreclosure investor with the opportunity to negotiate with the lender for the purchase of the REO.

To market the REO, lenders employ real estate brokers, although, some large banks holding many REOs have a separate department engaged in the disposition of REOs. REO is available for purchase by anyone with the means to pay the purchase price. Thus, these assets have moved beyond the more limited realm of foreclosure and should be considered to be a part of all properties listed for sale on the market. The foreclosure investor deals with REO as the investor would with any other property, except that lenders have a greater incentive to dispose of the real estate than many other sellers. This factor makes REOs an attractive asset for investors.

PART II - TYPES OF PROPERTIES

Many foreclosure investors limit their investments to residential properties, particularly single family residences where the homeowner is losing or has lost the home through foreclosure. This is natural because most people are familiar with residences and bring an innate expertise to the table.

Although investing in single family homes is an excellent way to amass wealth, a foreclosure investor who limits himself to single family residences may be forgoing other opportunities that can be quite profitable. However, multi-family residential projects, as well as commercial and industrial properties, require efforts that are not found in single family residential investments. The foreclosure investor should examine all available options, learn their requirements and then decide whether to limit or extend his investment horizons.

This Part of the book will examine different types of properties that the foreclosure investor may encounter. Different uses of property involve a myriad of different considerations. For example, the management of an office building differs from the management of an apartment building which differs from the management of a single user manufacturing plant. Each of these property types are marketed differently. Their revenues streams differ. A big box retailer provides one kind of revenue stream and experiences one kind of vacancy rate, while a four-unit apartment building with tenants on month-to-month leases generates an entirely different kind of revenue stream and maintains a different kind of vacancy rate. The operating costs vary for different types of properties. The successful foreclosure investor becomes familiar with these differences and tailors his due diligence to address them.

A property's location must be subjected to the same rigorous analysis. Residential properties should be situated in or near employment centers; the employment opportunities will attract prospective buyers or tenants. Similarly, commercial or industrial users seek to locate where there is a pool of prospective employees. The demographic profile of an area will help the foreclosure investor assess the viability of an investment. Economic developments can be important. If a major technical manufacturer is moving into an area, there is potential to attract highly educated employees, with the ability to afford higher rents and to patronize high end merchants.

The foreclosure investor needs to formulate his exit strategy. Then, the analysis of the property should be conducted with the exit strategy in mind. For example, if the strategy for a single family residence is to expand and then sell, but the zoning does not allow an expansion, the exit strategy will fail.

This Part II will identify many of the characteristics of properties that the foreclosure investor should take into account in formulating the investment plan.

CHAPTER II -1   RESIDENTIAL PROPERTIES

Residential properties are properties in which people reside. These include single family homes, duplexes and triplexes, townhouses, multi-family apartment buildings, condominiums, cooperatives, mixed-use properties, mobile homes, homes under construction on which work has halted and vacant lots in residential subdivisions that are only partially completed. They include residences built as part of a recreational development with a golf course or tennis courts or a recreational center. They include residences located in age-restricted developments, such as a seniors-only development. Residential properties can also be categorized by their purpose. For example, they encompass one's primary residence, second homes, vacation homes and time shares.

The foreclosure investor who drives through residential neighborhoods can see the vast variety of housing types. The investor who began in a downtown area and drove out to the suburbs would see high-rise residential apartment buildings, townhouses and row homes, duplexes and triplexes located on lots with about six feet of space between houses and an alley running behind the houses, single family homes with low fences closely adjacent to their neighbors with garages in the rear yard, brick Tudor-style houses with a quarter acre of yard, one-story ranch homes with a back yard and a swing set, colonial houses located on one-half acre lots with attached garages, subdivision developments dating from the years after World War II, large new homes of two-acre lots, a gated community with homes on a golf course and, in troubled times, neighborhoods with abandoned homes, subdivisions with some lots developed, some homes partially completed and some empty lots with streets and little else.

When acquiring real property, the foreclosure investor must investigate several factual matters affecting the property. The process of factual investigation is referred to as "due diligence." We will describe the elements of due diligence that the foreclosure investor should investigate for each type of real property. At this point, we will discuss the due diligence that generally ought to be conducted when acquiring residential property.

Undoubtedly, the most important element of due diligence is title. Title is important for at least two reasons. First, the foreclosure investor wants to know that the seller actually owns the real property. Under the Statute of Frauds, a law which dates from seventeenth century England, interests in real property must be evidenced by a written document. Owners of real property give notice of their ownership by recording the document which created their interest in the land records of the county or town in which the real property is located. It is a simple matter to discover who owns real property. One need only consult the land records.

Of course, it is never quite that simple. In order to search the land records, the foreclosure investor needs to be able to identify the real property. Ordinarily, the land will be identified by its legal description. The description might be by metes and bounds. A metes and bounds description describes the land by direction and distance. For example, the description might be North 30° West 50 feet, then West 45° South 70 feet, then South 3° East 14 feet, etc. The property might also be described by reference to a recorded map. For example, the land could be described as Parcel 2 on Parcel Map 469 recorded in Book 23 at Page 809. The property might also be described by reference to another recorded document. For example, it could be described as that certain 40 acres described in the deed from John Fletcher to George Washington recorded March 23, 1789. It is critical that the legal description of the land being researched is the same as the land that the foreclosure investor is investigating. If the foreclosure investor intends to purchase Parcel A, but accidentally searches title to Parcel D, the information obtained is not only irrelevant and useless, but also completely misleading.

The second reason for conducting a title search is that the foreclosure investor wants to know if the property is subject to other interests that could adversely affect the investor's interest in the real property. Earlier, we discussed the requirement that a purchaser conduct an examination of real property. A purchaser takes title to real property subject to all matters that are discovered by an actual inspection of the property and all matters in which the purchaser had constructive notice. A foreclosure investor is deemed to have constructive notice of any matter that could have been discovered by inspecting the property and all matters that could have been discovered by reviewing the land records in which documents are recorded. The foreclosure investor discovers interests that have been recorded by either examining the land records personally or by hiring a title company to do a title search of the land records. The location of the land records will vary from state to state and county to county. In some states, the land records are maintained for each county by the county recorder. In other states, the land records may be filed in the municipal offices in the city or town in which the real property is located. In some counties, the land records have been reduced to electronic form and can be searched either online or at the county recorder's office by computer.

A foreclosure investor making an initial evaluation of the prospective property might wish to conduct a personal title search in order to conserve funds. However, if the investor intends to actually purchase the real property, it is essential that the investor obtain title insurance. The title insurance company will insure the investor that the land is in fact owned by the person shown in the records and that there are no encumbrances on the title other than those that are described by the title insurance company in a preliminary title report. Because the title insurance company must search the records in order to enable it to issue insurance, it can be more economical to utilize the title insurer to conduct a search on the investor's behalf. The benefit of title insurance is that if the title insurance company has made a mistake, it will indemnify the investor for any losses suffered. The title insurance ordinarily insures against fraud in the record which the individual investor would not be able to discover. For example, if the owner preceding the current owner did not have adequate authority to sell the property but did so anyway, that fact would be impossible to determine from a search of the records. The title insurance company will insure the foreclosure investor against that improper conveyance.

Another reason to obtain title insurance is that every institutional lender will require that title to its mortgage be insured in the amount of the mortgage loan. The foreclosure investor who utilizes financing in the acquisition of real property must obtain title insurance.

In some states the title insurance company will issue a title report or preliminary title report showing the ownership of the real property and the encumbrances and other interests affecting the title. In other states, the title insurance company delivers a commitment agreeing to issue a title insurance policy when certain conditions have been fulfilled.

The foreclosure investor reviews the title report or commitment and determines which encumbrances are acceptable and which ones are not. Of course, knowing that a title search is an essential part of every real property acquisition, the foreclosure investor should reserve the right to approve the state of title in his purchase agreement.

The factors that a foreclosure investor needs to consider when assessing such properties varies as greatly from property to property as do the types of housing themselves.. We begin with the most common type of residential property foreclosure that investors acquire.

A.   Single Family Homes

A single family home is a house that is detached from any other residence or other structure (other than a garage) and situated on a plot of land owned by the owner of the residence. The land can range from a plot that is entirely covered by the structure to multi-acre properties, such as a house on a four-acre parcel with a horse stable and a tennis court. A single family home affords privacy to the occupants. It also requires the owner to perform (or at least pay for) all maintenance and repairs, mow the lawn, rake the leaves and shovel the snow off of the sidewalks.

While many single family homes were constructed individually, a significant number of single family homes were constructed as part of a planned development. In those developments, the lots are subject to recorded covenants, conditions and restrictions, commonly referred to as "CC&R's." The CC&R's regulate how the land can be developed and used. CC&Rs can regulate the height and other dimensions of structures, the distance between the lot lines and the house's footprint, the architectural style, the materials used and the colors of the materials. Any deviations must be approved by the development's architectural committee before they can be undertaken. The use of the property may also be regulated. For example, in a planned unit development in Southern California, a homeowner was prevented from setting up a basketball backboard and hoop next to the driveway in the front yard because they were prohibited by the development's CC&Rs. Some developers believe that uniform appearance of houses in a development increase the value of the individual lots in the development. Whether this is always the case is for each foreclosure investor to decide. However, an investor who acquires property subject to CC&Rs must be sure that the investor's plans for refurbishing the property comply with the CC&Rs.

One advantage of limiting investments to single family residences is that the foreclosure investor only needs to negotiate with one party. The borrower is usually an individual or a married couple. In other residential properties, there are tenants that the investor must take into consideration. In a duplex, the borrower shares a party wall with the owner of the adjoining unit which may raise issues. Also, most commercial, multi-family residential properties are often owned by a partnership or limited liability company with several members that have a say in how the property is dealt with and discarded.

Another advantage is that it should be easier to inspect and evaluate the condition of the structure. A knowledgeable home purchaser retains a professional inspector to inspect the property. Consequently, there are a large number of experienced inspectors that the foreclosure investor can hire to inspect the property. Items that a foreclosure investor needs to consider when inspecting the property include (i) presence of radon; (ii) termites; (iii) underground storage tanks for fuel oil; (iv) septic system; (v) quality of the water for properties served by a private water well (i.e., properties that are not on the municipal water system); (vi) condition of the roof; (vii) condition of the foundation; (viii) flooding in the basement; (ix) condition of heating and air conditioning system; (x) lead paint; and (xi) insulation. These are basic matters that the home purchaser investigates.

The foreclosure investor should not limit his inspection to the property itself. The neighborhood and the town are important considerations that should not be overlooked. If the neighborhood is in decline, the value of the house will be negatively impacted. If the neighborhood is being gentrified and is becoming more desirable, the investor can ride the upward movement of the neighborhood's attraction to greater profits. When evaluating the community, the investor should consider the school system and the property tax regime. The value of real estate benefits from a first rate school system. A community that watches its expenditures to manage its tax burden also benefits the real estate investor.

One disadvantage of a single family home is that, unlike the owner of a commercial or industrial property, the owner of a residence has a tremendous emotional investment in the property. The borrower may have lived in the house for many years and raised his children in that house. The property is not a house; it is the borrower's home. The borrower can be very unwilling to deal with a foreclosure investor, at least at the outset of the foreclosure. On the other hand, if the borrower is motivated to preserve his or her credit, the investor should be able to gain access to the property to conduct an inspection. One thing to consider is that a home owner who is motivated may not become motivated until the last minute. This circumstance requires the foreclosure investor to be ready to react quickly when the borrower decides to dispose of the property.

A phenomenon has arisen in the recent recession that can severely impact the foreclosure investor, so the investor must be aware of its significance. The foreclosure investor who invests in a single family home usually plans to either sell the residence or rent it to a tenant. Even if the investor intends to sell, but later finds that the market has frozen, the investor still has the alternative of renting the property. However, the new phenomenon eliminates the rental option. It has been reported recently that some towns and some planned developments have restricted or prohibited the rental of residential units. The stated reasons are that tenants are noisy or rowdy, neglectful of the property, messy, they vandalize the property and their presence detracts from the value and aesthetics of the town or subdivision. These restrictions have been imposed even in situations where property values have been hit hard and renting may be the only way that a homeowner can retain ownership of his home. Rental restrictions can devastate an investor's business plan. Therefore, the investor must determine whether any rental restrictions exist or are being considered.

B.   Duplexes and Townhouses

A duplex is a type of townhouse, as is a triplex. A townhouse is constructed as one of a series of residences connected together with party walls between each residence. There can be any number of residences connected together. If there are two units, the structure is called a duplex. If there are three units, the structure is called a triplex. The owner of each unit owns the land underlying the unit. The unit can have a front or rear yard, but, except in the case of duplexes, the adjoining unit occupies the space where a side yard would be located. Townhouses, sometimes referred to as row houses, can be found in the urban centers of older cities, such as New York and Chicago. Townhouses can also be found in new planned unit developments such as age-restricted senior developments clustered around recreational amenities.

Townhouses have the disadvantage of sharing one or two party walls, so there is reliance on the owner of the adjoining unit. If a foreclosure investor is considering a unit in a townhouse development in a depressed neighborhood, abandonment of the adjoining unit can negatively affect the unit that the investor is considering. The impact

58

can be direct, such as leaks through the party wall, or indirect, such as trash accumulating on the adjoining unit's front stoop.

In a planned unit development, the owner of the townhouse owns the land under the townhouse and probably a small yard. The owner acquires rights to use other parts of the development, such as the private roadways, and amenities such as a recreation center that will likely be owned by a homeowners' association in which the townhouse owner belongs to as a member. The townhouse and all other parts of the development will be subject to CC&Rs and governed by the homeowners' association.

A foreclosure investor who wishes to lease a unit to a tenant will have the comfort of greater security because of the adjoining units. That is, even if the tenant is away from the unit, it is likely that the occupants of the adjoining units will be present and able to discourage vandalism.

Purchasing a townhouse has most of the same advantages and disadvantages of purchasing a single family home. One similar advantage is that the foreclosure investor needs to negotiate with only one party. The borrower is usually an individual or a married couple. However, as noted above, the nature of a townhouse includes the owner of the adjoining unit with whom the investor may have to be concerned.

The inspection is similar to that of a single family house. The structure itself, the neighborhood and the community should all be investigated.

The disadvantages are also similar. The townhouse is the borrower's home, and that can give rise to both difficulties and opportunities, just as it can with a single family home.

C.   Condominiums and Cooperatives

Condominiums and cooperatives are usually multi-family residential structures in which each resident occupies a unit or an apartment.

Under a condominium scheme, the unit owned by the borrower consists of air space plus an undivided interest in the common elements (described below). The unit owner also acquires ownership shares in the condominium association, which may be a limited liability company or a corporation. These shares go with the unit. The air space is the space within the interior side of the four walls, floor and ceiling of the unit. If the unit contains more than one floor, the air space is that space contained within the interior side of the outermost walls, floor and ceiling of the unit. The unit owner has the right of exclusive occupancy of the unit. The physical parts of the building, the utilities that serve more than one unit and the land underlying the structure are owned by the condominium association. The association also owns and operates any amenities such as a recreation center or tennis courts. These physical parts are owned and used in common by all unit owners and are referred to as the "common elements." The unit owners share the right in common with other unit owners to use the common elements. The unit owners pay a monthly fee to the condo association, and the association repairs the building and performs the ordinary maintenance and landscaping. If there is a mortgage on the entire structure, the association pays that mortgage.

Condominiums are creatures of state and local law. They are formed by preparing and filing, or recording, the condominium documents in the local land records or other appropriate filing offices. The condominium documents are comprised of a declaration of covenants, conditions and restrictions that complies with the requirements of the applicable law, a plat or plat showing the land and manner in which the air space is divided among the units, the articles creating the association, the association's bylaws and any other rules and regulations that the association may adopt from time to time. A foreclosure investor who is considering acquiring a condominium unit needs to become familiar with the declaration governing the condominium.

The condominium is operated by the condominium association. The condominium unit owners are the members of the association. The association is governed by a board of directors who are members of the association and elected by members. The condominium declaration prescribes how the association is governed, the procedure for electing the board and the responsibilities of the board. It may also describe the rights of the unit owners if a fire destroys all or part of the building. For example, if the condominium is a large apartment building, the unit owners each own a block of air space suspended above the ground. If the building burns to the ground, it would be difficult to reconstruct the building in the precise location it was originally built, so the air spaces need to be collapsed into the land and re-created when the building is completed. Alternatively, the unit owners may elect to retain the fire insurance proceeds and abandon the condominium.

Condominium unit owners must comply with the declaration of covenants, conditions and restrictions (sometimes referred to as the "CC&Rs").
Since the association is responsible for the maintenance and repair of the exterior, it makes the determination on certain matters affecting the exterior of the owner's unit. For example, a unit owner must get the association's approval to install a window air conditioner because the air conditioner impacts the appearance of the building's exterior. Any interior modifications that affect the structure, such as installing an indoor spa with expanded plumbing to the basement of the building, require association approval. The declaration also describes any limitations on the use of the unit. A condominium in a mixed-use zone may permit ground floor units to be used for commercial purposes. It may also prohibit the leasing of any units, or occupancy of any units, to any persons other than the owner's family. If a foreclosure investor is acquiring a condominium unit for the purpose of renting it out, this kind of restriction is extremely relevant. The foreclosure investor should investigate any restrictions on the use of the unit.

The units are owned individually by the unit owners. They can be sold, leased (if permitted), mortgaged and passed down to the owner's heirs. However, it should be noted, that there may be an approval process that the seller and buyer need to complete in order to transfer the unit. In addition, the unit owners are responsible for the maintenance and repair of their own units, and the association is responsible for the maintenance and repair of the common elements.

Foreclosure investors need to investigate the financial health of the condominium. Condominium buildings recently constructed in hot real estate markets now stand partially occupied. The unit owners and the developer must bear the costs of maintenance, repair and taxes. If the developer goes bankrupt, the unit owners will be saddled with costs far greater than they originally anticipated. Similarly, even if the building is fully occupied, a condominium without adequate reserves will assess charges to the unit owners for any major work that is necessary. That assessment is in addition to monthly association fees.

Notably, a condominium association will place a lien on the unit for any unpaid fees and assessments.

Under a cooperative scheme, the borrower owns shares in the cooperative corporation, or limited liability company, and leases the unit from the cooperative. The cooperative owns the building. The borrower's interest is that of a tenant in the building and a shareholder in the cooperative. The cooperative also owns and operates any amenities. The unit owners pay a monthly fee to the cooperative, and the cooperative uses those fees for routine maintenance, repairs and to pay taxes and insurance. If there is a mortgage on the entire structure, and there often is, the cooperative makes the mortgage payment.

The cooperative documents comprise of the proprietary lease, the certificate of incorporation and the bylaws of the cooperative. The bylaws may contain the rules and regulations for the building. The proprietary lease is the same for every tenant. The unit occupants cannot negotiate different deals with the cooperative, which is the landlord.

The building is operated by the cooperative. The tenants are the shareholders of the cooperative. The cooperative is governed by a board of directors who are shareholders and elected by the other shareholders.

Borrowers finance the purchase of units by pledging their leasehold interest and shares of stock as collateral. Cooperative boards ordinarily require a larger down payment than is required for a condominium. In some buildings, financing is prohibited; the foreclosure investor must pay the entire purchase price in cash.

Cooperative tenants must comply with the terms of the proprietary lease. The lease determines whether the tenant can make modifications to the unit. Ordinarily, such work requires approval of the board of directors.

The units are owned by the cooperative. The tenant can sell its proprietary lease and shares in the cooperative, but the cooperative's board must approve the buyer. This can limit the marketability of a unit. Also, the cooperative may prohibit or restrict subleasing. It may also prohibit occupancy by any persons other than the owner's family. If a foreclosure investor is acquiring a cooperative unit for the purpose of renting it out, the investor must inquire about this kind of restriction. The foreclosure investor should know the terms of the proprietary lease and the cooperative's rules and regulations.

The advantages and disadvantages of dealing with a condominium unit or a cooperative unit are somewhat more complicated than with a single family home. To begin with, the foreclosure investor who is considering the acquisition of a cooperative unit must obtain the approval of the cooperative board. The cooperative's rules may prohibit or strictly limit the investor's ability to finance the purchase. A condominium may also place restrictions on the sale of a unit, and those restrictions can make the transaction more difficult for the investor. Like a single family house, the unit is most likely the borrower's home invoking emotional attachment. If the building is only partially occupied, the unit will bear a disproportionate share of the costs of operating and maintaining the building. Condominium units, especially in vacation areas, are often owned by investors who rent out the units. During a recession when travel is restricted, the owners of those units may have difficulty making their mortgage payments, and the units may go into foreclosure. That may be the very reason that the unit you are considering is coming onto the foreclosure market. For this reason, the foreclosure investor should find out the ratio of owners to tenants who are occupying the building. If most occupants are tenants rather than owners, that could be a red flag for the investor. Of course, in recessionary times, when the cost of travel overseas is too expensive, vacationers may find appeal in renting a condominium unit in a in a desirable vacation location closer to home. This suggests that if the foreclosure investor is relying on vacation rentals to make a profit, the unit must be in a desirable location. Another reason for the red flag when there is a high ratio of tenants to owners is that owners who do not occupy their units may have less interest in maintaining the building in first class condition. They may vote in favor of a lower maintenance budget. Also, there may be financing concerns in a building only partially occupied by its owners. Mortgages on units in condominium projects where more than half of the units are rented out by the owners cannot be underwritten by Fannie Mae or Freddie Mac, who refuse to underwrite mortgages in condo projects where a majority of units are rentals.

In a constricted economy, purchasing condominium units, even in fully occupied buildings, carries other risks. It has been reported that in the recession beginning in 2008, condominium owners began to default on their common charges. These defaults occurred in buildings that had been recently constructed. In these buildings, the unit owners did not have enough time to build up equity in their units, and in many cases, the units went underwater. The condominium association had liens to secure the payment of the common charges, but they were ineffective. If the association foreclosed on the unit's lien, the due on sale clause would be triggered for the unit. The mortgage holders would have had the right to foreclose which would have wiped out the lien the condo association was trying to enforce. If the association desired to preserve the lien, it would have been forced to pay off the mortgage on the condo unit. Understandably, associations were not willing or able to do that, so the liens went uncollected and the remaining unit owners had to shoulder the unpaid common charges. Those owners were not able to sell their units because no lenders would finance units in a building with a substantial number of defaults on common charges or a considerable number of vacant units.

In formerly hot markets, where there are many single family homes on the market at depressed prices, the attractiveness of condominium or cooperative units are negatively impacted. Families that could not afford a single family home during boom times can now afford one during depressed times. During the boom, they could have purchased a cooperative or condominium, but during the recession, they can buy a single family home. Even so, the cost of a unit is usually less than comparable space in a single family home, so the unit may be affordable to a wider range of prospective purchasers.

An advantage for the foreclosure investor that intends to rent out the unit is that the condominium or cooperative board manages the building. The foreclosure investor need not concern himself with many maintenance issues. Another advantage is for the foreclosure investor is the possibility that condominium units may be available at discount prices. Lenders that foreclose on condominium units must pay the common charges. This obligation may spur the dumping of units at depressed prices at auctions. Also, if a majority of the units are sold to investors and rented to tenants, the investors can take control of the association's board of directors and seek to improve the return on their investments by electing to defer maintenance. This result can both benefit and negatively impact a foreclosure investor. The deferral reduces costs and improves the rate of return on the investment. However, the deferral reduces the value of the unit, and the transient nature of tenant occupancy may hurt the quality of the building which affects the value of the unit. The foreclosure investor must carefully consider all of these possibilities when contemplating purchase of condominium or cooperative units.

Regardless of the condition of the economy, there are other due diligence items for the investor when purchasing a condominium or a cooperative apartment. The investor needs to carefully review the declaration creating the condominium or the proprietary lease governing the use of the unit in the cooperative. Do these documents prohibit any activities that are important to the investor or that might make the unit less desirable to a tenant or a buyer? Is renting permitted or restricted? The investor should examine the financial condition of the condominium association or cooperative corporation. Are any major repairs being contemplated? Has a reserve fund been established to pay for major repairs? Is it adequately funded? The foreclosure investor should review the minutes of the board meetings where these kinds of matters are recorded. Do the common charges cover all of the costs of operating the building or complex? Do the common charges seem to be reasonable or excessive? Have there been any defaults in the payment of common charges? The investor should consider the management of the building or facility. Did the condominium elect to manage itself, or did the association elect to employ a professional manager? The foreclosure investor needs to know the status of the development. Has the developer completed the project and sold all of the units? If not, the developer will continue to have ownership interests for its unsold units and will have votes on the board. In some cases, the developer retains control of the board until all units have been sold. This can impact the desirability of the project, especially if the developer defaults and a lender forecloses on the unsold units, thereby taking control of the development.

The foreclosure investor should be able to find answers to many of these questions by reviewing the condominium declaration, the association's bylaws, the rules and regulations governing the common elements and the most recent audited financial statements.

D. Multi-family Apartment Buildings

A multi-family apartment building is a residential structure composed of apartments and may feature amenities such as a swimming pool or exercise facility. The apartments are leased or rented to tenants. The borrower owns the building and the underlying land.

Acquiring a multi-family apartment building differs in one fundamental way from the acquisition of a single family home or townhouse or condominium. Usually, the foreclosure investor intends to rehabilitate and sell the residence. On the other hand, the foreclosure investor who is contemplating the purchase of a multi-family apartment building intends to become a landlord. . Of course, a foreclosure investor can always turn around and sell an apartment building, but any prospective purchaser would intend to keep the property and operate it as an apartment building. Therefore, an apartment building must be analyzed not as a quick sale but as a long-term hold. The tenants create the property's value.

The value in a multi-family apartment building, as in any commercial or industrial property, derives from the income stream. The income stream is the result of the rents generated by tenants occupying the building minus the costs of owning and operating the building. An apartment building in foreclosure presumably has an inadequate income stream. A foreclosure investor should evaluate the income stream to determine if the revenue can be increased or the costs can be decreased. Revenue can be increased by raising rents, increasing the occupancy level of the building or by attracting new tenants that will pay higher rents. Costs can be decreased through efficient management of the property, by shifting some of the operating responsibilities to the tenants, by renegotiating contracts with third party service providers, such as the cleaning company that cleans an apartment after it is vacated, by installing energy efficient fixtures, such as a new furnace or air conditioning system, or by installing double or triple pane windows to reduce heating costs. Thus, one essential element of an investor's due diligence when examining rental property is the income stream. The foreclosure investor should review the rent roll for the property. If available, the investor should review the income and expense statements for the property. Also, a review of the property's vacancy rate will give the investor a sense of the attractiveness of the building to prospective tenants.

The critical part of the income stream is the leases. Without enforceable leases, there is no income. If the leases place an undue economic burden on the landlord, the costs cannot be managed. Accordingly, the foreclosure investor considering the purchase of an apartment building needs to review all of the leases. The investor should also examine the borrower's records on the tenants' financial condition. The tenant financials can be found in the applications that tenants completed when they entered into the leases which should be located in the tenant files. After the investor acquires the property, the investor should ask prospective tenants for references from their previous landlords and recent pay slips to show that the tenant is employed at a salary adequate to pay the rent. The investor should also order a credit report on prospective tenants. If possible, the investor should obtain estoppel certificates from any commercial tenants in the property. Estoppel certificates are discussed in more detail below. The investor should confirm that the landlord has all security deposits. These should be transferred to the investor. Otherwise, the investor will be liable to the tenants for the amount of all security deposits not applied to defaults or the last month's rent.

This level of due diligence may not be possible in a foreclosure setting. If the borrower is not cooperative, it can be risky to bid on an apartment building in which no financial due diligence has been conducted. The foreclosure investor needs to have a cooperating borrower for the purchase of an apartment building to make any sense.

Of course, the foreclosure investor will make the same kind of physical inspection of the structure as would be done in the purchase of a home. However, in apartment buildings, code compliance can be more of an issue because the welfare of the tenants becomes a concern. There may be reports of code inspectors available for review at City Hall. Also, a building is usually larger and more complex than a house so the inspection is more demanding. For example, the investor may decide to retain a structural engineer to inspect the building. The investor should also do an environmental inspection of the property.

The location of the property is important. A building located close to an employment center may be attractive to potential tenants, but a building that is the only apartment building in the area can have equal appeal due to its uniqueness. The investor needs to evaluate these factors.

The means of valuing a multi-family apartment building differ from the way a foreclosure investor would value a single family residence. An appraiser values a residence by using comparable sales. In the comparable sales approach, an appraiser looks at recent sales of homes that are comparable in size and location to the residence being valued. The appraiser estimates the value of the property through those other sales. As noted above, an apartment building's value derives from its income stream. The income stream is used to calculate a capitalization rate, often referred to as the "cap rate." The capitalization rate is the investor's return on his or her investment, calculated as if the property in question were purchased with all cash. To calculate the cap rate, the investor first calculates the net operating income from the property. The net operating income is the revenue from rents and any other revenue, such as monies earned from the operation of a laundry room, minus the costs of operating and maintaining the building. The net operating income is then divided by the purchase price of the building.

For example, if a foreclosure investor is contemplating paying a price of $2,500,000 for a building that has a net operating income of $350,000 per annum, the cap rate would be 0.14 or 14 percent. That, in effect, is the return on the capital invested in the property. There are more sophisticated formulae (such as those that take into account the effects of borrowing) for calculating rates of return on investment that can be found by searching the Internet.

E.   Undeveloped Residential Lot

Another possible residential investment is the purchase of an undeveloped lot in a residential subdivision. A number of developers of residential subdivisions have lost their financing, and their developments are standing unfinished.

Investing in an undeveloped lot is the riskiest and most costly investment. The foreclosure investor must be sure that all streets and utilities have been installed or he must pay for their installation. The investor then must either develop the lot, or find a buyer willing to purchase and build his own home in the unfinished subdivision. For the typical foreclosure investor, this is not a promising route to follow.

CHAPTER II - 2   COMMERCIAL PROPERTIES

Commercial properties are the second category of properties that a foreclosure investor should consider. Commercial properties are buildings, including shopping malls and neighborhood shopping centers, occupied by tenants conducting their businesses in the buildings. Similar to multi-family apartment buildings, the rental stream is the critical element to consider.

The value in any commercial property derives from the income stream. In order to finance an investment in a commercial property, the foreclosure investor must demonstrate that the income stream is sufficient to cover the debt service. This analysis is vital to the lender and the foreclosure investor. Debt service means the amount of the payment for principal and interest of the loan. If the income stream does not cover the debt service, then the investor must pay a portion of the debt service and operating costs out of his or her own pocket. To determine whether there is sufficient debt service coverage, the investor adds up all of the operating expenses. These expenses include the costs of maintenance and repairs, property taxes, insurance premiums, building utilities, management fees and a vacancy factor such as five percent of the rents. The total operating costs are subtracted from the total income to determine the net operating income, referred to as the "NOI." Debt service is not included in the operating expenses. If the numbers are based on monthly figures, the investor multiplies the monthly net operating income by 12 to determine the annual NOI. Finally, the investor divides the annual NOI by the annual debt service on the loan. The result of this division is the debt service ratio. The foreclosure investor should expect a lender to require a debt service ratio for commercial properties of at least 1.25 to 1. In other words, the annual net operating income from the commercial property should be at least 1.25 times the amount of principal and interest that the investor will pay annually on the loan.

If the income stream is insufficient to generate an adequate debt service coverage ratio, the investor needs to either reduce the purchase price or increase the net income by increasing the rental stream.

If the commercial property is in foreclosure, it is likely that the property has an inadequate income stream. There are ways that a foreclosure investor can improve the income stream by either increasing the revenue or by decreasing the costs. There are basic ways of increasing revenue: raising the rents or increasing the building's occupancy level or renting to a class of tenants able to pay higher rents. There are customary ways of decreasing costs: improving the property's management, entering into lower cost contracts with new service providers or improving the efficiency of the building's fixtures and installations. In all cases, the objective is to reconfigure the property to produce an adequate net income stream. To help analyze whether the property can be reconfigured, the foreclosure investor's financial due diligence of a commercial property should include a review the income and expense statements for the property and a review of the property's vacancy rate.

The foreclosure investor's financial due diligence of a commercial property should also include the property's income and expense statements, the rent roll, the leases, the property's insurance premiums and utility bills. These are all documents that the investor's lender will require.

Because the source of the income stream is the rents, and the rents derive from the leases, the investor must focus with special care on the leases with the tenants. The foreclosure investor considering a commercial building needs to review all of the leases. An experienced investor usually makes an abstract of each lease as it is reviewed. The abstracts can be shared with the investor's lender. The abstract can be on a form prepared by the investor that contains all of the information important to the investor and to the investor's lender. By using a standard form, the investor can identify leases that are missing an important element or that have unique provisions. Notable items include the term of the lease. If the majority of leases will expire within six months after the closing of the acquisition, there may be a problem. On the other hand, if the rents are well below market rates, an early expiration date permits the investor to increase the rents when the term expires. Another item of importance is the rent. Is the rent below market? Is the rent subject to an escalation clause that causes the rents to increase over time? Is there a consumer price index escalator?

Reviewing the leases is futile if the tenants deny that they are subject to the leases, deny owing any rent, or claim that the borrower as landlord is in default. For this reason, the investor should obtain estoppel certificates from each of the tenants. An "estoppel certificate" is a written document signed by each tenant in which the tenant confirms that the lease is currently in effect, that the lease has not been amended (or describing the amendments), that the landlord is not in default under the lease (or describing the defaults), that the tenant has not prepaid the rent (or describing the prepayments) and describing any options the tenant may hold to purchase the property, lease additional space or extend or terminate the lease. If the landlord is required to perform any obligations such as constructing leasehold improvements for the tenant, the estoppel certificate will confirm that the landlord has completed its obligations. The term "estoppel" comes

71

from the legal concept of "estopped" which means that the person making a statement or representation cannot later be allowed to deny that statement or representation. Why would a tenant complete an estoppel certificate? The tenant completes the certificate because most commercial leases contain a provision requiring the tenant to sign and deliver such a certificate and authorizing the landlord to do so on the tenant's behalf if the tenant fails to do so. The lease usually authorizes third parties, such as lenders and purchasers, to rely on the tenant's estoppel certificate.

Although the value of a commercial property derives from the income stream, it can also be affected by the quality of the tenants. Strong tenants with long-term leases support a higher valuation than weak tenants with long-term leases. Unfortunately, in a major economic crisis, it can be a true challenge to identify companies that are strong.

When the foreclosure investor acquires a commercial property, the investor becomes liable to the tenants for the security deposits. Accordingly, the investor should confirm that the landlord has all of the security deposits, and arrange to have the deposits transferred to the investor, or reduce the purchase price by the amount of the deposits.

Since the value of the property depends on the rental income stream, the foreclosure investor needs assurance that the stream will not be interrupted. Rents stop when a tenant leaves the property and that cannot be prevented. Rents also stop if there is a casualty, such as a fire, that causes the tenant to leave the premises during the period of repair. Foreclosure investors that are acquiring commercial property must carry rental insurance that will insure against an interruption in the rental income stream for the duration of the tenant's absence from the property.

There are matters, in addition to the financials, that a foreclosure investor should investigate when contemplating the acquisition of a commercial property. One very important matter is the lawful uses of the property. A building can be used only for the uses specified in the certificate of occupancy for the building. The certificate of occupancy is often referred to as the "CO" (pronounced "See Oh") or the "C of

O." The foreclosure investor should not assume that the purposes for which the tenants are using the property are authorized uses. There are reported cases where the municipal government shut down the use of a building after the building inspector discovered that a tenant was using its premises for something inconsistent with the C of O. The investor must review the C of O. The investor's lender will conduct such a review, and the investor should do likewise.

Another area of concern is the building's compliance with the requirements of the Americans With Disabilities Act (commonly called the "ADA"). Buildings constructed after a certain date or modified in a certain way must be made accessible to disabled persons. If the ADA applies to the building the investor is examining, and the building does not comply, the investor will incur additional costs to bring the building into compliance by making it handicap accessible. The foreclosure investor should become familiar with local building code requirements and the federal regulations that implement the ADA's Accessibility Guidelines. The investor should note that the regulations distinguish between commercial buildings that have public accommodations, such as restaurants, health clubs, doctors' offices and retail operations that are open to the general public, and commercial buildings that are not open to the general public such as private offices that open to the tenants' employees. The use of the commercial building affects the accessibility requirements.

Accessibility to high-rise commercial buildings can be an issue if the elevators or escalators do not function properly. The foreclosure investor should therefore include on his due diligence checklist the elevator and escalator maintenance contracts.

A cost that commercial properties bear that is not present in residential properties is the cost of building out the space. Most residential units are in a form that is acceptable to nearly everyone. The unit may not be as elegant as the buyer or tenant desires, but if it has a kitchen and a bathroom and a living room and a bedroom, the basics are covered. In contrast, commercial space that is suitable for one tenant is not suitable for another tenant. For example, the layout and furnishings of a clothing store are unsuitable for a bookstore. Even if the shape of the space works for two different tenants, each tenant may have its own "look" that its space must convey, and the shelves, counters and display cases must be acceptable to the tenant. Thus, an open rectangular space could house either a grocery store or a pharmacy, but the grocery store will need stoves and meat lockers and freezers and display cases that the pharmacy would not use. The cost of building out the space or installing the tenant's trade fixtures must be negotiated. Even if the tenant pays the cost of the build-out, the premises will be vacant for a period of time while the build-out proceeds and there will be no rent stream during that time.

There are certain matters that the foreclosure investor should review regardless of the property type. These are title review, the physical condition of the property and maintenance and operation of the parking lot or parking garage. The economic prospects of the area also take on importance. The foreclosure investor needs to evaluate the area's demographic composition and income levels. The foreclosure investor can obtain information on unemployment rates by going to the web site of the Bureau of Labor Statistics. The BLS shows unemployment rates and other relevant information by regions within the United States.

We have noted that the value of commercial buildings derives from their income stream. In a distressed economy, the demand for space will usually contract. Some commercial tenants may cut back or go out of business. Other tenants may decide not to renew their leases. This frees up rental space, increasing the number of vacancies and making the supply of space greater. The increase in available space is combined with a reduction in demand for the space. This combination results in lower rents. In other words, the property values go down, and the foreclosure investor can acquire them cheaper than in boom times. Also, with an increase in available space, developers of new commercial buildings will postpone or abandon their development plans. As a result, when the economy starts to recover, there will be fewer buildings to compete for tenants.

Another area of due diligence that the foreclosure investor needs to address is the cost of operating the property. In some foreclosure settings, the actual operating costs may not be made available to the investor. The investor would then prepare his own "pro forma" financial statements. A "pro forma" is one or more financial statements that contain assumptions or are based on conditions. For example, the investor may have a copy of the rent roll which alerts him to the amount of monthly rents. However, if several leases are due to expire, the investor can assume the amount of rent that new leases may generate and prepare a budget using a revenue amount based on the assumed rental amount. The resulting budget would be a "pro forma" budget. The investor will estimate the costs. If available, historic records provide a good starting point. If they are not available, an investor can consult with a property management company with experience in the area. It must be noted that costs vary from property to property, not only because one property may have more efficient operating systems, but also because the amount and type of costs borne by the tenants in one property can differ substantially from another property. Investors should also be mindful of the effect the acquisition will have on the real property taxes, which will change based on the purchase price.

The foregoing concerns apply to all commercial buildings. However, different types of buildings have their own concerns.

A.   Office Buildings

Office buildings can have a single tenant occupant or multi-tenant occupancies. Some office buildings may have retail or other non-office uses such as a bank on the ground floor. The typical office lease recognizes that an office tenant may find that the way the prior tenant had laid out or decorated the premises does not suit the present tenant's requirements. Therefore, the new tenant needs to remodel the space. The work of remodeling usually entails the demolition of the existing installations and the construction and installation of new improvements. These types of improvement are referred to as "tenant improvements." The office lease usually provides a period of time during which the tenant improvements are constructed. That period will normally be rent free. The work can be done either by the landlord or the tenant. If the landlord does the work, the cost can be included in the rent and spread over the term of the lease.

Office building tenants demand more services from landlords. The premises need to be cleaned every evening. The landlord will likely want to control access to the building's utilities and similar areas, so he will probably prefer to provide the cleaning service himself. The landlord provides utilities including heating, ventilating and air conditioning ("HVAC"). Howver, there may be a separate charge for these services, especially if the tenant places a large demand on the HVAC system, such as in the case of a specially air-conditioned computer room.

Office space is normally leased based on the amount of square footage contained in the space. There are several measurements of square footage. One pertinent measurement is the rentable square footage and another is the usable square footage. The usable square footage is the amount of space that the tenant can actually use for its business in its premises. The rentable square footage is the useable square footage plus, on a multi-tenant floor, the tenant's share of corridors, elevator lobbies, restrooms and other common spaces. Landlords charge rent based on the rentable square footage which is measured differently in every building.

Sizable high-rise office buildings are too costly and management intensive for the typical new investor to start with. However, in suburban neighborhoods there may be one or two-story office buildings that can be suitable for the foreclosure investor. In normal market conditions, the investor in an office building runs the risk that an economic downturn may drive away tenants and impact the office building's cash flow. In a major recession, that risk has already occurred, and the investor may be in a better position to evaluate the soundness of the building's cash flow.

Office properties tend to be more volatile in value than other commercial investments. One reason is that office leases tend to have shorter terms than leases for major retailers or manufacturers. Since there is a more frequent turnover of tenants, the rental revenue stream can be interrupted. Also, office properties tend to be more responsive to market conditions that can vary over time, and therefore the rental stream and the value of the property is more volatile.

B.   Restaurants

Properties that contain restaurants carry risks that do not apply to other kinds of properties. Restaurants consume water and power at a much higher rate than other commercial properties, and the foreclosure investor needs to address the consumption of utilities. Restaurant businesses have a much higher rate of failure than do other commercial businesses. If the building contains both a restaurant and offices or other retail uses, there could be an issue with cleanliness. A vigilant health department will keep a restaurant clean, but even well inspected restaurants have been known to generate roaches and other critters that can invade the premises of other tenants. The success of the investment depends on the acumen and skill of the tenant. Of course, even in ordinary offices, if a business tenant mismanages its business, it can go into default. National chain restaurant operators have a greater chance of success

Restaurant properties in suburban areas need adequate parking. If the property does not have sufficient parking, the investor should pass on the deal.

C.   Retail

There are different kinds of retail tenants. There are the national chain stores that occupy the entirety of a large, stand-alone building which is usually situated either on its own lot or in a strip mall or shopping center. These are customarily referred to as "big box" retailers because their stores resemble big boxes with a single occupant. There are national chain stores that occupy smaller space in a strip mall or neighborhood shopping center. One example of such a retailer is Radio Shack. There are also local or regional retailers that occupy space in a strip mall or neighborhood shopping center. There are national, regional and local grocery stores or pharmacies. Some may be stand-alone, while others may be the largest store in a strip mall or neighborhood shopping center. There are stores on the ground floor of a row building in which there may be offices or apartments on the second floor. Each type has its own unique concerns.

A big box property typically has a major national retail chain store as the tenant. Most big box or small box tenancies involve a "triple net" lease. Such a lease will involve a credit-worthy tenant who undertakes to pay real estate taxes, maintenance and insurance. A net or triple net lease should be contrasted to a gross lease. A gross lease requires the tenant to pay rent but not operating costs. The landlord pays operating costs, and therefore the rent received by the landlord represents a gross profit. The rent becomes a net profit only after the landlord pays these periodic costs. However, because the tenant pays these costs under a triple net lease, the rent is net to the landlord. Hence, the lease is called a net lease. Sometimes a tenant pays just one of these costs, such as insurance. Sometimes a tenant pays two of these costs. Often, a tenant pays all three of these costs. The type of lease in which the tenant pays some or all of these operating costs can be referred to as a "net" lease or a "net net net" lease or a "triple net" lease. The rent stream is a steady amount that does not vary even if taxes or insurance premiums increase. This helps make the lease more financeable. Because the tenant handles the maintenance, the landlord has minimal management responsibilities. In return for the benefits, the amount of rent is less than in the case of a gross lease. There are also hidden risks relating to the nature of the tenant and the building.

With a major, credit-worthy tenant, the ability of the landlord to negotiate the lease may be more limited than in the case of lesser tenants. The foreclosure investor should give any triple net lease a careful review and look for non-standard provisions.

An advantage of big box properties is that they typically have more credit worthy tenants. A tenant with a high credit rating will give value to the property. On the other hand, a retailer with a lower credit rating will produce a retail property with a lower market value. Naturally, as all investors are learning, a tenant with a national presence can still either go bankrupt or elect to close a store. Therefore, the foreclosure investor must evaluate a big box property both on the basis of the tenant's credit worthiness and on the basis of standard real property analysis, such as the terms of the lease, the condition of the building and the property's location. A disadvantage of a big box tenant is that if the tenant does go bankrupt, the big box will be harder to lease because there are fewer major retail tenants.

The building may not be configured to another retailer's specifications. If there are no big box tenants in the market, the big box might need to be subdivided into a multi-tenant configuration that can be costly.

First floor retail store tenants want street traffic. Accordingly, the more exposure they have to the street, the more value the premises possess. This street exposure is referred to as "front foot." The rent payable for a retail premises will increase with the amount of front footage. Similarly, retail premises on the second floor are less desirable and have a lower rental value.

Any shopping center, including a neighborhood shopping center or strip mall, should have a good mix of tenants. A center with six stores, five of which are dry cleaners and laundromats, will not maximize the value of the retail space because the tenants will be competing with each other and taking revenue from each other. It is preferable to have retail tenants that complement one another. In larger shopping centers and malls, the leases with the retailers will often have a clause limiting the goods and services that a tenant can offer so that the tenants do not compete with one another and cannibalize sales.

One reason commercial landlords want to protect the revenues of their tenants is that many commercial leases have a percentage rent provision that includes as a part of the rent a percentage of the tenant's sales from the premises. Typically, the tenant will pay a minimum rent plus a percentage of sales above a base amount. An issue to be negotiated between the landlord and tenant is the definition of sales from the premises. With sales being made over the Internet and merchandise ordered in one store but shipped from another, the question of sales can get complicated. Also, if sales are made by a concessionaire that is operating under a sublease or concession agreement, the landlord will try to include those sales in the rent calculation. Add in sales taxes collected by the tenant, returns of merchandise, dispositions of obsolete fixtures and bad debts, and the negotiation can become quite interesting. In any case, if the tenant's business is successful, the landlord benefits. If the tenant's business falters, the minimum rent provides a floor for the landlord.

In a multi-tenant commercial property, tenants need to ship their merchandise by truck to the property. Accordingly, these tenants need to have access to a loading dock or docks. If there is a single loading dock that is used by multiple tenants, the foreclosure investor should investigate whether each of the tenants has access to the loading dock and whether the lease covers the use of the dock.

A disadvantage of a multi-tenant commercial property is that it is more management intensive than some competing investments. The building must be maintained and repaired. The trash must be removed. The parking lot and landscaping must be kept in first class condition. Vacancies occur more frequently because lease terms are usually shorter. In recessionary times, tenants are under greater stress and more likely to default under their leases.

In analyzing multi-tenant properties with tenants that are not highly credit-worthy, special attention should be paid to the nature of the space. It should be generic space usable by many different types of tenants. Then, when one tenant fails and departs, the space can be easily leased to another tenant. Lenders are reluctant to finance the acquisition of properties leased to tenants with low or no credit ratings that will require substantial rebuilding at the end of the lease.

D.   Multi-purpose or Mixed-use Properties

Multi-purpose or mixed-use properties are those that are used for both residential and commercial purposes. A very common example can be seen walking down the main street of a typical American town with one or two story buildings lining the street. The two-story buildings have a store on the ground floor and an apartment on the second floor. Such buildings are multi-purpose. In this example, the purposes are commercial on the ground floor and residential on the upper floor.
The analysis of these properties involves a review of the principles for each use of the property.

CHAPTER II - 3   INDUSTRIAL PROPERTIES

Industrial properties are properties devoted to industrial uses. Industrial uses include the manufacturing of goods, ranging from an automobile assembly plant to pharmaceutical plants to clean facilities, such as a microchip fabricating plant, or the extraction of resources, such as gravel or oil, or the processing of materials, such as food processing or a machine shop for the shaping of metals or a steel mill or a refinery or wholesale and distribution facilities for the storage and shipping of materials and products, such as a warehouse, or ethanol plants or solar energy arrays or similar uses.

Industrial properties can be categorized as light industry or heavy industry. Light industrial properties include light assembly, warehousing and shipping, often which are conducted in one-story buildings. Light industry has the advantage of a broad and diverse range of tenants that the foreclosure investor can negotiate with. There should be less need for extensive leasehold improvements, and maintenance costs should be less than many other commercial tenants or heavy industrial users. However, industrial properties are no more resistant to a severe recession than other types of properties.

Industrial properties should be analyzed similarly to commercial properties. The value of most industrial properties derives from the rental stream. However, there are industrial properties whose value is not necessarily dependent upon the tenant occupying the property. For example, a gravel pit has value independent of any operator of the property because the owner can extract and sell the gravel with or without a tenant. Presumably, the foreclosure investor will be considering properties that are leased to an industrial tenant, and therefore we will focus on those kinds of properties.

The purchase of an industrial property requires the foreclosure investor to consider many of the factors that arise in the purchase of a commercial property, but it also requires the investor to consider a number of other factors. This part will discuss these additional factors.

A.   Factors Relevant to Industrial Properties

Many of the factors that a foreclosure investor takes into account when considering a commercial property also apply to an industrial property. However, industrial properties have additional concerns.

The first consideration involves utilities and services. A manufacturing operation certainly draws much more power than the typical commercial operation. Different tenants have different power requirements, necessitating the installation of new power panels, conduits and wiring. The requirements for heating, ventilation and air conditioning, commonly referred to as "HVAC," are more demanding for manufacturing. Some manufacturing operations require fans and ventilating systems that are situated on the roof of the building. Many manufacturing operations utilize boilers and pressure vessels and pipes. The consumption of water can be substantially greater in an industrial property than at a residential or commercial property. If the plant utilizes furnaces or kilns, there will be a greater demand for propane, natural gas or oil. Manufacturing plants will need fire extinguishing systems.

Maintenance is a second factor requiring special attention. A manufacturer will receive deliveries of raw materials, packaging and shipping materials, spare parts and the like. A manufacturer will ship finished goods to its distributors and customers. These shipments will be made by truck. Truck traffic causes considerable wear on driveways and parking lots, particularly in those parts of the country that experience snow and ice during the winter. During daily operations in a manufacturing plant, the tenant may be operating forklifts and other heavy-duty vehicles. Those can cause wear on the floor of the building. Additionally, if a forklift bangs into a wall or column, it can cause damage to the building. Industrial tenants typically have machinery and may have heavy duty equipment. Installation and removal of these items may cause damage to the premises.

The presence of machinery and equipment can also impact future leasing. If the tenant abandons the premises, removal of the machinery and equipment and its disposition in an appropriate location will be the landlord's responsibility and cost. Some of the equipment may be contaminated by waste oils, lubricants and other hazardous substances that increase the complexity and cost of disposal. In some situations, the machinery and equipment may be so integral to the operation of the building that they become parts of the building. This integration can facilitate, or it may impede, future leasing to a tenant in a different business.

It is not uncommon to find industrial properties located in industrial parks. These parks may be similar to residential planned developments in that the entire park will be subject to a declaration of covenants, conditions and restrictions that regulate use and occupancy of the buildings within the park. If the foreclosure investor is intending to purchase one of the buildings within the park, he or she needs to review the CC&Rs.

If the foreclosure investor discovers goods and materials stored on the property during an inspection of a multi-tenant property, the investor must determine whether or not the tenant who is storing those goods and materials has the right to do so and whether such storage interferes with other tenants' operations and their rights under their leases.

Location is an important issue, although the focus is different from that of commercial properties. When a foreclosure investor is evaluating commercial properties, he wants to be sure that the properties are located in an area that will be attractive to customers of the tenant. For industrial properties, the attractiveness of the neighborhood is not as important. However, location is still important. A well situated industrial property is near transportation facilities, such as an airport, a seaport, a freeway or interstate highway or a railroad station. The location should facilitate the movement of goods. If the tenants' businesses are tied to one industry, the property should be convenient to that industry. Proximity to fuel can be a factor to consider.

The quality of the building will be important to certain types of tenants. For several reasons, including just-in-time inventory control and the growth of Internet commerce, there has been a growing demand for warehouse space. Warehouse space can be a separate space in a separate building, or it can be included as a part of the main industrial facility. Warehousing requires buildings with higher ceilings. Some industrial tenants install conveyor belts and other material handling systems. Other industrial tenants utilize automated forklift systems. These new systems require better quality buildings with flatter floors. Industrial tenants that store considerable amounts of inventory require early suppression fast response fire systems. Such systems have come into existence in the last few decades, so older buildings may not have them. A foreclosure investor seeking to lease to more sophisticated industrial users must ascertain whether the building under consideration meets these technical standards. On the other hand, if the foreclosure investor is considering industrial properties with smaller or older buildings with lower ceiling heights, then the investor needs to be certain that there are tenants who have the potential to utilize such a building. Additionally, consolidation in certain industries has reduced the demand for certain kinds of facilities, and that should be taken into account in the investor's analysis.

Manufacturing operations tend to be more hazardous than retail or office uses. Accordingly, there is a greater risk of damage to the property or injury to persons on the property. As a result, liability insurance premiums will be higher. Also, liability insurance policies will be more specialized for industrial uses. In a multi-tenant property, the landlord insures the building against casualty damage, but the individual tenants maintain insurance on their goods, machinery and equipment. In a single tenant property, under the gross lease, the landlord insures the building, and under a net lease, the tenant insures the building.

B.   Single Tenant Occupancy

Industrial properties can be occupied by a single tenant or by multiple tenants. A multi-tenant industrial property might consist of a single building with parts of the building exclusively used by individual tenants, and other parts of the building such as the loading dock shared by all tenants, or it might be an industrial park with individual buildings occupied by individual tenants. In the case of an industrial park, the park may be owned by a single landlord, or each individual building may be separately owned with the park being subject to a set of covenants, conditions and restrictions. A single occupancy industrial property might be a manufacturing plant located on a parcel of land surrounded by parking lots and loading facilities. It may also be a small building on the street front, housing a business like a printing press or a wholesale bakery.

In the case of a single occupant industrial property, the foreclosure investor must first be concerned with the credit-worthiness of the tenant. The tenant's credit-worthiness plays a large part in setting the value of the property. The greater the credit rating of the tenant, the greater the value of the property, assuming that the lease provides for a market rate rent. Concomitant with a highly rated tenant is a higher price. There is greater competition to acquire an industrial property with a triple A tenant.

These kinds of properties are often leased for longer terms, such as fifteen to twenty-five years with options on the tenant's part to extend the term of the lease. Consequently, the foreclosure investor should view single occupancy industrial properties as long term investments, contrasted to the lease of an apartment where the term could be as short as one month. Thus, one advantage of the single occupant industrial property is the prospect of a steady income stream for several years. A disadvantage is that when the lease term finally expires, the building will be old and in need of refurbishment, which can be costly.

C.   Multiple Tenant Industrial Occupancy

A typical office building usually has many tenants, whereas the typical multi-tenant industrial property is likely to have only a few tenants. The disadvantage of this is that the loss of one tenant affects a larger percentage of the property. The corresponding advantage is that the investor is able to devote a greater amount of time to analyzing the financial condition of a prospective tenant. With fewer premises to lease, the foreclosure investor may also find it easier to lease the entire property.

In a multi-tenant industrial property, tenants that have different kinds of operations are likely to consume utilities and services in different amounts. Accordingly, the foreclosure investor must be certain that each tenant pays its fair share of utilities and services. In addition, the utility systems must be kept in good operating condition and repair.

In a multi-tenant industrial property, each tenant should have separate meters to their premises. The leases should allow access to utility runs for the tenants. If two or more tenants require fans and ventilating systems situated on the roof of the building, the foreclosure investor must assure himself that the operation of one of these systems does not interfere with the use of another tenant's system. Moreover, the foreclosure investor should ascertain a tenant's need for such a system, and if required, the presence of the system at the property.

Like a multi-tenant commercial property, a multi-tenant industrial property provides services to most, if not all, of the tenants. Hence, there are costs that affect the entire property which should be shared between the tenants. The foreclosure investor should search the leases to determine if there is a provision for the payment of common charges.

In a multi-tenant industrial facility, there may be a single loading dock that will be used by multiple tenants. The foreclosure investor must ensure that each tenant has access to the loading dock. It is possible that one tenant has exclusive access of the dock which affects the marketability of the other spaces. Further, the investor should learn if the leases govern the access and use of the dock, including its hours of operations.

In multi-tenant industrial properties occupied by tenants without an investment-grade credit rating, lenders scrutinize the financial condition of the tenants. The foreclosure investor should do the same. The tenants must have a history of profitability, sufficient cash reserves and be engaged in a business that has a substantial probability of continued viability.

D.   Industrial Property Leases

When acquiring industrial property, the analysis of the leases is as important as any other aspect of the investor's due diligence. There are four basics kinds of leases employed, depending on the kind of property. If the property is a single occupant property, the lease will be either a single occupant gross lease or some form of single occupant net lease. If the property is a multi-tenant property, the lease will be either a multi-tenant gross lease or some form of multi-tenant net lease.

The American Industrial Real Estate Association, now known as AIR, has published a series of form leases for industrial and commercial properties. These leases have been used for decades and are fairly balance landlord and tenant interests. The forms include leases for the following kinds of industrial properties: multi-tenant gross lease, multi-tenant net lease, single tenant gross lease and single tenant net lease.

Regardless of the type of lease utilized, the foreclosure investor should review the concerns applicable to a particular property type and be certain that the leases in effect address those issues. For example, if the property is a multi-tenant property, and all of the tenants use the loading dock, each tenant's lease, as well as the property's rules and regulations, should contain provisions laying out specific instructions regarding the use of the loading dock. Moreover, the provisions need to be consistent among the leases. If the leases are silent on the matter, a conflict between tenants may arise. If the leases are inconsistent, not only could a conflict occur, but the landlord may incur monetary liability to one or more tenants on the ground that the landlord failed to perform his covenants under the lease.

Gross leases are leases where the basic costs of operating and maintaining the building are paid by the landlord. The landlord pays for expenses such as real estate taxes, insurance premiums and maintenance. The landlord can recover these costs in one of two ways. First, the landlord can charge a rent that he believes will reimburse him for these costs. This is a risky approach because costs could escalate unexpectedly. The second way is to require the tenants to pay, as additional rent, a common charge that covers these costs. The common charge is calculated as the costs become known to the landlord.

The alternative to a gross lease is a net lease, which can take different forms. A net lease is a lease in which the tenant pays one or more of the basic costs of operating and maintaining the building. These basic costs include real estate taxes, insurance and maintenance. However, there might be other forms such as a lease under which the tenant pays the utilities. Typically, the term "net lease" is loosely used and does not have a firmly defined meaning. However, in general terms, a lease in which a tenant pays one of these costs is referred to as a net lease. A lease in which a tenant pays for at least two of these costs is considered a double net lease, and a lease in which the tenant pays for all of the expenses is referred to as a triple net lease. However, some people use the term "net lease" to include double and triple net leases. The foreclosure investor should learn the specific costs that the tenant is responsible for under the lease.

Another term sometimes used is "bond lease." A bond lease is a lease in which the tenant pays for all of the costs of operating and owning the property. It is called a bond lease because the rent is received by the landlord without any deductions, similar to the payment of principal and interest under a bond. It is also like a bond because the risk assumed by the foreclosure investor is the financial stability of the tenant. This is in contrast to the value of residential property which is based on the intrinsic value of the real estate.

Since industrial uses can impact the costs of operation and value of the property much greater than residential or commercial uses, investors tend to find that net or triple net leases predominate in the industrial market. As described above, triple net leases usually require the tenant to pay for taxes, utilities, service contracts, maintenance and repair and insurance. The landlord may impose responsibility for other aspects of the property on the tenant as well. The lease of a single occupant industrial property will often be a triple net lease.

CHAPTER II – 4   WHY THE TYPE OF PROPERTY MAKES A DIFFERENCE

There are certain constants that apply to every type of real property. Title is an example of such a constant. No matter the use of the property, the foreclosure investor must carefully consider title. A detailed discussion of title appears below. However, as noted at the beginning of this chapter, each type of property carries different concerns that distinguish one type of property from another. This chapter discusses the distinctions between the different kinds of property uses.

A.   Differences among properties

A major difference is the investor's exit plan. The foreclosure investor may decide to purchase a single-family home and then sell it. There are new rules either in place or under consideration that can affect an investor's ability to make a quick sale. These will be discussed in more detail below. At this point, it is sufficient to note that the ability to sell a property at a profit will depend on the market for similar properties. In an area that has been hard hit by residential foreclosures, the investor may be better able to rent a house than to sell it. In that case, the investor may elect to look elsewhere for residential property or may decide to look into other kinds of properties that are more marketable.

Another difference is management. Management concerns arise on at least two levels – occupancy and use. The first involves occupancy of a property. Management of a multi-tenant apartment building entails much more involvement than the management of a single family residence that has been rented to a family. Also, management of a multi-tenant property probably cannot be turned over to a tenant because of all the tenants involved. One exception is the multi-tenant apartment building where the manager is paid by receiving a reduced-rent or rent-free apartment. In office buildings and shopping centers, the tenants do not have the expertise or interest to manage the building for the benefit of all occupants. In these cases, the foreclosure investor must determine whether to manage the property personally or to hire a management company. The investor whose principal interest is in developing a portfolio of properties may be better off concentrating on property acquisitions and hiring a professional manager.

Management concerns also arise regarding the use of the property. The expertise needed to manage a neighborhood strip mall differs from the expertise needed to manage an industrial building. Before deciding to spend time on a particular type of property, the foreclosure investor should evaluate the level of management involvement that the property will require and whether the investor is prepared and able to provide that level.

Revenues vary among property types. Rent from a single family residence is a relatively straight-forward matter. If the tenant departs, there is usually a market of replacement tenants for the property. A new tenant will not require major improvements to the property. The building may need some repainting, carpet cleaning and window washing. This work can be completed fairly quickly. This work can also be undertaken even if a new tenant has not yet been identified because this kind of work is done for most new rentals. If there is a market of ready replacement tenants, there should not be a prolonged interruption in the rent. The same applies to apartment buildings. Rent from commercial and industrial properties can be a different matter. When a commercial tenant moves out of an office building or a neighborhood shopping center, there may be a period of time spent locating a new tenant. Tenant improvements cannot be completed during that time because the investor does not know what improvements the new tenant requires. If the property was outfitted for a unique use, it may take considerably longer to find a new tenant, and the rental stream will be interrupted for a longer time. This is more likely to occur with retail tenants than with office users.

Vacancy rates will vary. An apartment building has a regular turnover of tenants, requiring the investor to spend time and money advertising the availability of space, conducting credit checks of prospective tenants and cleaning apartments. Rents rise or fall more frequently as the market changes. Therefore, it is more problematic for the investor to project future rents. However, apartments tend to be somewhat generic and should be easier to rent. In contrast, the big box retailer who has a strong credit rating provides a steady rental stream for several years. The rent tends to be somewhat insulated from market fluctuations. However, when the lease expires, the building may be obsolete, requiring extensive and costly rehabilitation that cannot be undertaken until a new tenant has been identified. There could be a long period of vacancy.

Operating costs are dependent on the uses of the property. An industrial property is likely to consume utilities at a much higher rate than a residential facility. A single occupancy property can allow the investor to enter into a form of net lease under which the tenant pays the cost of utilities. Common area charges can be a means of capturing operating costs in multi-tenant properties. However, investors need to manage properties efficiently to avoid above market common charges that will affect marketability.

The marketing of rental space differs with each type of property. If the investor has expertise in marketing one kind of space, he or she may decide to stay with that kind of use.

The condition of the neighborhood affects different types of properties differently. Some communities may have residences located adjacent to industrial parks. The industrial nature of the area will not impair – and might very well improve – the value of an industrial building. However, the industrial character of the area could negatively affect the value of the adjacent residential properties. An announcement by state government that a new campus of the state university system will be constructed in a community should result in increases in the value of all kinds of properties. However, the value of industrial property suited for technical uses will benefit more than industrial property suited for automobile body shops. This is an example of how the foreclosure investor can analyze the way the condition of a neighborhood can affect the value of different uses.

B.   Is There Such a Thing as
Recession-Proof Property?

In a recessionary climate, investors seek recession-proof properties. The question for the investor is whether any such property exists.

There is one sure property investment – an office building leased to the General Services Administration or other agencies of the Federal Government. Dealing with the Federal Government means accepting many of the government's standard documents and terms, but in a difficult economy, the benefit may outweigh the burden.

Many other uses had been considered recession-proof. For example, dry cleaners were considered recession-proof because people need to have their clothes cleaned. In a normal recession, that would be the case. In a severe downturn, people who have lost their jobs do not need to have their clothes cleaned as frequently as before they were laid off. Some luxury goods merchants were considered sound investments, but when a stock market collapse takes away wealth, people cut back on luxury items. Some commercial properties that feature food stores and other basic retailers seem to be recession-resistant, but retailers at every price level are vulnerable to severe recessionary pressures.

Another type of sound property investment involves residential property with a tenancy subsidized by the government. This type of investment is described in more detail in Chapter VI – 1.

Our review of the different kinds of properties should help a foreclosure investor identify the uses that he or she might consider acquiring. Now, we will turn to the means that an investor can utilize to identify and locate these properties.

PART III – FINDING AND ANALYZING PROSPECTIVE INVESTMENT PROPERTIES

The foreclosure investor must do some spadework to locate properties that are potential acquisitions. Information on such properties' availability can be found, but the sources of this information will vary with each stage of the foreclosure process.

As noted in Chapter I-6, we noted that foreclosures can go through up to four stages. The four stages are:

(1) the "pre-foreclosure stage"

(2) the "default and sale stage"

(3) the "redemption period"

(4) the "REO stage"

Sources of information are identified in each stage, and then the ways that the investor can utilize that information is addressed.

CHAPTER III – 1   SOURCES OF INFORMATION ON DISTRESSED PROPERTIES

A.   Pre-Foreclosure Properties

The first time that a property becomes a potential foreclosure acquisition arises when the borrower begins to have difficulty making the mortgage payments. How does an investor learn that a borrower is experiencing difficulties? There is no public source for this kind of information. The lender may not even know at the outset. The borrower rarely announces these facts. Hence, the approach for a foreclosure investor is to advertise the investor's interest in dealing with a particular kind of property or properties.

Advertising can be done by using the local media. The investor can publish ads in local daily and weekly newspapers. The investor should review the ads that are placed in these newspapers to see what size, typeface and placement are most effective at catching the reader's eye and then formulate a similar advertisement. The text should be brief, directly to the point and contain the investor's phone number. The investor can also place commercials on the local radio station. The investor can create a website advertising his or her investment aspirations and requirements. Newspaper ads can refer to the website.

Another way to make the investor's interest known is to distribute flyers throughout a likely neighborhood. During some recessions, communities and residential neighborhoods are publicized as suffering waves of foreclosures, and those neighborhoods may be good targets for flyers. The investor may consider putting up signs. The legality of signs depends on local law, so the foreclosure investor should check local ordinances. .

Other means of searching include reviewing the court records for divorce or bankruptcy filings. These filings indicate transitions and possible financial stress that may be a harbinger to a foreclosure. On the other hand, divorce filings do not necessarily indicate financial difficulties. Spending time checking these filings may not be the most efficient use of an investor's time. One advantage of getting early information about a prospective foreclosure is that there are fewer persons competing to acquire the property. An investor needs to decide whether this advantage is sufficient to justify the time gathering information that has a lesser potential of turning up a prospect.

At some point there will be a default by the borrower, and the lender becomes aware that the borrower is in the pre-foreclosure stage. At this point, other sources of information become available. One potential source of information on defaulted borrowers is a real estate broker who specializes in foreclosure properties and short sales. These brokers have information on potential properties through the borrower and through the lender. Borrowers who are in default, or nearing default, may decide to list their properties with a real estate broker. Brokers specializing in short sales or foreclosure properties may have notice of these listings before they appear on the Multiple Listing Service ("MLS"). Similarly, brokers who specialize in these kinds of properties probably have relationships with lenders. If a borrower is negotiating to obtain approval of a short sale from the lender, the broker may learn from the lender about the existence of the default. Obtaining notice about the existence of a default is an advantage to the foreclosure investor because there are fewer investors competing for the property.

An additional source of information is found in short sale specialists or consultants. There are companies, that can be found on the Internet, that will provide consulting services to borrowers who wish to dispose of their properties through short sales. Short Sales Scholars, which maintains a website that can be found at http://www.shortsalescholars.com/?gclid=CJDTw4Pr6ZgCFSXBDAo dbF1X2Q advertises that it will assist any borrower who wishes to dispose of distressed property through all of the stages of the short sale, including to go shooting with the lender, at no cost to the borrower. Short Sales Scholars is a registered trade name of Continental Real Estate Group, Inc. Notably, a point of great interest to a foreclosure investor is that the company advertises that it will market the property to short sale buyers and investors. A foreclosure investor who has made his interest known to this and similar companies will presumably be contacted by them when property becomes available.

B.   Default and Auction Properties

Identifying potential foreclosure properties becomes much easier when a property enters the default and sale stage. It is at this point that public notices are posted, broadcasting to the world that a property is in distress. These notices can be found in public records, in published announcements and on the Internet.

In states where mortgages are foreclosed by a judicial proceeding, the lender begins a foreclosure by directing its attorney to commence a lawsuit to foreclose the mortgage. The attorney files an action against the borrower. This is the first public notice that a property is entering the foreclosure process. A foreclosure investor can obtain notice of

95

the lawsuit by visiting the local courthouse each day and reviewing the record of suits filed that day. The investor can check the filings at the appropriate court. The name of the court may vary, but it is the trial court as opposed to an appellate court. It can be called the county court or the superior court or the circuit court or the municipal court. The investor can consult with the office of the clerk or the prothonotary of the appropriate court. In addition to searching court records, there is another way to get notice.

Since a foreclosure suit affects title to real property, it is important that anyone who might be dealing with the property have notice that the suit has been filed. Recall that real property investors are charged with constructive notice of any title matters that they could have discovered by consulting the land records. In order to give constructive notice, the lender will record a notice of the lawsuit in the appropriate land records. This notice is called a *lis pendens*. The term *lis pendens* means "suit pending." A *lis pendens* describes the real property, the court and the parties. Because the *lis pendens* gives constructive notice, persons who subsequently deal with the property will be bound by the results that emanate from the law suit.

In title theory states, the lender contacts the trustee under the deed of trust and directs the trustee to issue a notice of default and record it in the appropriate land records. The purpose of the recording of the notice of default is the same as recording the *lis pendens*. Recording the notice of default gives constructive notice that the borrower is in default and any action taken by the trustee regarding the default binds subsequent purchasers of the property and lenders to the borrower. The contents of a notice of default will vary from state to state. In California, the notice of default must contain the name of the borrower, a description of the mortgage or deed of trust or a description of the property, a description of the default, the lender's election to sell the property and any right of the borrower to reinstate the debt.

The recording of a *lis pendens* or a notice of default is a public event and thereby provides a means for foreclosure investors to identify potential acquisitions. The foreclosure investor could review the filings in the appropriate land records periodically to find *lis pendens* or notices of default. The foreclosure investor who wants to search the public record must find the location of the appropriate land records. That location varies from state to state. In some states, the land records are maintained on a county by county basis, and there is one governmental office charged with maintaining the records. In states where there are no county governments, land records are maintained by the individual municipalities within the state. The office could be called the county recorder's office or the county register's office. Investors can find a nationwide listing of tax assessors' and recorders' web sites at a website maintained by Nationwide Environmental Title Research, LLC at http://www.netronline.com/public_records.htm .

Title companies obtain copies of all documents recorded daily and enter the documents in the company's plant records; an investor can establish a relationship with a title company (which is advisable even without considering the *lis pendens* issue). A *lis pendens* or a notice of default is also required to be published in newspapers of general circulation within the area where the real property is located, so the investor can subscribe to newspapers covering any areas in which the investor is interested and review the public notices each day. Then, there are services to which an investor can subscribe that will do the search for the investor and report its results. Finally, there are websites that offer this information on a local, regional and national basis.

The foreclosure investor can find websites by employing a search engine using search terms appropriate to the information the investor is seeking. If the investor searches for "New York foreclosures" on Google, the first site listed in the search results is a website maintained by Profiles Publications Inc. In this website, the operator offers information on the New York State foreclosure process. If the investor clicks on "Learn The New York Foreclosure Processes" and then clicks on "Step 1: Lis Pendens Filings: The Case Begins," a description of the foreclosure process appears. Regarding *lis pendens,* the website states that a subscriber to its *lis pendens* reports will receive the following information:

> . . . the names of the plaintiff and defendant, the property address, block and lot number, neighborhood, zip code, NYC

Building Classification Code, the date and amount of the mortgage, tax lien or common charge in default, the index number of the lis pendens file and the Plaintiff's attorney and telephone number. . . plus the Plaintiff's attorney and telephone number!   .   .   .   .
http://nyforeclosures.com/mastering/process_step1.html

The third entry on the search results is a website maintained by RealtyTrac, a nationwide source of extensive information on foreclosure properties. Other websites that are frequently noted by investors include RealtyStore.com, Zillow.com and Foreclosuredata.com. Additional web sites that will provide the investor with information on pre-foreclosure properties, foreclosures, sheriff sales, sales by owners, REOs and bankruptcies are www.foreclosure,com, www.forecloses.com, www.realtyforecloses.com and www.freeforeclosurereport.com. The foreclosure investor need merely sit down at a computer and quickly find his favorite site for researching the filings of *lis pendens* and notices of default.

Another source of information is the online tax assessor records. If the investor has the address of the property or a name of the owner, the investor can go into the assessor's records to obtain other relevant information. An excellent source of tax assessor websites and many other public records is PublicRecordFinder.com. This website lists all of the states and links to their public record websites.

A foreclosure investor can consult a website that lists addresses, phone numbers, and URL's of county recorders. One such website is Zanatec.com. The investor can find the name of the owner of a prospective property. The investor could also look up the lender. Once the investor has the names of the owners, the investor can use a name finder website such as WhitePages.com to locate more information on the owner. Also, tax assessor sites provide information on the owner. With this information, the foreclosure investor can begin the investment process described below.

Information on pre-foreclosure properties can be found at the websites maintained by real estate auction companies. These companies conduct nationwide auctions and dispose of large numbers of properties. Some of the companies that an investor may want to investigate include (i) Real Estate Disposition LLC, whose website can be found at http://www.ushomeauction.com; (ii) J. P. King Auction Company, Inc. whose website can be found at http://www.jpking.com; and (iii) United Country Auction Services whose website can be found at http://www.ucauctionservices.com.

Another critical filing is the notice of sale. This notice gives the details on the date and place of the auction or sale of the property. The notice of sale can be found in the same way that the *lis pendens* and the notice of default are found.

Finally, some owners of distressed property list their properties with real estate brokers. It is always a good idea for a foreclosure investor to have a relationship with a real estate broker, especially one that specializes in short sales and other foreclosure sales. These brokers usually have connections to the REO departments of lenders and may have information on properties that are about to be offered on the market before the properties become generally known.

If the foreclosure investor is unable to negotiate a deal with the owner prior to the actual foreclosure, the investor may still want to attend the auction and, if there is sufficient equity in the property, participate in the bidding. The investor can also confirm whether or not the lender purchases the property at the auction. If the lender purchases the property, the investor can move into the last stage of foreclosure discussed in Subchapter III-1-C below.

C.   Redemption Properties and Post-foreclosure REOs

The stage of foreclosure following the default and sale stage is the redemption and REO stage. At this phase, the lender is the owner of the property. The lender may be a private lender, or it may be a governmental entity like the Department of Housing and Urban Development.

A lender acquires real property in a foreclosure sale by making the highest bid at the auction. The lender will not bid more than the amount of the debt secured by the mortgage or deed of trust. If the lender is outbid, that means there is equity in the property. If the lender is the highest bidder, that may mean that there was no equity, or it may mean that there was equity but not enough to attract competing bids. In any case, title to the property transfers to the lender.

In states that grant the borrower a right of redemption, there will be a period of time prescribed by state law during which the borrower has the right to repay the lender and recover the property. Any investor who purchases a property from the lender during the period of redemption runs the risk of losing any funds invested in the property. Assume that a foreclosure investor purchases a single family residence and installs a new roof on the building. Then, the borrower redeems the property. The investor loses the money he spent on the roof. To avoid this, the investor must either wait until the redemption period has expired, or must make a deal with the borrower to purchase the borrower's right of redemption. Accordingly, during any redemption period, an interested investor needs to deal with two parties – the lender and the borrower. After the period of redemption expires, the investor only needs to deal with the lender.

Properties acquired by lenders are referred to as "Real Estate Owned" or "REOs." These properties are not assets that benefit an institutional lender. They are non-performing assets that the lender needs to dispose of, usually by a sale. The foreclosure investor can capitalize on the lender's desire to dispose of Real Estate Owned to negotiate a favorable deal for the purchase of the property. Now, who does the investor contact?

Institutional lenders with large inventories of REOs often have a separate department charged with disposing of the real property. This department may be referred to as the "REO Department" or "Special Assets Department." Hence, one good source of information on REOs is the lender's REO Department. The foreclosure investor who has been conducting careful research into opportunities at other stages of the foreclosure process has probably identified several lenders that are in the mortgage lending business and that have conducted foreclosures.

The investor might have attended an auction and watched the lender outbid everyone for the property. The lender has a list of properties available for sale that the investor can review. Some lenders have posted their REO list on the Internet. For example, Countrywide Bank has a website that allows the investor to search by state, county, city, property type and price. The listings include the contact person at Countrywide. Another example is Wachovia Bank, which has its REOs listed on its website. However, Wachovia does not provide contact information on its listings. Other institutional lenders have retained service companies to handle the disposition of their REOs. The Veterans Administration, as an example, retains Ocwen Financial Corporation to handle their REO sales. Investors can also contact local lenders and advise them that the investor has an interest in pursuing Real Estate Owned. In this way, investors can become a part of the local lenders' group of persons to contact when REO is acquired.

A listing of many institutional lenders and their REO departments or servicers can be found at the Mortgage News Daily website at http://www.mortgagenewsdaily.com/wiki/REO_Database_List.asp . Sales of homes held by the Federal Government can be found at homesales.gov.

Foreclosure investors should ask real estate brokers for information about REOs. Real estate brokers may be able to assist the foreclosure investor in identifying brokers that specialize in REO, if there are any in the area. Moreover, real estate brokers may be aware of the availability of foreclosed real property from lenders. They can also identify private lenders that are holding foreclosed properties. Brokers can also help with institutional lenders because institutional lenders retain real estate brokers to market their properties. This includes the Federal Government. If the investor goes to the website GovSales.com, which lists both real property and personal property for sale, clicks on buildings and land, and then selects a property, the website of the broker handling the sale appears. The Department of Housing and Urban Development ("HUD") lists its houses on the HomeSales.gov website, but if the investor is interested in a property, he must operate through a real estate broker to submit an offer. After a period of time elapses, called the Offer Period, HUD reviews the bids it has received and accepts the highest offer. The kinds of properties that HUD offers are described by HUD on its website as follows: "A HUD home is a 1 to 4 unit residential property acquired by HUD as a result of a foreclosure action on an FHA-insured mortgage." The Veterans Administration also uses real estate brokers to handle the disposition of its REOs.

There are also more traditional avenues of information. Foreclosure investors can review the classified ads in their local newspapers to see what properties may be available from lenders.

We have discussed the most basic information –the properties that may be available to a foreclosure investor. There is a second tier of information – property specific due diligence.

CHAPTER III -2   ANALYZING PROSPECTIVE PROPERTIES

The foreclosure investor should not simply arrive at a foreclosure auction and start bidding. That is a road filled with potholes. The investor must conduct an appropriate level of due diligence on the properties the investor is considering.

Due diligence is the act of examining all relevant aspects of a property to ferret out information necessary to make a decision to make an offer, settle on a specific price or agree to other terms of the deal. Relevant aspects vary depending on the type of property. A foreclosure investor usually does not have leases to review when considering single family residences but will when he is considering an office building.

A.   Physical Condition of Property

The physical condition of the property impacts the investment analysis. If the property needs repairs, the return on the investment is lower unless the price is reduced proportionately. If the property is not well located, marketing the property is more challenging.

The investor should evaluate the physical condition on several levels. The nearest level is the overall appearance. The investor may ask: Does a single family residence have "curb appeal?" Does it look good at first glance? Does a commercial building look inviting to potential customers? Is the landscaping attractive? Is there an appealing viewscape or does the residence face an interstate highway? Is there excessive noise from traffic or a nearby airport? Is there a school nearby with an athletic field that has lights which may interfere with the peaceful use of the backyard?

These are matters that the foreclosure investor and his real estate broker can assess visually. Other matters need the input of an expert.

In a typical home purchase, the buyer hires an inspector to examine the residence. The buyer may also hire specialized inspectors, such as termite or radon inspectors, to examine the building. A foreclosure investor should do no less than the normal home buyer.

The foreclosure investor must remember that the condition of a property can change in a short period of time. Assume that the owner of the property occupies the residence during the inspection. The owner is distraught over the foreclosure and before departing, takes revenge by removing the refrigerator and washing machine, pulling out the light fixtures and trashing the house. If the foreclosure investor does not conduct a final inspection just prior to the closing of the sale, there may be shock when the investor enters the house after the closing.

Other items to inspect include the foundation, the roof, septic and water wells, power and utility boxes, appliances, furnaces and central air systems. In addition, the investor should do a visual examination for mold throughout the house.

If the property needs repair or rehabilitation, the investor needs to estimate the cost and factor it into the calculation of the purchase price. Also, the investor must estimate the amount of time the repairs require because the house cannot be rented while the work is performed, and the investor must still make mortgage payments and tax payments. The value added to the property by the repairs should not be offset by the cost of holding the property.

B.   Rental Property – Leases and Financial Condition of Tenants and Trade Fixtures

Residential property can be valued by sales of other comparable properties or replacement cost. Commercial and industrial properties are valued primarily on their revenue stream. The revenue stream from real property is generated by the rents. The foreclosure investor who is considering the purchase of commercial or industrial property must evaluate the revenue stream. This is done by reviewing the leases and the financial condition of the tenants.

When reviewing a lease, the foreclosure investor focuses on the amount of rent paid by the tenant, rent adjustments that track increases in inflation, tenant payments for some portion of the operating costs and real estate taxes, security deposits, the term of the lease, any options the tenant has to extend the term, the amount of rent during the extended term (is it fixed or will it be set by a contemporary appraisal), the amount of space occupied by the tenant, any options the tenant has to add other space to the leased premises, the tenant's rights and obligations regarding trade fixtures, any landlord obligations and other relevant factors. The investor reviews the rent roll and vacancy reports. This review is much more beneficial to the investor if he can compare apples to apples instead of apples to oranges. To produce an apple report, the investor should prepare a template that is be used to review every lease. The template lists all the information that the investor needs from the leases. The benefits of using a template are manifold. First, if there are several persons reviewing the leases, they are all seeking the same information. Second, it is easier to identify a lease that differs materially from the others. As an example, if most of the leases increase the rent by five percent each year, but the lease for the largest tenant does not contain a rent increase, that fact will be very apparent. Third, unusual provisions stand out. If the largest tenant is paying the lowest rate for rent, and has an option to expand into the space occupied by the tenant paying rent at the highest rate, the exercising of the option can reduce the revenue stream but this analysis would not show up in a rent roll. Fourth, the investor knows that each provision of every lease has been considered. Also, written reviews can be provided to the investor's lender for its due diligence.

The foreclosure investor should know if any tenants have a history of late payment or other types of defaults. Are there any tenants currently in default that will need to be evicted? What are the economic prospects of the tenants? Is one of the tenants a subsidiary of a company that is threatening bankruptcy? All of these are questions the investor should ask.

The foreclosure investor should consider any trade fixtures installed in the leased premises. Trade fixtures are personal property, owned by the tenant for use in its trade or business, which are affixed to the real property. Examples of trade fixtures include a pizza oven in a restaurant, shelving and display cases in a clothing store or conveyors in a warehouse. The lease determines whether the investor is able to retain these items at the end of the lease term, whether the tenant is obligated to remove them if requested by the landlord or whether the landlord must bear the cost of removal and repair. The presence of trade fixtures can extend the time required to outfit the premises for the next tenant.

An important part of any lease review is to obtain the tenants' concurrence with the facts presented to the foreclosure investor. Concurrence is established by the use of estoppel certificates. Estoppel certificates are described above in the introduction to Chapter II-2. The investor must review them carefully to ensure that the tenants agree with the data on which the investor will be basing his economic analysis.

C.   Physical and Economic
Condition of Neighborhood

The condition of the area where the property is located is important to the foreclosure investor. This factor covers the physical and economic.

On the physical side, the presence of abandoned and boarded up buildings are a negative factor in evaluating residential and commercial properties. Some industrial properties may be better suited for that kind of neighborhood. Also, the area's prospects may be better than appears at first glance. The foreclosure investor probably does not have sufficient time to develop a deep understanding of an area's prospects. However, if the investor is familiar with a degraded area, the investor may be able to spot some real bargains. Historically, there are areas in major cities that were deteriorated and then experience gentrification which increased property values across the board. Unfortunately, an investor seeking financing may have difficulty convincing a lender that gentrification is on the horizon.

Prospects can be dependent on the presence and movement of major employers or cultural and educational establishments. The foreclosure investor can speak to the local chamber of commerce to get an overview of an area if the investor is not personally familiar with it. Financial publications can be mined for news on the plans and prospects of companies already present in the neighborhood, and local magazines and newspapers may have articles on expected inflows of residents and employers.

The percentage of renters to owners may be a significant statistic. In a college town with many students living in apartments, the high percentage of renters would not raise a red flag. In the average residential neighborhood, if the percentage of renters is high compared to owners, then many residences are held by investors. A high percentage of investors might mean that the area has passed muster for investors and is a good place to invest. In contrast, if the investors become over-extended or seek larger returns elsewhere, there may be a sell-off resulting in a decrease in property values.

There are real estate services that, for a fee, provide an investor with a neighborhood report listing future developments that have received public notice. For example, such services report if a developer has applied for a building permit to construct a high-rise which will block the view from a residence. These reports also cite articles on neighborhood nuisances, such as bars and discotheques that stay open until the early hours of the morning with noisy patrons hanging around outside the door. The investor can ask a real estate broker about such services in a given community.

Demographic information can be very useful. It can be found for many communities online. At a website maintained by Onboard Informatics at http://www.onboardnavigator.com/WebContent/OBWC_Search.aspx? AID=108 , the following information, among other things, can be found for 3,000 communities: the population growth (since 2000), the density of the population, the size of households, the percentage of households with children, the annual residential turnover, the number of families in residency more than five years, the median year in residency, the percentage of residential dwellings, the population of the community broken down by age group, the highest level of education attained, the composition of the workforce, the number of workers and the income by dollar range.

Crime rates affect the ability to sell or rent properties. Lower rates will benefit the investor while higher rates can have a negative effect. Crime rates for certain cities can be found online.

Proximity to hazardous waste sites or nuclear reactors affects the value of properties. Proximity to sources of power can benefit industrial properties. If the property is in a flood plain, the cost of insurance is impacted. If the property is located in wetlands, the ability to remodel or redevelop is subject to stricter governmental control.

The condition of the neighborhood may be reflective of the economic prospects for the community in which the property is located.

In a severe recession, there are many layoffs, bankruptcies of businesses and company closures. In a mild recession, these factors are present but to a lesser degree. In a burgeoning economy, these factors should not be present. If the economy is strong, but they exist in the community the investor is considering, that is a serious red flag.

Some cities have fared very poorly in recent recessions. They can be identified by searching the Internet. They offer the opportunities of lower prices, but the prospects of short-term recovery are slight.

D.   Financial Analysis of the Property

A foreclosure investor can choose from a few financial goals when investing in foreclosure property. The first is to realize a profit through appreciation in the value of the real property. The second is to realize a profit from revenue generated by the property. A third goal is to obtain tax benefits. Achievement of the first two goals depends on the investor making a reasonably accurate assessment of the value of the property. In order to accurately estimate a property's value, the foreclosure investor needs to know how real property is valued and where to find the relevant data. We will first discuss valuation methods.

The methods of valuing a property vary depending on the type of property. A residential property is usually valued by comparing it to sales of similar properties in the same neighborhood. This method is referred to as the "comparable sales" method. An appraiser examines the property being valued and ascertains its date of construction, square footage, the number of bedrooms and bathrooms, the size of the lot and other relevant factors. The appraiser then looks for other residences with comparable physical features that have sold recently. The theory is that if people are willing to pay a certain price for a comparable property, the market will pay approximately the same price for the property being valued. Sometimes there are no comparable properties. In that case, an alternate method of valuation is to estimate the cost of constructing the building from scratch. The appraiser adds up the cost of the materials and labor required to duplicate the building or, in other words, to replace the building. The appraiser then depreciates the existing building over its remaining useful life and applies the same depreciation rate to the hypothetical replacement building. Finally, the value of the underlying land is added to the depreciated value to produce a current value of the property. This method is called the "replacement cost" method. Construction cost estimators can be found online. One example is get-a-quote.net. Another technique to estimate construction cost is to consult with an insurance broker who represents casualty insurers. An insurance agent has information on replacement costs because that is one form of commonly issued casualty insurance. The method most commonly used to value rental property is the income method. The income from the property is capitalized to derive a value.

The value of a commercial or industrial building is measured by its income stream. The income stream is capitalized to produce a market value for the property. To capitalize an income stream, the investor determines the amount of the income stream and the capitalization rate, often referred to as the "cap rate." For purposes of valuation, the income stream is referred to as the net operating income or NOI. To determine the net operating income, the foreclosure investor adds together the annual rental income and annual income from other sources such as vending machines and laundry facilities. The investor reduces the gross revenue by an estimated vacancy figure. This number is the gross operating income. The investor then subtracts the annual operating expenses of the property. Operating expenses are those costs that must be paid to maintain the property and enable it to continue to produce income. These expenses include real estate taxes, management fees, insurance premiums, repairs and maintenance. Operating expenses do not include capital expenditures, mortgage payments of principal and interest, depreciation and income taxes. Gross operating income less operating expenses equals "net operating income" or "NOI."

The net operating income is the actual return that a foreclosure investor receives on his investment. The cap rate is the rate of the investor's return on his investment. The effect of excluding financing costs from the calculation is to identify the capitalization rate if the property in question were purchased with all cash without any financing.

To calculate the cap rate, the investor takes the net operating income from the property and divides it by the purchase price of the building. For example, a foreclosure investor who is contemplating paying a price of $1,250,000 for a building that has a net operating income of $200,000 per annum would obtain a cap rate of 0.16 or 16 percent. That in effect is the return on the capital invested in the property. Now an investor can conclude that a return of 16 percent is acceptable and formulate an offer based on that return. However, that does not establish the value of the property.

The value of the property is the amount a willing buyer will pay to a willing seller. In a given market, prospective buyers may be willing to accept a cap rate of 10 percent. Assuming under our hypothetical that the net operating income is $200,000, the value at a cap rate of 10 percent would be $2,000,000, derived by dividing the net operating income by the cap rate. In this example, the formula would be Value = NOI / Cap Rate.

As we have just demonstrated, the cap rate can be used both to establish a value for the property and to determine the rate of return on the investment. If the rate of return is not acceptable, the investor may elect to pass on the property or offer a lower price.

If an investor always has the option to offer a lower price, how does the cap rate determine value? This is done by the investor reviewing sales of other, similar properties. If the market rate for strip mall shopping centers in the area is 8 percent, the foreclosure investor should offer a purchase price within reason of that range, or the seller will reject the offer. Of course, in the foreclosure context, sellers have other motivations that outweigh valuation by capitalizing the revenue.

The foreclosure investor who desires to apply a very sharp pencil to this financial analysis can find more sophisticated formulae for calculating capitalization rates, including ones that account for the effects of borrowing, by searching the Internet.

The second ingredient in an accurate estimate of value is the ability to find relevant data. Data can be obtained from public records and the Internet.

Valuation of residential property depends primarily on finding comparable values. There are different means available to foreclosure investors for finding comparable values. One source is the Internet. An example is the website maintained by Zillow.com. When the investor enters the address of a property, Zillow shows other (presumably comparable) residential properties that recently sold along with with the sales price and the date it was sold. It also shows relevant data about the details of the house. It can be used to search for foreclosure properties. Yahoo's real estate website also offers free information on recent sales in the neighborhood (Yahoo's information is compiled by Zillow, according to Yahoo's website). Another website that the investor can try is maintained by HomeGain.com, Inc. This site gives free information on neighborhood sales. Simply enter a zip code to get the data. Other foreclosure websites offer similar information for a fee with a free initial trial, often seven days.

A second source of information is public records. In many jurisdictions, this information can be obtained online. The foreclosure investor who has identified a prospective property can go to the local tax assessor's office or to a website such as PublicRecordFinder.com to get the assessor's website and then access the assessor's records. The assessor may act for an entire county or for a municipality or a township. The tax assessor determines the assessed value of property within his jurisdiction. The governing body sets the mill or millage rate. Then, the tax collector sends out the tax bills and collects the tax. Both the assessor's office and the collector's office can be sources of useful information.

Once at the tax assessor's website, the investor can type in the address of the prospective property. If the investor has the tax assessor's parcel number or name of the owner, that data can also be used. The address gives the investor access to the tax assessors' records on that property, which in most instances will include the names of the property owner and the mailing address for the real estate tax bill. It also shows the tax assessment and recent sale sales. It may also show construction details, such as the date of construction, the square footage and, in the case of a residence, the number of bedrooms. This information can be used to do comparisons of comparable properties. The investor can repeat this search for other properties on the same street, or within several blocks, to learn of any recent sales and to gather details on assessed values in the neighborhood. If the assessed value of the property is considerably higher than its neighbors, this would be a red flag. If assessed values have been declining, that would be a caution. The tax collector's office may have information about delinquencies and special assessments. A special assessment differs from a tax. The tax is levied on all real property within the community. A special assessment is used to pay for a municipal improvement that does not benefit the entire community, such as a sewer that serves just one neighborhood. Only the properties that benefit from the improvement are charged with paying for the improvements through a special assessment.

When undertaking this analysis, the foreclosure investor must remember that the assessed value is not the market value. The assessed value is usually a percentage of the actual value as determined by the tax assessor. The percentage is usually established by law. If the investor can learn the percentage and apply it to the assessed value, that would yield the value ascribed to the property by the assessor. However, the assessor's valuation is not likely to be accurate. This result arises because the assessor has to value every parcel of real property within his jurisdiction, and most assessors' offices simply do not have the personnel to re-assess each property every year. Hence, the valuations are usually not up to date with the market.

If the transaction is in the pre-foreclosure stage or the default and sale stage, when the borrower still has title to the property, the foreclosure investor needs to estimate the property's value and the borrower's equity. This information is necessary to effectively negotiate with the borrower. For example, if the borrower has $15,000 in equity, and investor A offers to purchase the property at a price that yields nothing to the borrower, it is unlikely that the offer will be accepted. However, a better informed investor B will offer a price taking the information into account and successfully make the deal.

To calculate the amount of the borrower's equity, the foreclosure investor begins with the market value of the property and then deducts all liens (except non-delinquent tax liens and assessments) encumbering the property. This includes the foreclosure costs that the borrower must pay to reinstate the loan, plus the amount due under the mortgage, plus any second mortgages and delinquent tax liens. The investor should then deduct any costs of repairing the property. The result will be the borrower's equity. The investor intends to capture some part of that equity, so the offer made by the investor must be priced accordingly. This exercise will also help the investor determine if the property is underwater.

One question that the foreclosure investor needs to answer is whether to retain an appraiser to help determine the value of the real property. If the investor intends to finance the acquisition, the lender answers that question affirmatively for the investor (although some lenders will use their own appraisers and not one retained by the investor). The advantage of an appraiser is that the investor can be confident that the offer price is in the correct range. Also, if the investor runs its own appraisal, then the investor knows that the price is likely to be appropriate when the lender runs a second appraisal using its own appraiser. The advantage is that in a foreclosure deal, time can be of the essence. If the lender's appraisal were to come in below the price, the loan may be denied, or the investor will have to put more of his or her own money into the deal. There may not be time to adjust or redo the appraisal, so having an idea of the value before the lender finishes its own valuation can be beneficial for the investor. Further, the price a lender may be seeking for REO could include the costs incurred in foreclosing on the property and, thus, exceed the market value of the property. An appraisal can help the investor assess value. On the other hand, if the investor has done a thorough and careful estimate of value and is not intending to finance the property, then the investor could consider foregoing an appraisal.

E.   Environmental Concerns

Most residential purchasers do not give much attention to environmental liabilities. In most cases, that does not cause a problem. However, commercial and industrial properties carry environmental risks that the careful investor covers in the due diligence effort.

As a general rule, the owner of real property is responsible for damage caused by hazardous substances located on that real property. The owner is liable even if he was unaware of the hazardous substances and had nothing to do with their creation or disposition on the real property. Accordingly, foreclosure investors need to include hazardous substances in the property analysis.

The first step for the investor is to retain an environmental professional to conduct a Phase I Environmental Site Assessment. The contents of a Phase I are prescribed by law. The assessment includes a physical inspection of the entire property, interviews with persons who have knowledge concerning the property, a review of state and federal lists of known contaminated sites, hazardous materials users, spills and underground storage tanks, the evaluation of nearby operations to determine if they could affect the property, a review of topographic maps and aerial photographs, a review of any environmental documents that apply to the property, an examination of the current and historic uses of the property and a survey of the history of the record owners of the property. If this assessment produces evidence of the presence of hazardous substances, a Phase II Environmental Site Assessment is conducted. The Phase II assessment is designed to address the kinds of contamination suggested by the Phase I review. It involves taking samples and doing an analysis of the property in order to determine if contamination exists and the nature and composition of any contamination.

Although industrial properties are obvious candidates for such an assessment, some commercial establishments can also be contaminated. Dry cleaners and gasoline service stations are classic examples of properties that should be carefully evaluated.

In commercial properties with tenants engaged in risky uses (both present and historic), the foreclosure investor needs to confirm that the leases with those tenants place responsibility for any contamination on the tenant.

CHAPTER III – 3   TITLE AND TITLE INSURANCE

What is the most essential aspect of investing in real property? The one item that the foreclosure investor must resolve is title. Acting without knowing the condition of the title to the property can be a very expensive proposition for the foreclosure investor.

Some people argue that if the price is low enough, the title becomes less important. Of course, if the investor can acquire a property for one dollar or one peppercorn, then that argument carries a great deal of weight. However, even in a severe recessionary economy, few properties are sold for a nominal price. Moreover, even if the price is unbelievably low, if the seller does not own the property, the investor loses the money paid to the seller, the time spent on the deal and any expenditures made during the examination of the property.

Failure to track title can also result in unforeseen expenses. Properties purchased at a foreclosure sale can be subject to tax liens, second mortgages and various other claims. If the property is subject to an unknown mortgage or other lien, the value is reduced by the amount of the encumbrance. The foreclosure investor will be forced to make some arrangement to satisfy the lien.

Failure to examine title can also impact the investor's ability to utilize the property. For example, a local governmental agency may have filed an action to condemn a part of the property. That portion of the property may be necessary for the use that the investor contemplates for the property. Without that component, the property may not be suitable for the investor's planned use.

In short, failure to secure good title can cause many problems. This chapter describes the kinds of title problems that a foreclosure investor may encounter when considering the acquisition of a parcel of real property.

A.   Types of Title

Ownership of real property is frequently described as a bundle of rights. To better understand this analogy, picture a bundle of sticks all tied together. An example would be a "fasces," a symbol of ancient Rome. A fasces consists of a bundle of rods or sticks bound together into a cylinder. The entire bundle comprises all of the rights and interests that make up the title to the real property. Each separate stick represents a different interest or right. The interests and rights include different forms of ownership, rights of occupancy, encumbrances and encroachments.

There are several types of ownership. The most complete ownership is known as "fee simple absolute," often referred to as "fee simple." Fee simple title can be conveyed by the owner without restriction to anyone. There is no greater form of ownership than fee simple. However, there are lesser forms. One example is "fee simple determinable." An owner whose title is fee simple determinable has full ownership of the real property but the title comes to an end upon the happening of some specified event, and upon that occurrence, title transfers to another owner. For example, a deed can convey title to the owner so long as the property is not used for the consumption of alcohol. If alcohol is consumed on the property, then title is transferred. A life estate is ownership that ends on the death of the owner or some other person named in the conveyance.

If the foreclosure investor encounters title in any form other than fee simple, the investor should either pass on that property or, if the deal is attractive, consult with an experienced real estate attorney for advice on the consequences of accepting such title and ways, if any, to address any problems. In the case of a life estate, for example, the foreclosure investor could contact the holder of the future rights and purchase those future rights from the holder. The cost of the future rights and the present rights should not exceed the value of the property if title were held in fee simple. After all, fee simple is equal to the present rights and the future rights, so the value of the present and future rights together should not exceed the value of the two combined.

The type of title found in most properties is fee simple absolute. This is seldom an issue for foreclosure investors. The more common issues will be either title vested in a person or entity other than the seller or title subject to unacceptable encumbrances.

One occasional problem is the vesting of title in a person other than the seller. In some instances, this arises because the seller acquired the property under the wrong name. Some well-known companies are better known by their fictitious business names than by their official names. However, fictitious business names are not the real name of the company. Other instances arise in the context of fraud. It has been reported that in neighborhoods where several houses have been foreclosed and are standing vacant, scam artists have sold abandoned houses to credulous purchasers who did not bother to check the state of the title.

B.   Encumbrances to Title

Rights of occupancy include leases and easements. A lease gives to the tenant, or lessee, the exclusive right of occupancy to the premises (although occupancy is not truly exclusive because landlords reserve limited rights to enter the premises). If the real property has been leased to a tenant, the foreclosure investor who purchases the property takes the property subject to the rights of the tenant for the term of the lease, at the rent specified in the lease. Leases can be beneficial to investors who are purchasing commercial or industrial properties. Without the leases, there is no income stream. An easement gives the easement holder a right to enter and pass over the real property. The most typical easements are rights-of-way for roads or driveways, but easements can also include conservation easements that prohibit development of the land. Easements may run across parts of the property that the investor intends to use for a beneficial purpose. The easement may prevent the investor from implementing that use.

Assuming that title is vested in the seller, the foreclosure investor must still ascertain whether the title is subject to acceptable encumbrances. Encumbrances are claims or liabilities that affect the property and impair its value or utility. Almost all real property is subject to encumbrances. The most common form of encumbrance is a real estate tax lien. A "lien" is a right that secures an obligation and gives the lien holder the right to sell the property if the obligation is not paid or performed. Counties and municipalities levy real estate taxes on real property within their jurisdictions. Real estate taxes typically are payable in installments over time and are secured by liens on the real property. The liens are imposed when the taxes are levied and are released when the taxes are paid. Because there are always real estate taxes to be paid, most real property is always subject to a tax lien. However, in some places, the government has exempted real property owned by nonprofit corporations and religious institutions from the obligation to pay real estate taxes. Those properties are the exception to the rule that real property is always subject to some form of lien. However, if the property is sold to an individual or a for-profit entity, the tax exemption terminates.

In the foreclosure context, real property is subject to a mortgage or deed of trust (assuming that the lender has not yet foreclosed). Some properties are subject to just one mortgage or deed of trust. Properties where the owner has borrowed on a home equity line of credit will be subject to a second mortgage and possibly a third mortgage or deed of trust. If the foreclosure investor acquires an encumbered property, and the mortgages and liens continue in effect, the investor must pay the mortgages or run the risk of being foreclosed upon.

An owner who has been unable to keep current on the mortgage payments is likely to be delinquent on other debts. The creditors of those other debts may have a right to file a lien against the debtor's property to secure payment of these debts. A foreclosure investor who purchases real property before the liens have been discharged may have to pay the debts to preserve the investor's purchase if another solution is not found.

Encroachments are interests that intrude upon a parcel of real property. For example, in a residential subdivision, consider two houses – a ranch house and a colonial house - that have abutting back yards. The owner of the ranch house has constructed a fence along the rear property line but has located the fence three feet into the yard of the neighboring colonial house. In this hypothetical, the ranch house's fence encroaches onto the colonial house's back yard. The foreclosure investor purchasing the colonial house may never know about the encroachment unless the investor has the property surveyed.

C.   Notice of Title Issues

Centuries ago, in 1677, England's Parliament adopted a law known as the Statute of Frauds. The Statute of Frauds identified certain types of contracts that were considered so important that they had to be in writing and signed by the parties, or one of the parties could refuse to perform the contract. Among these contracts were agreements to transfer title to, and interests in, real property, and also agreements that could not be performed within one year. At the time of the statute's adoption, leases were not considered to be interests in real property so leases of less than one year were not required to be in writing. As a consequence, almost all deals involving real estate were reduced to writing. Because all deals were in writing, the terms could be preserved by being transcribed in a public record.

A public record works very well if information recorded in it is accessible to the public. Documents relating to a certain parcel of land can be made accessible because land is permanent and immovable. Accordingly, if a parcel of land is accurately described, it can always be located. This characteristic has enabled governments to establish a system that keeps track of all persons who own and have owned the land over time and all persons who have owned an interest in the land or an encumbrance on the land. This system is referred to as "recording." Although each state has the authority to set up whatever system it desires, all states have adopted systems that are similar in operation. Depending on the state, either all counties or all municipalities within a state have an office where copies of relevant documents are placed on the public record. These are often referred to as "recorder's offices."

Purchasers of real property are obligated to consult the land records to ascertain the condition of title. The reason for this requirement can be explained by an illustration. Consider a person who owns an easement that enables him to cross over Parcel A to reach his own isolated Parcel B. The owner of Parcel B wants to be sure that the owner of Parcel A will not sell it to an innocent purchaser without disclosing the existence of the easement. If that were allowed, the new owner of Parcel A can prevent the owner of Parcel B from using the easement. This has two undesirable results. First, it would cheat the owner of the easement out of a valid right. Second, it leaves Parcel B isolated and unreachable which makes it unproductive. The common law judges did not favor creating unproductive properties. Accordingly, they required purchasers, as well as mortgagees and any other person acquiring in interest in real property, to consult the land records.

In the example of the easement crossing over Parcel A, the existence of the easement might well have been discovered by a purchaser if he made a physical inspection of the Parcel. If the easement is recorded, of course, it can be discovered by a search of the land records. But what about the tenant under a month-to-month lease? That type of document is not recorded and cannot be found by a search of the records. No, but a physical inspection of the property would disclose the presence of a tenant. Rights and interests in real property can be discovered by a physical inspection of real property. When the tenant's existence is discovered, a purchaser can ask the tenant to describe the agreement that gives the tenant the right of occupancy.

From these characteristics of real property, the common law courts developed the concept of notice. Actual notice is anything that the foreclosure investor actually knew about. Constructive notice includes (i)anything that an inspection of the property and inquiry regarding the property would have revealed, such as the presence of tenants, or the existence of wetlands, or roads running across the land; and (ii)anything that has been recorded in the appropriate land records.

As a consequence, under the recording laws, a foreclosure investor who acquires an interest in land and improvements takes that interest subject to everything in which the investor has actual notice and everything in which the investor has constructive notice.

D.   Searching Title

It is clear that encumbrances can limit the value of a property, and faulty title can result in losses. How, then, does a foreclosure investor examine title?

Title can be examined by the foreclosure investor, by a title insurance company or by a professional retained by the investor. Although it is highly recommended that a foreclosure investor purchase title insurance on any property that he purchases, when making a preliminary inquiry, the investor may decide to perform a title search himself to conserve funds. Where then, would the investor find the land records? Similar to many other items in real estate, the answer varies from state to state. In some states, the town clerk of the municipality in which the property is located maintains the land records. In other states, the county recorder maintains the land records for the entire county. Some county recorders have reduced the land records to electronic form that can be searched electronically, either online or at the county recorder's office.

The property can be described in the land records by its legal description or, in some cases, by its street address, or by the name of the current owner in the grantor/grantee index. To obtain names, the foreclosure investor can consult the records of the local tax assessor. The tax assessor probably has a property tax role which lists the properties, their owners and the assessed value. Properties are identified by a unique identifier, usually a number. In some areas, the tax assessor's number can be used to access the land records for a particular property.

E.   Title Insurance

If the foreclosure investor intends to purchase the real property, it is essential that the investor obtains title insurance. The title insurance company insures the investor that the land is in fact owned by the person shown in the records, and that there are no encumbrances on the title other than those described by the title insurance company in a preliminary title report. Since the title insurance company must search the records in order to enable it to issue insurance, it can be more economical to utilize the title insurer to conduct a search on the investor's behalf. The benefit of title insurance is that if the title insurance company makes a mistake, it indemnifies the investor for any losses suffered. Also, title insurance ordinarily insures against fraud in the record which the individual investor is usually not able to discover. For example, if the borrower purchased the property from someone who did not have adequate authority to sell the property, that fact would be impossible to determine from a search of the records. The title insurance company insures the foreclosure investor against that improper conveyance.

Title insurance can be issued to insure the investor's title or to insure the lien of the lender's mortgage or deed of trust. A title insurance company reviews the state of the title and issues insurance in which it agrees to indemnify the insured if the title to a property is not in the condition represented by the title insurer. Even if the foreclosure investor does not desire title insurance, every institutional lender demands that its mortgage or deed of trust be insured in the amount of the mortgage loan. Since the investor will have to purchase title insurance to satisfy the lender, and pay for the title company's search, the investor might as well buy owner's title insurance. The premium for the two policies will not exceed the cost of the owner's policy.

At the opening of a transaction, the title insurance company searches the land records and other relevant public records. Modern title insurance companies maintain title plants on their premises that contain all of the documents that are found in the public land records, and those plants are accessible electronically. The title insurer issues a preliminary title report or a title commitment in which the property is described by its legal description, the record owner is named, all liens encumbering the property are described and all other encumbrances such as leases and easements and CC&Rs are described. In a commitment, the insurer states the events that must occur if title is to be insured in the name of the new owner or lender.

Whether the title insurance company issues a title report or a title commitment depends on the state in which the property is located.
After reviewing the title report or commitment, the foreclosure investor will identify those encumbrances that are acceptable and those that are not. To protect the investor's options, the purchase agreement entered into by the investor will have as a condition the right to approve or disapprove the condition of the title.

If the property is acquired after a foreclosure sale, the title insurance has the additional effect of insuring that the foreclosure sale was properly conducted. If the purchase occurs just before a foreclosure sale by auction, the investor needs to update any title search to be sure that no other lenders or claimants have filed liens against the property since the original search was conducted. A title insurance company will conduct such a last minute search.

PART IV   HOW PURCHASING THE PROPERTY AT DIFFERENT STAGES OF FORECLOSURE AFFECTS THE INVESTMENT PROCESS

As we have discussed in preceding chapters, the foreclosure process goes through four stages. These are the pre-foreclosure stage, the default and auction stage, the redemption stage and the REO stage. Each of these stages has its own advantages and disadvantages. This Part IV will examine the circumstances, advantages and disadvantages that a foreclosure investor would encounter in each stage.

One thing to note is that the owner of the property differs from stage to stage, and the person with whom the foreclosure investor negotiates will differ from stage to stage. The person controlling the negotiation will have different motivations at each stage, and understanding these motivations can be advantageous to the foreclosure investor.

CHAPTER IV-1   PRE-FORECLOSURE STAGE

The opportunities available to a foreclosure investor during the pre-foreclosure stage are mixed. First, the amount in default is at its lowest amount because the borrower has not missed a large number of payments, and the lender has not incurred foreclosure costs. The advantage this gives the foreclosure investor is that if the owner has elected to dispose of the property, the amount that the foreclosure investor needs to pay is less during this time than it is at a later stage. On the other hand, because the amount in default is the least, it is easier for the borrower to cure and bring the loan current. Second, the borrower, particularly a residential borrower, may be in denial of his financial circumstances and, hence, unwilling or unable to deal with the crisis he is facing. Third, if the property is underwater or upside down, the foreclosure investor is not making a sound investment by paying the full amount of the loan. Therefore, he needs to negotiate a short sale. A "short sale" is a sale by the borrower to the investor at a price below the amount due on the loan. Short sales are discussed in greater detail below.

A.   Finding Prospective Properties

Defaults involving properties that have not yet reached the default and auction stage are not publicly noticed. Consequently, the foreclosure investor must rely on the methods described above in Chapter III-1 to obtain information about prospective properties.   If the closure investor has implemented these techniques, he has a network of real estate brokers and foreclosure lenders, or he has his interest in pre-foreclosure properties, or he has made short sale specialists aware of his interest. Any of these techniques can give the foreclosure investor notice of the availability of a prospective property.

When a foreclosure investor identifies a prospective property, the investor must complete the due diligence described above in Chapter III-2. Part of the due diligence involves contacting and dealing with the borrower.

B.   Negotiating with the Borrower

Foreclosure investors may identify a target property but have difficulty finding the names and addresses of borrowers in default because there has been no public notice of the default and the borrower may reside elsewhere. There are several websites that offer names, addresses and possibly telephone numbers.   Some   of   the   sites   include einvestigator.com, intelius.com, addresses.com, querydata.com and knowx.com. Many of these sites charge a fee for the information.

When discussing matters with the borrower, it is important for the investor to speak to the actual borrower. It has been reported that in one area, where there was a large number of foreclosures, individuals began occupying abandoned homes and posing as the owners. Investors entered into deals with these scam artists who absconded with the investors' money. Therefore, it is important to know with whom you are dealing. From the borrower's perspective, the borrower wants to know that the investor is who he purports to be. In an age of identity theft, one cannot be too cautious.   Accordingly, before progressing too far into discussions, it is advisable for the investor to show the borrower his driver's license or other government-issued photo identification and ask to see the same of the borrower.

When speaking with the borrower, a foreclosure investor should be understanding and helpful. This approach eases the negotiations with the borrower.

In the pre-foreclosure stage, the borrower is at the beginning of the default process. The borrower may have missed one, or maybe even a couple of payments under the mortgage. The mental state of the borrower ranges from anger to optimism to desperation. The payments might have been missed because of a temporary glitch in the borrower's cash flow. There may be sufficient equity in the property to justify the borrower's efforts to cure the default and retain title to the property. The borrower may be optimistic that the default can be cured. In contrast, the payments might have been missed because the borrower has just lost his job, has suffered a debilitating illness or has just completed a divorce. In these circumstances, the borrower may feel anger or desperation. The property may be underwater and the borrower cannot see any benefit to continue making payments on the mortgage. The willingness of the borrower to negotiate a sale varies greatly under each of these mindsets. Accordingly, it is beneficial to the foreclosure investor to try to get an idea of the borrower's situation early in the process.

An investor must remember the reasons for a borrower to enter into a pre-foreclosure transaction. First, this transaction can avoid the negative impact on the borrower's credit rating. A foreclosure can tarnish a borrower's credit rating. Similarly, a short sale has a negative effect on the borrower's credit rating. Therefore, the borrower has an incentive to arrange a deal that eliminates, or at least mitigates, these negative effects. Second, the borrower may simply be overextended and desire the relief from the burden of a particular mortgage. Allowing an investor to take over the property and the debt may be welcomed by the borrower.

Conversely, the investor must also understand reasons why a borrower may not be willing to enter into a pre-foreclosure transaction. One major reason for the borrower to decline includes the prospect of new federal programs that provide for mortgage modifications to help borrowers stay in their homes. The borrower may think that he qualifies under such a program. However, the reasoning for a borrower's inclination to enter into a sale at this stage will nevertheless return to the facts of the situation.

If the borrower has defaulted and takes no measures to cure, the situation goes from bad to worse. The amount of principal in default will mount, there will be default interest on the principal, late payment fees, and if the loan goes into foreclosure, there will be trustee and attorney fees. The situation worsens with each month that goes by, and the amount required to cure the default becomes greater. Some lenders work with the borrower in order to work out the loan or modify the payment terms. In a particularly severe recession, where there is government pressure on lenders, the efforts to modify the loan are greater. However, when the property is underwater, or the borrower has suffered a serious economic setback, these efforts may not be fruitful, thereby creating an opportunity for the foreclosure investor. Because borrowers usually place priority on retaining their homes, they might have used their available cash to make mortgage payments and maximized the charges on their credit cards. If there is equity in the property, they might have taken out a home equity loan or second mortgage. It is likely that the borrower is in default of the obligations under this additional debt.

The foreclosure investor's intervention can benefit the borrower who is able to dispose of the property without going through a foreclosure. If there is equity in the property, the borrower may be able to walk away from the deal with some money. One of the foreclosure investor's most important jobs at this point is to engage the borrower in a manner that gives the borrower confidence that his financial difficulties can be resolved. . A borrower who does not have confidence in an investor has little incentive to deal with that investor.

Depending on the state of the loan, the foreclosure investor may have several different options to propose to the borrower. If there is substantial equity in the property, the foreclosure investor can acquire the property by bringing the loan current, or even paying off the loan with new financing, and purchasing the borrower's interest. If the property is underwater, the foreclosure investor can assist the borrower in negotiating a short sale with the lender. The level of creativity to approach the situation depends upon the investor and the parties. In any case, the borrower should see that the investor's actions benefit the borrower. In executing any of these strategies, the foreclosure investor must keep in mind the other factors that have been discussed. For example, acquiring the property may trigger the due on sale clause, and therefore, the investor needs to address that with the lender.

Also, when the foreclosure investor meets with the borrower, one goal of the meeting is to establish a rapport with the borrower. Another goal is to obtain information necessary to carry out the purchase. Therefore, the investor needs to ask questions. The investor should develop a list of questions for the borrower prior to the meeting. Questions that the investor should ask include: (i) What is the amount of the loan and the amount of the monthly payment; (ii) Does the borrower want to stay in the property (if it is a residence); (iii) What is the amount in default and what fees and costs have been charged against the borrower; (iv) Is the borrower planning to declare bankruptcy; (v) How much does the borrower think the property is worth; (vi) How much equity does the borrower think exists in the house; (vii) Is the borrower able to access the loan account online; (vii) Is the property on the market; (viii) Have any offers been made to purchase the property; and (ix) Is there a home equity loan or second mortgage on the property.

If the borrower can access the loan account online, the investor has a means of quickly obtaining or confirming information. Also, the investor should not assume that the absence of a "For Sale" sign means the property is not on the market. Some communities forbid the posting of such signs. Lastly, if there is a home equity loan or second mortgage, the investor needs to ask all of the same questions about the second mortgage.

C. Advantages to the Foreclosure Investor

One principal advantage to the foreclosure investor of acting at this stage is less competition. Since there is no public notice of the default, there are fewer investors competing for the property. When defaults are noticed, borrowers receive inquiries from potential investors, brokers, bankruptcy consultants and debt consolidation consultants. The borrowers probably have difficulty distinguishing you from all of the other potential investors. When the default has not yet been noticed, the borrower may feel more comfortable with the investor who has sought out the borrower and acted in a helpful manner.

Another advantage arises in the context of commercial properties. The value of commercial properties flows from the rental stream. When a borrower defaults, the lender is likely to exercise its assignment of rents so that it may begin to collect the rents itself. The lender first applies the rents to pay down the debt, so there may be insufficient revenue to maintain the property. In that context, when the property is finally acquired, the foreclosure investor incurs additional rehabilitation costs. If the investor acts during the pre-foreclosure stage, the rents will flow to the investor upon acquisition of the property.

Another advantage of acquiring a property in the pre-forclosure stage is that the investor can develop a good relationship with the borrower. This allows the investor to have an opportunity to inspect the property which can be very important if there are problems with the property.
Even if the foreclosure investor does not initially develop a working relationship with the borrower, the investor who starts during the pre-foreclosure stage has more time to develop such a relationship. The borrower continues to be the owner of the property until the foreclosure sale. The investor has that time from the first contact until the sale to develop a relationship and strike a deal. This is an advantage over other investors that do not meet the borrower until later in the foreclosure process.

There are other advantages to acquiring property at the pre-foreclosure stage. At the auction sale, the only option available is to purchase the property and pay cash in the amount of the highest bid. Once the investor has made a bid, the investor is legally obligated to pay the bid amount. In contrast, during the pre-foreclosure stage, the investor may be able to negotiate a price which is less than the potential highest bid. The investor can also negotiate a transaction that does not involve paying the full amount in cash. In addition, the investor may be able to strike a deal that leaves the existing financing in place. This obviously minimizes the investor's risk and saves the time and money required to find new financing.

During the pre-foreclosure stage, if the foreclosure investor is obligated to make a down payment, the payment is likely to be in a small amount. This is because the amount in default is at its lowest amount, and it is the easiest time for the borrower or the investor to bring the loan current. Other than a deposit in escrow, no cash should change hands until the closing when the borrower has vacated the property, the investor has completed a last-minute inspection, and all other due diligence matters are satisfied.

D.   Disadvantages to the Foreclosure Investor

At the pre-foreclosure stage, one of the more difficult problems to overcome is convincing the borrower to allow the investor to negotiate the settlement on the borrower's behalf. During the default and auction stage, many people contact the borrower, such as the lender, the lender's collection agency, attorneys, real estate brokers, mortgage brokers, investors and debt counselors. It is possible that during the pre-foreclosure stage, the same individuals contact the borrower. This may cause the borrower apprehension in allowing the investor to immediately negotiate a deal with the lender. This also exemplifies the importance of establishing a good working relationship with the borrower early in the process.

Another disadvantage of the pre-foreclosure stage is that the borrower may not wish to speak to an investor because he is in denial about the situation or his inability to cure the default. It has been reported that one of the major problems lenders have in trying to resolve foreclosure problems is that borrowers refuse to talk to them. This is typical of many people in default, and it can be a disadvantage to the investor who is seeking to become involved early in the process.

Another disadvantage of purchasing real property directly from the borrower prior to foreclosure is that encumbrances which are junior to the mortgage are not wiped out like they are when the foreclosure proceeds. A borrower who is in default under the mortgage is probably in default under other obligations, including tax liens and judgment liens. The investor who acquires property directly from the borrower will have title subject to these junior liens.

Another possible disadvantage is that the borrower may be negotiating with the lender while he is negotiating with the foreclosure investor. This means that the investor may incur expenses and spend time working on a deal to later learn that the default has been cured through a modification. Prior to undertaking pre-foreclosure negotiations with the lender, the investor should reach an agreement with the borrower that the borrower will not deal separately with the lender.

E.   Legal and Practical Restrictions on Investors

The Federal Government and some trade associations began developing practices that can restrict the ability of a foreclosure investor to acquire property in the pre-foreclosure stage. One example of a government restriction appears in the Department of Housing and Urban Development ("HUD") single family mortgage insurance programs. The rule effectually prohibits flipping of certain properties. The following rules apply to properties that are eligible to be financed with Federal Housing Administration ("FHA") mortgage insurance. If these rules are not followed, the properties are not eligible for FHA insurance.

To be eligible for FHA insurance, the following must be followed:

(1) The property must be purchased from the record owner and not through an assignment of the contract of sale;

(2) The mortgagee must document that the seller is the owner of record and must submit this documentation to HUD;

(3) Any property sold within 90 days of the seller's acquisition is not eligible for FHA mortgage insurance;

(4) Any property sold between 91 days and 180 days following the seller's acquisition is eligible for FHA mortgage

insurance except that if the re-sale price is 100 percent over the purchase price, there must be documentation establishing that the increased value results from the property's rehabilitation;

(5) Any property sold between 91 days and 12 months following the seller's acquisition is eligible for FHA mortgage insurance except that HUD may require that the lender document the re-sale value of the property if the re-sale price is 5 percent or greater than the lowest sales price of the property during the preceding 12 months.

This rule only affects properties that are eligible for FHA insurance. An investor is affected by this rule if he intends to sell the property to a purchaser utilizing FHA insured financing.

A group of trade associations, comprising the Mortgage Bankers Association of America ("MBA"), the American Land Title Association ("ALTA") and the American Escrow Association ("AEA") has published a draft of a document, dated December 8, 2008, entitled the *Uniform General Closing Instructions*. The intent of this initiative is to establish a set of rules that govern real estate closing procedures across the nation. Under the proposal, the individual charged with conducting the closing must postpone the closing and contact the lender to obtain its permission to proceed if, at any time during the closing, the employee discovers that (i) the transaction is part of any other sale or financing of the real property, such as a flip, a double closing or a pass through; or (ii) the real property was transferred within the past 180 days. These rules can disrupt closings in which foreclosure investors intend to flip a property. Foreclosure investors should determine the current status of these rules and ascertain whether or not they affect any intended transaction.

F.   Loan Information

Regardless of whether the foreclosure investor has any dealings with the lender, the investor must learn the amount of the loan and any charges in default before finalizing a deal with the borrower. Otherwise, the investor can take title subject to a loan considerably in excess of the amount expected.

In order to get this information, either the borrower or the foreclosure investor should request that the lender issue a mortgagee estoppel letter. The concept of this estoppel letter is similar to the concept of a tenant's estoppel certificate. Here, the lender is prevented from making claims that are contrary to the facts set forth in the letter or certificate. Accordingly, the investor should verify that the estoppel letter covers all relevant information. The investor should ask the mortgagee, or lender, to confirm the unpaid principal balance of the loan, the current interest rate, identify any applicable default interest rate, the total monthly payment, the arrears amount, and the sum needed to cure all defaults to reinstate the loan. As a practical matter, if the investor has been dealing with the lender's representatives, the investor can send the request for a mortgagee estoppel letter directly to the lender. If the investor has not been dealing directly with the lender, the borrower needs to authorize the lender to send the estoppel letter directly to the investor.

CHAPTER IV-2   DEFAULT & AUCTION STAGE

The default and auction stage is that period of time beginning at the point where the lender gives formal notice of the borrower's default and ends at the completion of the foreclosure auction. Since the borrower continues to be the owner of the property until the end of this stage, a number of factors that apply to the pre-foreclosure stage also apply to the default and auction stage. However, now that the lender is taking action, the lender plays a greater role in the process. Additionally, the foreclosure investor may have to deal with the lender's attorneys and with the trustee under the deed of trust.

This stage is bifurcated because it can proceed in the direction of striking a deal with the borrower and lender or it can entail a sale at auction involving different opportunities. The first part of this stage is similar in many ways to the pre-foreclosure stage. However, there are some significant differences.

A.   Contacting Borrowers during the Default and Auction Stage

Identifying prospective properties is easier to accomplish, but that ease is accompanied by greater competition with other investors. The identification is easier because the defaults are publicly noticed. In a lien theory state, the lender files a foreclosure lawsuit and records a *lis pendens* in the land records. In a title theory state, the lender notifies the trustee under the deed of trust to record a notice of default in the land records. Both of these recordings give public notice to the world.

This public notice creates a disadvantage for the foreclosure investor because it increases the number of investors who are competing for the property. The foreclosure investor may be shut out of a deal by the competitors. Along these same lines, the borrower may use an offer from one competitor to try and exact a better deal from another investor.

Another consequence of this public notice is that there are more people contacting the borrower. These people are not just competing investors. They include the lender, the lender's collection agents, the lender's attorneys and any other number of interested persons. The borrower may receive inquiries by mail or telephone or possibly even personal visits. One challenge to the foreclosure investor is to distinguish himself from the multitude of persons contacting the borrower.

The foreclosure investor will need to decide which technique works best for him. One technique is to contact the borrower by a cold telephone call or by knocking on the borrower's front door. One problem with knocking on the borrower's front door without any advance notice is that you never know who will answer the door. A borrower who is responding with anger to a notice of default is likely to respond with anger to an unwelcome knock on the door. Regarding cold telephone calls, many borrowers who are in default try to avoid the lender or the lender's collection agency. If the borrower's telephone does not have caller recognition, the borrower is likely to avoid picking up the telephone when the investor telephones the borrower.

Another less intrusive technique is to contact the borrower by writing a letter and sending it to the address found in the notice of default or *lis pendens*. Even if the investor feels that a telephone call or personal contact is more effective, it is advisable to make the initial contact in writing. The foreclosure investor should consider mailing letters to all borrowers with properties in which the investor has a true interest. On the other hand, investors should be careful not to overdo it. If, unexpectedly, several borrowers reply affirmatively, the investor may have more properties than can be handled efficiently. When the borrower responds to a letter inquiry, the foreclosure investor can arrange to discuss the matter over the telephone or in a direct meeting. The foreclosure investor also needs to decide whether to send follow-up letters and how often to do so. A letter that is sent just after the initial filing of the public notice may be thrown away because the borrower expects to cure the default or work something out with the lender. The letter sent just 10 days before the foreclosure sale may arrive too late because there may not be enough time to act or because some other investor's offer has been accepted.

The letters should be carefully written, free of typographical errors and certain to contain the investor's contact information. Using a printed letterhead makes the letter look more professional. Once the investor has developed a form of letter that has proven to be effective, the investor can use a mail merge software program to reproduce any number of letters.

The foreclosure investor should endeavor to contact the borrower as soon as the investor becomes aware that the borrower has mortgage problems. In most states, the borrower has a period of time after the default in which to reinstate the loan. The foreclosure sale cannot occur until the reinstatement period has expired. This gives the foreclosure investor and the borrower time to negotiate and close the transaction.

To be effective, the letter must spell out in clear terms the actions that the foreclosure investor is prepared to take. The more research the investor has done on the property, and the more information the investor has developed about the property, the more detailed the investor's letter can be. If the investor knows nothing about the property except the fact that it is in default, the investor should not state in the letter that he is prepared to purchase the property for a specified amount. On the other hand, the investor should not spend too much time researching the property and miss the opportunity to acquire the property because another investor has moved more quickly.

This discussion about contacting the borrower also applies to the pre-foreclosure stage. However, because of the possibility of competing investors chasing the same property, the foreclosure investor should be prepared to act quickly at this stage.

The development of a good system to contact borrowers does not assure success. The investor must be able to do more. It is incumbent upon a foreclosure investor to strike a good relationship with the borrower. The borrower is probably distressed by his present financial condition and may be under great pressure from debts that are accumulating. Once the *lis pendens* or notice of default has been filed, the borrower has only a limited amount of time to decide upon a course of action, He can either try to save the property or dispose of the property in a beneficial manner. The clock's ticking will only make it more difficult for the borrower.   The challenge to the foreclosure investor is to overcome these negative circumstances and gain the borrower's trust. A second challenge for the investor is being able to walk away from a deal that cannot be structured to make economic sense. . This can be a blow to the borrower who has relied on the investor, but the investor must be prepared for this situation. If this situation is too difficult for an investor, he should consider skipping the pre-foreclosure stage and the early part of the default and auction stage.

When meeting the borrower for the first time, the foreclosure investor should ask the questions described in Subchapter IV-4.B below. The foreclosure investor should also ask for copies of the mortgage or deed of trust, the promissory note, any other loan agreement, any leases, condominium or cooperative documents, the escrow statement and any appraisal or surveys of the property that the borrower possesses. The reasons for reviewing these documents are discussed in Chapter III-2.

One key to success is persistence. The foreclosure investor who continues to make the effort may ultimately be rewarded with a deal. The investor who walks away will have spent time, and possibly money, with nothing to show for it. There is no guaranty that tenacity will pay off, but the investor can be assured that lack of persistence will not succeed.

If the foreclosure investor's efforts do not pay off, and contact with the borrower cannot be established, the investor is still able to purchase the property at the foreclosure sale. The techniques, advantages and disadvantages of a foreclosure sale are discussed in detail in Subchapter IV-2.C below.

When the foreclosure investor connects with the borrower, he must be prepared to deal with the lender. As noted above in the discussion of the pre-foreclosure stage, if there is equity remaining in the property, the investor has options that need not include the lender. However, for properties that are underwater, the foreclosure investor must involve the lender. If a default is filed, it can be presumed that the borrower has been unable to arrange a workout with the lender. Otherwise, the default would not have been filed. Consequently, unless there is equity in the property, which is unlikely in a severe recession, negotiating any arrangement with the borrower also includes the lender.

B.   Arrangements Involving the Lender

One of the difficulties of investing during the default and auction stage is that borrowers resist allowing investors to deal directly with their lenders. This is not surprising. The foreclosure investor is asking the borrower to entrust his financial well-being to a complete stranger.

If there is no equity in the property, the foreclosure investor cannot complete a deal that makes sense without involving the lender. The reason is that the foreclosure investor has no interest in purchasing a property which is encumbered by more debt than the property is worth. Therefore, the investor must strike a deal that reduces the amount of the debt which requires lender's involvement and consent. This is referred to as a "short sale." Short sales are discussed in more detail in Chapter V-2 below.

Another reason for contacting the lender is that the foreclosure investor must have an accurate statement of the debt, fees and charges owed by the borrower to the lender. The investor cannot calculate the borrower's equity without having the details of the debt. An investor who has not performed a careful due diligence may find himself having paid $150,000 for a property that is encumbered by a debt of $200,000 and additional fees and costs of $25,000. If the investor has not assumed the loan, the investor will not be liable for these obligations, but the property will nevertheless be encumbered by this debt. Investors should not rely on just the information contained in the *lis pendens* or the notice of default. These documents will not contain information on junior liens, tax liens or judgment liens.

For now, we will address the steps that the investor should take to contact the lender.

The borrower must provide the contact between the foreclosure investor and the lender. Institutional lenders with loans in default may assign these loans to special departments. These departments are sometimes referred to as "loss mitigation" or "loan loss mitigation" departments. Other terms that an investor may encounter when dealing with an institutional lender include the foreclosures department, the loan work-out or modification department and the loan reinstatement department.

The borrower should contact the lender's loss mitigation department in writing, authorizing the investor to receive information on behalf of the borrower and requesting that the lender provide the investor with all relevant information about the loan and the default. Many institutional lenders do not deal with an unrelated third party without the written consent of the borrower. Even if the investor can get loan information online, the investor should still require the borrower to order a written statement from the loss mitigation department to confirm the accuracy and completeness of the online information. The foreclosure investor should have the initial due diligence completed in

137

order to calculate whether there is any equity as soon as the lender returns the information on the loan.

The foreclosure investor should ask the borrower to instruct the lender to send a mortgagee estoppel letter to the investor. The mortgagee estoppel letter is described in more detail in Chapter IV-1.F.

The foreclosure investor should use the same approach with the holders of second mortgages and other junior liens. Before approaching the holder of a subordinate lien, the investor should calculate whether there is any equity that could be used to compensate the junior lien holders. If there is no equity, the junior liens will be wiped out in a foreclosure. Therefore, when talking to these lien holders, the investor should point out to them the likelihood of their liens being eliminated. If the investor is planning to structure a deal that involves the holders of subordinate liens, it is helpful to get their cooperation. One way to get their cooperation is to offer them something to either preserve their liens or otherwise compensate them. This is not to say that the investor should always accommodate the holders of junior liens. Sometimes, there is no equity or other reason to involve them, and there will be little the investor can do for them. Other times, when there is some equity but not enough (after subtracting the amount of the junior lien) to make the effort worth the investor's while, the investor could offer to purchase the junior lien at a discount. In this situation, the investor and the junior encumbrancers share the remaining equity.

C.   Purchasing at the Foreclosure Auction

If the foreclosure investor is unable to make a deal with the borrower and the lender before the foreclosure sale, the investor can always bid at the auction. However, depending on the reasons for not striking a deal, this can be a risky proposition. If the foreclosure investor was unable to make a deal because the borrower refused to meet with the investor, or because a competitor pushed the investor out of the picture, or there was any other matter preventing the investor from meeting with the borrower, then the investor can be at a disadvantage.

Properties in the auction process may not be open to public inspection. Unless the property has been abandoned, the occupant does not usually allow strangers or home inspectors onto the property. Even if the property has been abandoned, it is still owned by the borrower, and anyone who enters the property without permission may be trespassing. A drive-by inspection does not reveal mold, termites or leaky basements. The borrower may have trashed the property and removed the fixtures and appliances before the sale. A person who bids at the foreclosure auction without an inspection runs the risk of incurring substantial repair costs that are not reimbursed because the lender is selling without any warranties regarding the same. The problem is not as widespread in the auction of a commercial or industrial property because tenants under leases usually do not leave the property and have no reason to damage their own premises.

Another consideration of purchasing a property at auction is the degree of control over the price that the investor will pay. At an auction, the price is dependent on the bidders, and the investor's only recourse if the price goes beyond the investor's limit is to stop bidding. The investor needs to guard against the excitement that can accompany an auction in order to avoid over-bidding.

Another item to consider when purchasing a property at auction is that the foreclosure investor must have the cash to pay the bid price. The investor must demonstrate the ability to pay before being permitted to bid and must pay the bid price (or percentage) in cash at the sale. This requires financing the bid price. The investor must pay the amount of the loan, late charges and costs. This can be advantageous to the investor with funds. Competitors may not be able to comply with funding requirements, which eliminates them from the auction.

An investor purchasing a property at auction must realize the possibility that the property is occupied by the borrower or squatters. In that case, the investor is forced to bring an eviction action against the occupants. Depending on the law of the state where the property is located, the eviction process can take months to complete. In contrast, if the investor deals with the borrower, the investor can condition payment of the price on the borrower vacating the property. At a foreclosure sale, the price must be paid to the lender even if the property is occupied.

In some states, the borrower has the right to redeem the property for a period of time after the sale. This is discussed in Chapter IV-3 below.

Foreclosure sales can be postponed or canceled. A foreclosure investor can spend time and money on the due diligence effort and arranging the financing, only to have the borrower declare bankruptcy or cure the loan default at the last minute. Alternatively, a competitor may have purchased the property in a deal with the borrower. These events all cause a cancelation of the auction.

Buying at a foreclosure sale does have some advantages. For example, the sale eliminates all liens and encumbrances that were filed against the property after the recording of the mortgage or deed of trust. The foreclosure wipes out all of these junior liens. For investors that are unwilling to negotiate with the borrower, the sale allows the investor to acquire the property without having to deal with the borrower. An auction may give the investor the opportunity to bid with minimal competition. Some properties attract investors, others do not. For those properties that do not, the investor only has to outbid the lender.

The investor deals with the auctioneer. The auctioneer can be the trustee under the deed of trust, the sheriff or some other officer of the court.

After the auctioneer brings down the hammer on the highest bid, the bidder becomes the owner. The borrower no longer has an interest in the property except in states that give the borrower a right of redemption. The period of time in which the right of redemption is in effect is the third stage of the foreclosure process.

If the foreclosure investor elects to participate in an auction, here are the keys to success:

- The first few properties offer the greatest bargains. After the auction is underway, there may be many bidders. At the very beginning of the auction, however, other bidders have not yet arrived or are not yet warmed up or are waiting to see the lay of the land. The earliest parcels are the best buys.

- Never, never, never enter into a bidding war. Allow the heat and emotion of the action to lead your competitors astray. You must stay level-headed and true to your analysis of each property's value.
- Station yourself at the front of the line, in the first rows of seats or at the front of the standing room and dress for success. Dress in good business attire to give the auctioneer and your competitors a good impression of your confidence and capabilities.

As an example, I had targeted an office building located at 139 Glen Street, Glen Cove, New York as a property I wanted to acquire. The property was listed for sale at $1,000,000 but had not sold and was being offered at auction. This was an absolute auction with no reserve. The bidding started at $115,000. I made the second bid of $116,000. My bid was the second and last bid. No one else bid. After the closing of the auction, I was offered $100,000 for my right to purchase the property and eventually I sold a property for $550,000 that I had acquired for $116,000. About 35 people attended that auction, but only two bid and I was the high bidder. My approach and appearance sealed the deal for me. How you present yourself can mean a great deal at an auction.

CHAPTER IV-3 REDEMPTION STAGE

The statutory right of redemption is the borrower's right, after the closing of the foreclosure auction, to pay the redemption amount and recover title to the property. Only certain states permit redemption, and in some states, the availability to redeem depends on the kind of foreclosure proceeding that the lender utilized. In those states where a statutory right of redemption exists, the holders of junior liens may also have redemption rights.

In some redemption states, the borrower continues to own the property until the expiration of the redemption period. In those states, the high bidder at the foreclosure sale does not acquire title to the real property at the closing of the auction sale. Instead the high bidder purchases the right to own the property until the redemption period expires. Accordingly, in some redemption states, the borrower can continue to reside in the property if it is a residence or collect the rents from a commercial property.

A. Problems and Opportunities for the Foreclosure Investor

Redemption poses problems and opportunities for the foreclosure investor. The problems should be obvious. Title is not finally vested in the high bidder until the period of redemption has expired. If the investor is the high bidder, he cannot take possession of the property in some states until expiration of the redemption period. In that time, the borrower can strip a residence of its fixtures and appliances and could divert rents from commercial or industrial properties to the borrower's pocket. There are techniques to address these problems, but the investor must first become familiar with the state's redemption procedures in order to know what action to take.

Another problem is the restraint on the high bidder's ability to sell the property. Few purchasers buy property that a third party can redeem at any time. The high bidder must bide his time until the right of redemption has passed. Though, the high bidder can market the property subject to the redemption right.

A foreclosure investor who desires to acquire a property in the redemption stage must pay the entire redemption amount. Due to this requirement, redemption investing makes sense only if there is sufficient equity remaining in the property. The investor can calculate whether there is sufficient equity by adding together the redemption amount and any mortgage liens that remain after the foreclosure (if foreclosure done by junior lienor), and subtracting that sum from the market value of the property. If the remainder satisfies the investor's investment criteria, then the investor should consider a redemption investment. Redemption does not make sense if the property is underwater and the equity is non-existent or too small to be of any real value.

Assuming there is sufficient equity, the foreclosure investor may encounter redemption in one of two situations. The first is where the investor is the high bidder at the foreclosure sale and must deal with redemption rights held by other persons. The second is where another person was the high bidder at the foreclosure sale, and the investor wishes to exercise the redemption right. Either situation is addressed by the same technique.

Foreclosure investors who have purchased the property at the auction can protect themselves against redemption by purchasing the redemption rights from the borrower (or junior lien holders). In states where the right of redemption has been created by the courts rather than the legislature, the courts examine a sale of redemption rights so the foreclosure investor needs to be above board in his dealings. Similarly, foreclosure investors who wish to purchase the equity can also use the redemption rights to acquire the property by purchasing the rights from the borrower and then redeeming the property from the high bidder. This is a possibility when there is equity in the property, the borrower is in need of funds and there are no subordinate liens remaining after the foreclosure sale.

One interesting scenario that the foreclosure investor may consider is to purchase the redemption rights from the borrower when the value of the real property exceeds the amount of the first mortgage, any junior liens have been extinguished by the foreclosure, and the holders of those junior liens have no redemption rights. Assuming that the borrower is in difficult straits and welcomes a cash payment, the foreclosure investor can acquire the redemption rights, possibly for a nominal amount. In that case, the property is acquired for a discounted price without having to negotiate with the lender. If the junior lienors do have redemption rights, they may be willing to sell them for a nominal amount which permits the foreclosure investor to redeem the property from the lender at a small premium over the amount of the loan.

Another promising scenario for the foreclosure investor is to purchase the redemption rights from the borrower when a junior lien is foreclosed, there are no other junior lienors, and the value of the real property exceeds the amount of the first mortgage plus the redemption amount. This is similar to the pre-foreclosure stage purchase where the investor acquires the property subject to the first mortgage and continues to make the payments on the mortgage. In the redemption stage, the investor purchases the redemption rights from the borrower for a nominal sum and then redeems the property from the holder of the second lien subject to the first mortgage. The investor must still arrange financing to pay the redemption amount and to pay the borrower. However, the investor is able to premise a deal upon the property being vacated by the borrower, the investor can inspect the property and perform due diligence, and the investor should receive cooperation from the holder of second lien who is principally interested in disposing of the property. The investor must investigate the local laws to be sure that assignments and sales of redemption rights are permitted.

A variation on this last strategy is for the investor to make all the arrangements to acquire the redemption rights, but rather than completing the purchase, the investor assigns the package to another investor who actually completes the purchase of the redemption rights. This saves the investor the cost of new financing. The investor must strike a deal with the borrower to acquire the redemption rights and then market the property to a third party who becomes the ultimate purchaser.

B.   Advantages and Disadvantages
of Investing during the Redemption Stage

The foreclosure investor who understands redemption procedures can have an advantage over competitors who have not mastered the procedures. Competitors that are not familiar with the procedures will assume that they need to wait until the expiration of the redemption period before they can acquire the property. The knowledgeable investor can purchase the redemption rights from the borrower or a junior lienor during the period that other investors are waiting for the period to expire. Naturally, the investor needs to be sure of the applicable law.

Another advantage is that the foreclosure investor has the time and opportunity to inspect the property and secure necessary financing for the purchase. This assumes that local law provides for a redemption period sufficient to complete these tasks.

The redemption purchase can limit the risk of the investor. If the investor can acquire the redemption right for a nominal sum, that amount is the extent of the investor's risk. If all else fails, and the redemption period expires, the investor has lost only the nominal purchase price.

The borrower's right to occupy or control the property presents an important consideration if the investor purchases the redemption right from a junior lien holder. For residential properties, the borrower gets to remain in the house rent free, and for commercial and industrial properties, in some states if the lender has not exercised its assignment of rents, the rents would go to the borrower and would not be applied to taxes or maintenance.

CHAPTER IV-4   REO STAGE

The REO stage is the point in the foreclosure process after the foreclosure sale where the lender is the highest bidder, the redemption period has expired and the lender is now the owner of the property. The benefits of this stage arise, in part, because lenders are not in the business of owning real property, and every parcel of real property that the lender acquires is a non-performing asset. Lenders are prepared to dispose of foreclosed properties at bargain prices.

A.   Opportunities in the REO Stage

In the REO stage, the borrower has been removed from the picture. At this stage, the foreclosure investor deals with the lender or, in the case of some lenders and governmental agencies, real estate brokers retained by lenders to dispose of the Real Estate Owned.

Acquiring properties in this stage is basically purchasing real property from a seller. The foreclosure investor must identify a prospective property, negotiate a purchase, perform due diligence, arrange financing and close the acquisition. Of course, a major difference from an ordinary sale is the need of the seller to dispose of the

145

property. Hence, attractive prices can be negotiated in a recessionary environment.

The original purpose of real property collateral is to repay the lender the amount of a defaulted loan and all costs and fees. During the foreclosure, the lender does not bid more than the amount owed on the loan. Once the loan has gone into default and the lender has become the owner of the property, the lender can sell the property at any price it decides. In a hot real estate market, the lender may be able to set a price that includes a profit. In a recessionary environment, the lender's inventory of REO is increasing, and the need to dispose of the REO is also increasing. Real Estate Owned carries costs such as payments for taxes and insurance and opportunity costs, as the funds tied up in the REO are not earning revenue for the lender. In these circumstances, it benefits the lender to sell the REO as soon as practical.

B.   Advantages and Disadvantages
of Investing during the REO Stage

The title to a property in the REO stage is in sounder condition than before the foreclosure sale. The effect of the foreclosure is the elimination of all matters that were recorded after the recording of the mortgage, other than tax liens. This includes not only second mortgages and judgment liens, but any other interests such as leases, mechanic's liens and easements. Lenders pay any delinquent real estate taxes to assure that the property is not lost to the tax collector. When the investor acquires the property, the investor receives the benefit of this payment.

The property is likely to be vacated by the borrower, and residential properties are not likely to be occupied by any tenants. The investor need not deal with an eviction. Another advantage is that the amount of cash needed from the investor is less than in some other situations. The investor does not have to incur eviction costs or pay delinquent real estate taxes or pay the borrower any money for redemption rights. The amount of the down payment may be set at a lesser amount than an ordinary purchase as an inducement from the lender to make the deal.

In a severe recessionary climate, there is an abundance of Real Estate Owned that the foreclosure investor can consider. An investor who surfs the Internet foreclosure websites will find scores of REOs at sharply reduced prices. However, there are reasons why these properties are priced the way they are, and the investor needs to undertake the due diligence to winnow out the chaff from the bargains.

In order to facilitate a sale, the lender gives the investor time and opportunity to inspect the property and check the title. The investor should ask the lender for a copy of the most recent appraisal for the property. If the investor needs financing, the investor should inquire as to whether the lender is willing to finance the investor's purchase. Lenders are in the business of lending money to credit worthy borrowers, and the lender is familiar with the property, so there is a good possibility that the lender will agree to do so. The key for the investor is to get terms that allows the investor to make the level of profit that the investor requires. Some lenders actually allow an investor to take over the original loan. This makes sense only if the property has substantial equity remaining.

When the investor spots a prospective property, the investor needs to act promptly. If a property is attractive to one foreclosure investor, it is likely to be attractive to several competitors who can get the deal if they move faster.

A disadvantage to the foreclosure investor is that the abundance of properties makes it easier for other investors and prospective home owners to participate in the REO stage. Real estate brokers that specialize in REOs contact the investors they know are interested in Real Estate Owned, and if an investor is not on a broker's list, competitors get first notice of the availability of attractive properties. Another disadvantage is that, because the title is better established than at other stages, the risk is less and the discounts are less, reflecting the relative degree of risk.

The purchase is likely to be on an "as-is" basis. The investor assumes the risk of any defects in the property. Of course, the due diligence should be structured in a way to reveal these defects.

147

Some lenders employ real estate brokers to help dispose of their Real Estate Owned. Government entities, such as the Department of Housing and Urban Development ("HUD"), dispose of REOs through real estate brokers. The employment of brokers means that the lender incurs the obligation to pay a commission which has the effect of increasing the purchase price.

Lastly, even though the investor needs to move quickly, the lender is likely to move slowly. Institutional lenders can have bureaucratic processes to follow that can slow down the pace of the transaction.

PART V – PURCHASING THE PROPERTY

The foreclosure investor has identified one or more properties that can yield an acceptable profit on the right terms. The investor has performed the due diligence and is now prepared to take the next step – purchasing the property. This Part V addresses the means that investors can use to acquire foreclosure properties, including traditional methods used to purchase real property.

The discussion in this Part V concerns the foreclosure investor purchasing a property. The purchase can occur during any of the stages previously presented. The seller of the property can be the borrower or the lender or the holder of redemption rights. For purposes of this chapter, we assume that the seller is the borrower, but it could be any of the other parties that participate in the foreclosure process.

Purchasing includes setting the terms and arranging the financing. If the investor can negotiate terms that do not require financing, then that is one less step that needs to be taken. If the investor can negotiate terms that do not require the investor to commit his own capital to the transaction, that leaves money available for other deals. We will begin with a discussion of purchasing foreclosure property using "no money down."

CHAPTER V-1   NO MONEY DOWN

No-money-down methods are techniques that permit the foreclosure investor to acquire a property without reaching into the investor's own pocket to produce the necessary cash or by minimizing the cash that the investor must commit at the outset. This does not mean that the seller, who may be the borrower or the lender or the high bidder at a foreclosure sale, does not receive cash at the closing. It merely refers to the investor's cash outlay. Some of these methods depend upon thoughtful structuring of the financing.

Most of these methods minimize the amount of cash that the investor has committed to a particular property. This can be an advantage to the investor because the investor with limited resources can spread those resources over a greater number of investment opportunities. However, institutional lenders have become less willing to finance acquisitions in which the investor does not have a material stake. Therefore, when considering these methods, bear in mind that they may be viable in certain circumstances but not in others.

A.   Cash Out Borrower with a New Mortgage

One method that can be used if there is substantial equity in the property is cashing out the borrower with a new mortgage. In an economy that is severely restricted due to a collapse of a housing boom, many properties will be underwater and will not have any equity. However, even in those circumstances, there is a sizable number of foreclosures that result from financial strains on borrowers without regard to the amount of equity. For example, a homeowner who purchased a house in a stable community, who has owned the house for twenty years and who has enjoyed steady but not spectacular appreciation, is likely to have substantial equity. If that person loses a job, or goes through a difficult divorce, or contracts a debilitating disease, it may become impossible to continue making mortgage payments. The borrower may have become resolved to the need to dispose of the house but would like to retain part of the equity. If the equity is greater than twice the amount of the mortgage debt, this is a situation where this method can be applied.

Using this method, the foreclosure investor obtains a new mortgage loan in an amount sufficient to pay the existing debt plus the portion of the equity that goes to the borrower. An example makes this method clearer. Assume that the property has a current value of $275,000. The amount of the existing loan is $70,000. This means that the equity is $205,000. The investor and the borrower agree to split the equity so the borrower receives a down payment of $102,500and the investor receives that same amount as profit. The investor must come up with cash in the amount of $172,500 (the current loan of $70,000 + the down payment of $102,500). The investor obtains a new first mortgage loan for $172,500. The loan to value ratio (the ratio of the amount of the first mortgage loan to the value of the property) would be 62.7 percent. A conservative loan to value ratio for residential properties is 80 percent, so this hypothetical deal is extremely conservative. The property can lose 37 percent of its value and still be worth the amount of the loan. The investor pays the borrower $102,500 and takes the deed to the property. The purchase price equals $172,500.

The foregoing hypothetical is very simple. In some cases, the purchase price may be higher so that the borrower recaptures more of the equity. In those cases, the investor gives the borrower a second mortgage in an amount equal to the difference between the higher purchase price and the amount of the first mortgage loan. The borrower and investor must negotiate the payment terms of the second mortgage, such as the interest rate and the due date. This structure gives the foreclosure investor ownership and control of the property, and the default is cleared with little or no impact on the borrower's credit rating because the loan has been paid in full. The investor then makes payments on the first and second mortgages until the property is sold.

B.   Wrap-around Mortgage

Another method is to use a wrap-around mortgage. In title theory states, it is called an all-inclusive deed of trust. The wrap around mortgage became very popular in the late 1970's when interest rates went into the mid-teens and higher. In the late 1970's, sellers of real property typically had property subject to a mortgage or deed of trust that had been entered into several years earlier, and the loan bore interest at a rate substantially less than the then current rates. To avoid getting a new loan at a high interest rate, buyers paid the seller the down payment in cash and gave the seller a second mortgage or deed of trust to secure the balance of the purchase price. The existing loan would not be paid off. Instead, the seller agreed to continue to make the payments on the first mortgage loan out of the payments that the buyer made under the second mortgage loan. This kept the first mortgage loan in place, preserving the low interest rate. It was called a wrap around mortgage because the new mortgage wrapped around the original mortgage.

The wrap-around mortgage can be used to carry out a no-money-down purchase. One of the reasons this approach is attractive to a borrower is that it provides an income stream to the borrower. However, it does not cash out the borrower, so if the borrower needs funds to acquire a new residence or other property, this method does not work. Also, the method depends upon the mortgage being assumable. This means either that the mortgage does not contain a due on sale clause or that the lender agrees not to enforce the due on sale clause.

An example illustrates the benefit of a wrap-around mortgage. Assume that the borrower owns a commercial property worth $180,000, encumbered by a first mortgage in the amount of $72,000, bearing an interest rate of 6.5 percent. The monthly payments of principal and interest are approximately $455. If the purchase is structured as a no- money-down deal with the investor assuming the first mortgage of $72,000, the investor owes the borrower the balance of $108,000 which is paid by giving the borrower a second mortgage for $108,000. The interest rate is negotiated at 8 percent, making the monthly payment of principal and interest on the second mortgage approximately $790. The investor's monthly payments on the first mortgage ($455) and the second mortgage ($790) equals $1,245.

Using the wrap-around mortgage method, the investor gives the borrower a wrap-around mortgage securing a debt in the amount of the purchase price, in this example $180,000, bearing interest at the negotiated rate of 8 percent. The monthly payments under the wrap around mortgage are approximately $1,320. The borrower continues to make the payments under the first mortgage of $455. The borrower pockets the difference between the second mortgage and the first mortgage, in this example $790. On an annual basis, the borrower receives payments worth $15,840 (12 X $1,320) and pays the lender $5,460 ($455 X 12). The borrower receives and retains the difference of $10,380 ($15,840 - $5,460). Since the equity in the property is $108,000, the annual return to the borrower is 9.6 percent. Over time, the first mortgage is paid down faster and eventually in full, so that the proportion of the value of the property securing the second mortgage is increasing. If the rental stream from the commercial property supports the monthly payments under the wrap-around mortgage, the investor is able to acquire the property without putting up any of the investor's own capital and the borrower gets a valuable return on the wrap-around mortgage.

Wrap-around mortgages carry inherent risks to investors. As noted above, if the mortgage contains a due on sale clause, the investor must deal with that issue. Of equal importance, the investor relies on the borrower to continue making the payments under the first mortgage. If the borrower fails to pay the first mortgage, the lender can declare a default and the investor must bring that mortgage current. A risk to the borrower is that the value of the property can decline and the investor defaults. In that event, the borrower must bear the expense of evicting the investor and recovering possession of the property. In addition, the borrower loses some part of the equity as the property's value decreases.

C. Equity or Collateral Substitution; Cross Collateralization

This method depends upon the foreclosure investor owning other real property or other valuable assets in which the investor has substantial equity. Assume that the borrower owns a commercial property which the borrower is willing to sell for $125,000. The property is subject to a $100,000 mortgage, so the borrower's equity is $25,000. The investor wants to make a down payment of $10,000 on a no-money-down basis. Assume the investor owns other real property or other assets in which the investor has equity of at least $10,000. The investor offers the borrower a down payment in the form of a promissory note for $10,000, secured by a mortgage on the other property and a second mortgage in the amount of the remaining equity of $15,000 ($25,000 - $10,000). The down payment is paid by the equity in the other property. The documentation for the transaction reserves the right for the investor to substitute other collateral of equal value to secure the down payment.

If the borrower insists on receiving the down payment in cash, the borrower can sell the note for cash. However, purchasers of second mortgage notes do not pay the face amount; the notes are discounted. If the borrower is to get the full $10,000 in cash, the investor must give a note for an amount greater than $10,000, so that the borrower can sell the note and mortgage at a discount equal to $10,000.

This method has risks. If the equity in the other property declines, the borrower's collateral is worth less than the amount of the debt. Of course, the value of the original property can also decline, but at least the borrower is completely familiar with the original property and may not have that concern. If the other property is real estate and subject to a first mortgage, there is the risk that the investor defaults on the first mortgage and the borrower loses its collateral. The investor is loading other property with debt. In a rising market where equity grows through appreciation, this method allows the investor to expand his or her holdings, but in a declining market, the other property may go underwater.

One way to mitigate declining market risk is to substitute collateral that should retain its value. Of course, any collateral that is purchased on a market runs the risk of declining in value. However, there is one category of collateral that, in spite of fluctuation in value, can provide adequate security. That collateral is highly rated government bonds. Bonds are purchased at a discount to their value at maturity. As interest rates move up and down, the bonds' values move down and up. Nevertheless, on the date that the money is needed, the bond matures and the issuer pays the holder the face amount of the bond. The investor can provide bonds with maturity dates that match the dates payments come due under the down payment note. Certificates of deposit insured by the Federal Government may also serve as satisfactory collateral.

D.   Broker Financing

In a market in which few properties are selling, real estate brokers may facilitate deals by reducing required funds at the closing. A no-money-down investor can request the broker to take the commission in the form of a promissory note. The terms of the note must be attractive enough to entice the broker. For example, the interest rate can be set above the current market rates. If the broker accepts a promissory note, the amount of the down payment can be reduced.

In addition, the investor can ask the broker to loan the down payment to the investor or to discount the commission to make the deal happen.

E.   Like-kind Exchanges

Foreclosure investors with other properties may be able to find a borrower who is willing to exchange the foreclosure property for the investor's other property. If the borrower does not find the investor's property appealing, a three way exchange can be arranged with the borrower putting the property into the deal, and when an acceptable property is found, the third party delivers it to the borrower. Like-kind exchanges have significant tax benefits but they are complicated, and should not be attempted without the assistance of an experienced tax or real estate attorney.

F.   Hard Money Second

This method involves a borrower who is anxious enough to dispose of commercial property that he will do so at a price lower than market value. The investor must have access to private or non-institutional lenders, sometimes referred to as "hard money lenders." In this hypothetical situation, the borrower owns a property worth $80,000 encumbered by a $60,000 mortgage so the borrower's equity is $20,000. The property has been on the market for a substantial length of time, and the borrower is now willing to sell at a reduced price. The investor offers the borrower a price of $75,000 which is paid by the investor taking title subject to the $60,000 mortgage and paying the borrower cash of $15,000. The investor obtains the cash by borrowing $15,000 from a private lender and giving the private lender a second mortgage for that amount. The private lender has $20,000 in equity securing a $15,000 note.

G.   Assuming Borrower's Obligations

The borrower, particularly in troubled times, may be up to his or her neck in debt. The foreclosure investor could offer to assume the borrower's credit card debt in lieu of a down payment. The investor negotiates with the borrower's creditors for extensions of the time to pay the debts or to restructure the obligations.

H.   Lease with Option to Buy

If the foreclosure investor needs to move quickly to acquire a property but does not have the time to put together a financing package, the investor can offer to lease the property with an option to purchase the property. The lease terms must address the circumstances affecting the property. For example, if the first mortgage is in default, the investor can make payments on the mortgage in lieu of rent. When the investor has arranged the financing, the investor can exercise the option to purchase the property.

I.   Taking Property Subject to an Existing Mortgage; Desperate Borrower Syndrome

In those cases where the borrower is desperate to dispose of the property, the foreclosure investor can simply take title to the property subject to the existing liens. In this case, the investor either pays the borrower a nominal sum for the property or nothing at all.

Using this technique, the foreclosure investor takes over the property without having legal obligation for the mortgage. This does not mean that the lender is out of the picture. Depending on the state, the mortgage still gives the lender a lien or title to the property. Accordingly, in order to preserve title to the property, the investor needs to pay that debt. Hence, the investor does not want to take a deed to a property that is underwater. If the mortgage exceeds the value of the property, the acquisition may not be worth the investor's efforts.

In addition, the transfer can trigger the due on sale clause. The investor must handle this issue with the lender. However, in a recessionary environment, if the investor can make the payments, the lender has reason to leave the investor in place.

This approach works where the borrower has a strong incentive to avoid foreclosure and believes that the investor has the financial strength to make the payments. Additionally, the investor may agree to pay the borrower a sum which makes sense to the borrower. For example, in the case of a residence, the borrower must find rental property to replace the house. Accordingly, the investor may offer to pay for the borrower's moving expenses and rent for a certain number of months.

The foreclosure investor acquires the property by accepting a deed from the borrower. Borrowers who wish to quickly walk away from the property use a quitclaim deed to effect the transfer. A quitclaim deed is one in which an individual transfers whatever interest he has in the real property but does not make any warranties regarding that interest. If it turns out that the borrower did not actually own the property, the quitclaim deed imposes no liability on the borrower. For this reason, if a foreclosure investor accepts a quitclaim deed, the investor must be certain that title is fully vested in the borrower. Since there is normally time available to carry out the transaction, the foreclosure investor should consider purchasing title insurance.

J.   Borrower Financing; Purchase Money Mortgage

A slightly less desperate borrower with equity may be willing to accept a promissory note in an amount equal to a fraction of the equity. The note postpones and spreads out the down payment. The foreclosure investor offers to give a note equal to a fraction of the equity because the investor is seeking an acceptable rate of return.

Of course, the foreclosure investor can structure almost any kind of borrower financed arrangement if the borrower is willing to forego the receipt of cash at the closing and instead take back a promissory note for some portion of the purchase price. The risk to the borrower is that the investor has not made an investment in the property, so the investor does not have an incentive to make payments on the note given to the borrower.

An investor who is short of cash at the closing, but expects to obtain more funds later, can offer to take title subject to the first mortgage and give the borrower a balloon note and mortgage for the balance of the purchase price. A balloon note is a note that does not fully amortize over the term but has a large final payment. For example, the investor might offer the borrower a promissory note for $10,000,

157

payable in five years with annual installments of principal in the amount of $500, and a final installment of principal in the fifth year of $8,000. The risk to the investor arises if the investor is unable to raise the funds needed to pay the balloon installment and is unable to refinance the debt. Then the investor could lose the property.

In the commercial or industrial property context, the foreclosure investor could propose to the borrower that the borrower accept a promissory note for the down payment payable out of a portion of the rents from tenants. It must be a portion because the remainder of the rents must go to pay the lender and operate the property.

K.   Applying Closing Credits

At the closing of any purchase and sale of real property, the purchaser receives credits for various items. For example, in the sale of an apartment building, the tenants have paid security deposits, cleaning fees and sometimes the last month's rent to the landlord. The purchaser needs to have those funds delivered to it so that the purchaser will be able to return the security deposits to the tenants at the end of their leases and will have the last month's rent to apply to the rent. One way to accomplish this is to have the seller deliver a check for these amounts to the purchaser. The more typical way is for the seller to give the purchaser a credit against the purchase price equal to these amounts. Real estate taxes are another charge for which the purchaser can receive a credit. With commercial property, the rent is paid on the first day of the month. If the transaction closes on a day other than the first day of the month, the purchaser gets a credit for rent paid to the seller equal to the daily rental rate multiplied by the number of days remaining in the month. The credits can be applied to the down payment, and the balance of the purchase price paid by a new mortgage or by taking subject to the existing mortgage.

L.   Installment Sale Land Contract

Under this method, the investor agrees to purchase the property by making periodic payments to the borrower. The parties enter into a land sale contract. Under this contract, title remains vested in the borrower until the final payment is made and then the borrower deeds the property to the investor. The investor has the exclusive right to occupy and possess the property and collect any rents and profits from the property. All vestiges of ownership are held by the investor except the actual title. The parties establish an escrow account in which the deed is placed, and when the investor has paid the price in full, the escrow agent deeds the property to him.

Land sale contracts have legal complications. Because the land sale contract does not contain the provisions normally found in a mortgage, the foreclosure is complicated. For this reason, many land sale contracts give the seller a power to sell the property if the purchaser defaults. However, if mortgage provisions are included, the courts and taxing authorities can construe the transaction to be a present sale, further complicating matters. If the borrower goes bankrupt, the creditors may argue that the land sale contract is an executory contract and not enforceable against the borrower. Whether such an argument can succeed is irrelevant. The investor is forced to join the bankruptcy proceeding and defend the transaction at a significant cost to the investor. Any investor considering this method should first consult with an experienced real estate attorney in order to gain an understanding of the potential potholes.

The advantage of this type of deal is that the investor does not need a lot of money up front. In fact, the investor can usually acquire the property with just a couple months' payment. The disadvantage is that the investor can lose the property by failing to make just one payment. For example, the investor can enter into a land sales contract and make payment over the course of five years. If he defaults in one payment in the middle of the fifth year, the borrower can take back the property. In many states, laws have been enacted to curb this result, but that will depend on the particular state.

M.   Installment Sale Land Contract for the Downpayment

A foreclosure investor who does not have sufficient funds to pay the full amount of the down payment could offer the borrower an installment sale in which the investor pays a part of the down payment each month for a certain period of time. The borrower retains title until the down payment is fully paid. Then the borrower deeds the property to the investor who finances the balance of the purchase price with a mortgage loan. This will reduce the amount of cash needed at the closing.

N.   Partner Financing and Other Participation

The foreclosure investor who is not in a position to put money down at the closing can seek a partner who will provide the financing in exchange for a part of the deal. A typical arrangement is for the investor to find the properties and conduct the due diligence in exchange for an interest in the partnership. The money partner puts up the money, or other collateral, for an interest in the partnership.

In addition to straight-forward financing, the partner can also help with other forms of no-money-down transactions. For example, if collateral is to be substituted, the money partner can offer other real property that she owns to secure a promissory note given in lieu of the down payment. Alternatively, the partner can also post stocks or bonds as collateral. The role that a partner plays, and the terms in which the role is premised, are as boundless as the investor's imagination.

CHAPTER V-2   SHORT SALES

In severe recessionary times, some of the methods and strategies used when property values were rapidly appreciating simply do not work in a deflationary economy. There is no equity to purchase and sell. The mortgage loans exceed the value of the properties. Even if the borrower were to just give a property to an investor subject to the existing mortgage, save certain tax situations, the deal probably does not make economic sense for the investor. The investor is taking a property on where the total of the mortgages exceeds the property's value. The investor is in the hole the moment the deal closes. Therefore, for properties that have no equity and are underwater, the foreclosure investor must negotiate a purchase price that is less than the amount of the debt on the property. In other words, the investor must negotiate a short sale.

A "short sale" is a sale by the borrower to the investor, approved by the lender, at a price below the amount due on the loan. The lender must approve the sale because the lender accepts a discounted amount in payment of its loan and releases the lien of the mortgage from the property. Short sales occur during either the pre-foreclosure stage or the default and auction stage while the loan is still outstanding and the borrower owns the property. The amount due on the loan includes past due interest, late charges, legal fees, trustee fees and the unpaid principal balance of the loan.

A.   Parties to a Short Sale and Calculating Price

The parties to a short sale are the borrower, the foreclosure investor, the lender and the servicer of the lender's loan. The borrower has no equity in the property and is either currently in default or anticipates default in the near future. In fact, a number of borrowers who find themselves with properties underwater simply abandon the property and walk away. However, the borrower can benefit from a short sale. The borrower does not receive any money from the sale, but the unpaid balance is typically forgiven. In any case, it is always better for a borrower to discuss the problems with the lender than to remain silent or to abandon mortgaged property.

The foreclosure investor sees an opportunity to manufacture equity in the property. The investor must determine the value of the property. If the property is a commercial or industrial property, the investor can get information on the rental stream and calculate the value using techniques discussed in preceding sections of this book. If the property is residential property, it can become a rental property or it can be resold if the price is consistent with, or better than comparable properties. In any case, the investor calculates a value that he ascribes to the property. Then, the investor calculates the price that the investor is willing to pay. The difference between the value and the price becomes the investor's equity, and ultimately part of the investor's profit. However, as noted below, one of the factors that a lender takes into account when deciding to approve a short sale is the market value of the property. An unreasonably low offer may trigger a rejection.

Having derived the target price to acquire the property, the investor offers this price, or a lower price, to the borrower. The borrower has no equity so the price makes little difference because he will never see any money from the sale. The primary concern about price for a borrower is that the offer is high enough to secure the lender's consent. In addition, the borrower considers any remaining liability to the lender for the unpaid balance of the loan. The unpaid balance remaining after the sale of the property is referred to as the "deficiency," which the borrower wants to minimize. Even if the lender does not sue for the deficiency, it is possible that the amount of debt forgiven can be taxed as income to the borrower. This is explained in Subchapter V-2.D below.

In a short sale, the lender receives partial payment of its loan from the proceeds of the sale. The short sale request is usually directed to the lender's loan loss mitigation department. The lender has several factors to consider in deciding whether to approve the price offered in a short sale. These factors relate to the likelihood that the loan can be repaid in full. If the lender believes that there is a good possibility of repayment, either from the borrower, a foreclosure sale at auction, or from sale as Real Estate Owned, then the lender is not inclined to approve a short sale. Part of the foreclosure investor's challenge is to show the lender that there is little likelihood of repayment in full. The factors are described in Subchapter V-2.B below.

Notably, many institutional lenders that originated mortgages have sold them in the securitization market. Those mortgage loans are handled by a servicer acting on behalf of loan investors that purchased mortgage backed securities. The loan investor who owns the loan, which could include Fannie Mae of Freddie Mac, must approve the short sale. This can take a considerable amount of time, in some cases several months.

B.   Factors the Lender Considers in Deciding Whether to Approve a Short Sale

A lender presented with a request for a short sale will consider factors affecting the borrower, the property and the lender. The principal factor affecting the borrower is the ability to repay the loan.

If the lender believes the borrower is not able to repay the loan, the lender is more likely to approve the short sale. To reach this point, the borrower must demonstrate financial hardship. The borrower will submit a letter or statement to the lender explaining the reasons that the borrower is unable to pay the deficiency. Some reasons include: (i) the borrower has been laid off and has been unable to find alternative employment due to circumstances beyond the borrower's control, such as a severe economic crunch; (ii) the borrower or the borrower's family has experienced a catastrophic illness or injury that is not adequately covered by insurance and has left the borrower in severe economic straits; (iii) the borrower has been called to military duty, and the pay of a soldier or sailor cannot cover the mortgage payments; (iv) the borrower has died, become severely disabled or has suffered a debilitating injury prohibiting employment; (v) the borrower has gone through a divorce and cannot make the minimum payments required under the mortgage; or (vi) the borrower is insolvent, has exhausted the savings account and has no assets that can be applied to pay the loan.

Lenders also consider factors affecting the property. The lender makes its own analysis of the property, but the lenders also request professional opinions on its value. The lender may review the loan-to-value ratio. The lender knows when the property was purchased or refinanced. If that event occurred at a time when the market was frothy, and economic conditions have constricted since then, the lender can conclude that the property was overpriced or financed at more than 100 percent of value. If the area has been experiencing a freeze in home sales or a surge in foreclosures, the lender can conclude that the property's value has declined. If the Federal Government has reported significant job losses in the area and local businesses are closing their doors, the lender can expect a decline in commercial rental rates that impact the value of commercial property. The property needs to be worth less than the loan if a short sale is to obtain approval. Another factor that affects the property's value, and the lender's decision, is the property's physical condition. The lender inquires about physical damage that must be repaired in order to make the property marketable. Would that damage be costly to repair? What is the value in its current condition? The lender is also concerned about the cost of upgrading the property to make it saleable, and the value of the property if it were repaired. The lender considers the cost of selling the property if it became Real Estate Owned. Remember, that cost includes real estate broker's commissions, taxes, utilities, marketing costs and the opportunity cost of holding a non-performing asset. The foreclosure investor may have noted that these lender concerns are shared by the investor. The investor interested in a property has the same concerns and analyzes them from the investor's perspective and from the lender's perspective. The investor may have to demonstrate to the lender how these factors have caused the value of the property to fall below the amount of the loan.

Another set of factors that lenders take into account when considering a short sale is the condition of the lender and its REO inventory. A lender's decision is affected by the lender's own financial condition, the financial condition of any other party who has purchased an interest in the loan, whether the lender has a large inventory of REOs and other non-performing loans, the lender's and loan investor's policies regarding short sales, and the policies regarding foreclosures of federal regulators and the Department of the Treasury and the Federal Reserve. Loans guaranteed by the Federal Housing Administration or Veterans Administration have their own set of guidelines for short sales that the investor must understand and comply with.

C.   Short Sale Approval Process

The foreclosure investor should be prepared for the approval of the short sale to be a lengthy process. First, the servicer needs to be convinced that a short sale will benefit the lender. Then, the loan investor must reach the same conclusion. Waiting periods of several months have been reported.

The borrower has little incentive to pursue a short sale, so the burden of pursuing the deal comes to rest on the foreclosure investor's shoulders. In order to deal with the lender, the borrower must authorize the lender to deal directly with the investor and to release information to the investor. This is the same sort of authorization as discussed above in Subchapter IV-2.B. At some point, the investor may have to offer the borrower some monetary incentive to go forward, such as the payment of moving expenses and the first month's rent at the borrower's new residence.

Some loans have been insured by private mortgage insurance ("PMI"). Private mortgage insurance is normally purchased by a lender (and paid for by a borrower) for loans that exceed the 80 percent of the property's value. PMI is sold to lenders and trustees of pools of securitized mortgages to protect against the borrower's default. If a default occurs, the lender can recover a percentage of the loan from the insurance company. The terms of the insurance policy affects the lender's ability to approve a short sale. Some policies pay if there has been a loss from a foreclosure. Because a short sale is not a foreclosure, the lender must receive the insurer's approval of the short sale. Some insurance companies have established guidelines with the lenders they insure, enabling the lender to approve a short sale without the insurer's consent. If the investor's loan meets the guidelines, the lender can accept the short sale offer. If the loan does not satisfy the guidelines, the insurer has the right of final approval. The insurer considers the amount of the loss, the percentage covered by insurance and the value established by the BPO (described in the following paragraph).

The lender probably does not make a final decision on the merits of a short sale proposal without obtaining professional advice on value. The lender consults with either an appraiser or an experienced real estate broker. If the lender turns to a broker, the lender requests a broker's price opinion ("BPO"). The laws of some states prohibit this technique and require an appraisal. After the lender has reviewed all other required documentation, the lender will order a BPO. The opinion gives the broker's opinion of the property's value in its present condition, referred to as its "as is" condition, and the value after the property is repaired.

The BPO or appraisal is a critical document. The value needs to be within an acceptable range of the offered price for the deal to continue. The investor should try to meet with the broker or appraiser and share the information that the investor has collected regarding value so that the appraiser or broker is fully informed.

The foreclosure investor must submit to the lender a package of the documents that the lender requires before approving a short sale. Lenders usually require a HUD 1 Settlement Statement completed by the borrower and investor. This form can be found on HUD's website. This form details the purchase price, unpaid loan balances, real estate brokers' commissions and all other costs of the transaction. It should not show any money going to the borrower. Lenders may also have their own form of short sale application. If the lender has such a form, be sure to include it in the package. The other documents vary among lenders, but a typical package includes the short sale offer, the purchase and sale agreement between the investor and the borrower, the letter signed by the borrower authorizing the lender to deal with the investor, the borrower's financial statement with related documents such as several months of the borrower's bank statements and two years' worth of income tax returns, pay stubs or unemployment compensation documents, the borrower's statement describing the hardship that has brought the borrower to this point, documents that support the hardship statement, such as a divorce decree, death certificate or hospital bills, documents supporting the valuation of the property, such as a listing of needed repairs and estimates of their cost from one or more licensed contractors, a list of comparable properties recently sold and comparable properties currently on the market, photographs of the property and other documents that the investor uses to convince the lender to enter into the transaction. In some markets, the first mortgage lenders do not require much convincing, but other markets may test the investor's patience.

If the property is subject to multiple mortgages or liens, the investor must go through the approval process with each of the mortgagees and lien holders. Holders of subordinate mortgages should receive the complete package. Lien holders should receive a copy of the option agreement and HUD 1 Settlement Statement. Note that as the deal is negotiated with each party, the option agreement and HUD 1 must be updated to reflect current terms. In a foreclosure, holders of junior mortgages and liens are wiped out, so they are glad to receive something. Most commentators suggest offering junior mortgagees and lienors between five percent and 20 percent of the amount of their lien. If they do not agree, the investor has the option to complete the short sale, in which case the investor must pay off these liens or abandon the deal.

D.   Tax Consequences of a Short Sale

In past years, short sales had negative tax implications for borrowers, and in future years they may have the same implications. However, the rules causing tax problems have been modified for the calendar years 2007 through 2012. In order to fully understand the issue, we will discuss the normal rules and then the exception.

Under the rules of the Internal Revenue Service ("IRS") concerning forgiveness of debt, debt that is forgiven becomes income to the debtor. Income to an individual is taxed. A loan is not income because it must be repaid. However, if the loan is forgiven, it need not be repaid. The borrower gets to keep the funds, and the IRS treats those funds as ordinary income. (Debts forgiven when the borrower is insolvent, and debts forgiven through a bankruptcy proceeding, are not taxed as income.)

Forgiveness of a nonrecourse loan has a special set of rules. A "nonrecourse loan" is a loan for which the borrower has no personal liability and, if the borrower defaults, is repaid by a sale of the collateral. Many commercial and industrial loans are non-recourse by their terms. In some states, certain types of loans are made recourse by state law. The foreclosure investor needs to ascertain whether the loan is recourse or non-recourse. The investor interested in acquiring property encumbered with nonrecourse debt should become familiar with these rules. The rules are explained in IRS publication No. 4681.

The difficulty that the forgiveness of debt rules cause is that the loan was spent to acquire the property, the borrower is now financially strapped and the borrower receives no funds from the short sale. Under these rules, the short sale will cost the borrower. For example, in the hypothetical situation where the borrower owes the lender $225,000 secured by a mortgage on the property and the lender accepts a short sale for $175,000, the borrower owes income tax on the difference of $50,000. However, all of the proceeds from the sale are paid to the lender. The borrower has no cash, no title to the property and owes the United States Treasury income tax on ordinary income of $50,000.

This result was modified by the Mortgage Debt Relief Act of 2007. The act provides tax relief for forgiveness of indebtedness up to $2,000,000 or $1,000,000 for married couples filing separate tax returns. It is in effect for the calendar years 2007 through 2012. According to the IRS's website, the act allows

> ". . . taxpayers to exclude income from the discharge of debt on their principal residence. Debt reduced through mortgage restructuring, as well as mortgage debt forgiven in connection with a foreclosure, qualifies for the relief. . . ." http://www.irs.gov/individuals/article/0,,id=179414,00.html

The act applies only to debt secured by the borrower's principal residence. For the debt to qualify, its proceeds must have been used to purchase, construct or substantially improve the borrower's principal residence. Refinancing of this kind of debt also qualifies. The exception created by the act is referred to as "qualified principal residence indebtedness."

More information on the effects of the act can be obtained from IRS publications and from the IRS website. The investor should be sure to inform the borrower of the debt forgiveness consequences of a short sale.

E.   Caveat - Home Equity Purchase Laws

California, New York and other states have laws designed to protect persons who are losing their homes to foreclosure. Foreclosure investors that operate in these states must comply with these regulations. These laws are frequently referred to as Home Equity Purchase/Sales Acts or Home Equity Theft Acts. Under these laws, purchasers of residences (including one to four unit buildings if the borrower resides in one of the units) under foreclosure must comply with various requirements designed to assure that a borrower deciding to sell his residence to an investor is making an informed decision. These laws give borrowers the right to rescind the deal for five days, which the investor must notify the borrower of this right. The investor cannot take any action to carry out the purchase until the rescission period has expired. Failure to comply allows the borrower to cancel the sale and makes the investor liable in damages to the borrower.

F.   Finder's Fee or Wholesale Flipping in a Short Sale

A variation on the traditional short sale that can produce an immediate return to the foreclosure investor is the finder's fee. The investor does the normal search for a prospective property, locates a property that is eligible for a short sale and negotiates the terms of a short sale transaction. A website maintained by Ameraco, Inc. states that it has over 10,000 private real estate investors. The site advertises that it pays a fee to the person locating an acceptable foreclosure deal.

A variation of the finder's fee is wholesale flipping. Flipping is the practice of purchasing a property and quickly selling it. In most cases, the sale of the property is concurrent with its acquisition. Wholesale flipping is where the investor arranges the acquisition and then assigns his contract to another investor instead of closing the purchase.   In this scenario, the investor finalizes the deal with the borrower and reduces it to writing. Then the investor assigns the entire deal to a new investor, or assignee.   The assignee arranges his own financing because no sensible lender allows an assignment of a loan agreement to an individual that has not been approved. Assignees range from foreclosure investors to persons looking for a property to rehabilitate. The investor can receive a fee for arranging the deal or he can market the sale of his contract.   Wholesale flipping results in the investor making less profit than the investor may have made by flipping the property, but the investor does not need to put up any cash.

An investor who intends to engage in wholesale flipping needs to assemble a team before the first deal. Finding a title company, brokers and lenders is fairly straightforward. Assignees can be located by searching local classified ads for persons looking to purchase "fixer uppers." Assignees can also be found by attending foreclosure sales and networking with bidders. Another possible avenue is attending a local real property investment club. Information on investment clubs can be found online. A website maintained by CRE Online, Inc. lists investment clubs in all fifty states.

A prime property for the wholesale flipper is one with equity equal to about half of the market value and in need of substantial repairs which the borrower cannot afford to make. This combination works well for wholesale flipping to assignees that intend to rehabilitate a property because the amount of equity allows the assignee to make a profit after acquiring the property and making repairs. .

The purchase agreement that the investor negotiates with the borrower must expressly permit the investor to assign the agreement without the consent of the borrower.

G.   Impact on Borrower's Credit

The investor should understand that a short sale has a significant effect on the borrower's credit rating. For some purposes, such as eligibility for purchase by Fannie Mae, the impact is not as severe as a foreclosure, but the short sale lowers the credit rating of the borrower.

CHAPTER V-3   FINANCING THE PURCHASE

If the foreclosure investor does not have a pool of cash partners to provide funding for acquisitions, the investor must arrange financing for the acquisition of foreclosure property. This applies even if the investor intends to flip a property at the closing or assign the purchase contract to a third party. The need to arrange financing arises because parties to a foreclosure acquisition must be convinced that the foreclosure investor has the financial wherewithal to conclude the transaction. If the investor cannot establish that capability, the borrower or lender will deal with a competitor. Moreover, the amount of money needed, in most cases, may be considerable. In Chapter V-1, we discussed some no-money-down methods, but those methods required some technique to accommodate the existing mortgage. Some methods assume that the property has substantial equity. In a booming economy, that assumption may be correct. In a constricting economy, equity is harder to find. Other methods involve the investor assuming or taking subject to the mortgage. Acquiring the lender's consent to an assumption, or taking subject to the mortgage, is easier in an era of less restrictive loan standards and more difficult in an era of heightened scrutiny. Other methods call for the investor to substitute collateral in which the investor has sufficient equity. Assuming that the investor does have equity, the investor is still putting up items with substantial value. In short, no matter what method is used, the foreclosure investor must be prepared to dig into the investor's pockets for cash or to obtain financing.

The amount of the financing ranges from the sum required to reinstate a loan in default to the purchase price of a short sale to the purchase price of Real Estate Owned.

Financing can be arranged with institutional lenders such as banks, private lenders, the investor's own resources or through partners. In the case of REO, it is possible to possible to get financing from the bank that owns the property. There are different kinds of loans that an investor can obtain from institutional lenders. This chapter examines these financing sources and types of loans.

The difference in residential real estate loans mainly derives from the practices and policies of agencies and companies created by the Federal Government. The relevant agencies are the Department of Housing and Urban Development ("HUD"), the Federal Housing Administration ("FHA"), and the Department of Veteran Affairs ("VA"). There are also two government sponsored enterprises ("GSE's"). The GSE's are the Federal National Mortgage Association, commonly known as "Fannie Mae," and the Federal Home Loan Mortgage Corporation, commonly known as "Freddie Mac."

A.   Federal Agencies and Enterprises

The Federal Housing Administration, or FHA, was created in 1934 in the depth of the depression. It is now a part of the Department of Housing and Urban Development, or HUD. The FHA insures the payment of mortgage loans made to finance the acquisition of residential real property. The primary mortgage insurance program is referred to as Section 203(b). Section 203(b) covers one-to-four family homes and can be used to insure the purchase or refinancing of existing one-to-four family homes. This program is designed to assist first-time home buyers and certain other purchasers who cannot afford mortgages made under conventional terms. For example, as of the beginning of calendar year 2009, a borrower under a loan insured by the FHA can put down as little as 3-1/2 percent and finance 96.5 percent of the purchase price. The borrower pays mortgage insurance premiums as part of the loan. The FHA also accepts debt-to-value ratios that are higher than conventional loans. However, a borrower whose mortgage is insured by the FHA must reside in the property. FHA insured loans are not available to investors. Accordingly, if a foreclosure investor's strategy rests upon assuming a mortgage, the investor must be sure that the loan is not insured by the FHA because the investor is not be eligible to assume the loan. Nevertheless, residences that the FHA has foreclosed upon can be purchased by investors.

The Department of Veteran Affairs, or VA, guarantees repayment of a percentage of mortgage loans made by non-governmental lenders, such as banks, to eligible veterans. The guarantee is provided to veterans without payment of any premium. The mortgage proceeds must be used to purchase a residence that is personally occupied by the veteran.

The Federal National Mortgage Association, or Fannie Mae, and the Federal Home Loan Mortgage Corporation, or Freddie Mac, have the same mission which is to provide stability and liquidity to the United States housing market. As of September 2008, the two GSE's had $5.4 trillion of guaranteed mortgage-backed securities ("MBS") and debt outstanding. That number equaled the publicly held debt of the United States. Fannie Mae and Freddie Mac carry out their mission by purchasing from lenders the mortgages that the lenders have made to finance the purchase or refinance of a residence. Fannie Mae and Freddie Mac fund their purchases of mortgage loans by using securitization-based financing. The GSE's issue mortgage-backed securities and then provide a guarantee of the payment of principal and interest on all securities. The GSEs also purchase mortgage loans and mortgage-related securities and hold them as investments. On

172

September 7, 2008, the Federal Housing Finance Agency ("FHFA") placed Fannie Mae and Freddie Mac under the FHFA's conservatorship.

B. Types of Residential Real Estate Loans

There are three types of loans that investors in residential properties commonly obtain. There are so many different types of loans that an investor in commercial or industrial property can negotiate that the discussion is beyond the scope of this chapter. The commercial or industrial investor should discuss the possibilities with the investor's advisors.

The three types of residential real estate loans are (i) conventional mortgage or deed of trust loans; (ii) Federal Housing Administration ("FHA") mortgage or deed of trust loans; and (iii) Department of Veteran Affairs ("VA") mortgage or deed of trust loans.

Conventional loans are loans made by lenders that are not guaranteed or insured by an agency of the Federal Government. However, conventional loans can be purchased by the two government sponsored enterprises ("GSEs") -- Federal Home Loan Mortgage Corporation, commonly known as "Freddie Mac," and the Federal National Mortgage Association, commonly known as "Fannie Mae." Fannie Mae and Freddie Mac influence the residential mortgage market by specifying the terms of the mortgages they purchase. A loan that complies with these terms is called a "conforming loan." Conventional loans include both first and second mortgage residential loans. The maximum amount of a conforming loan is set by law and the GSEs or their regulators. In 2008, the Housing and Economic Recovery Act modified the definition of a "conforming loan" to establish two maximum limits – one for high-cost areas and one for the rest of the country. The Federal Housing Finance Agency prescribes the high-cost areas in which the maximum loan amount is greater than the remainder of the country. A residential loan that exceeds the maximum amount is called a 'jumbo loan." These loans are not purchased by Freddie Mac or Fannie Mae but are purchased and securitized in the secondary market. Jumbo loans bear higher interest rates than conventional loans.

173

Fannie Mae and Freddie Mac's underwriting standards limit the number of loans that an investor can have outstanding at any time (either individually or as a joint owner) to ten mortgages. In the second half of 2008, Fannie Mae and Freddie Mac imposed a limit of not more than four 1-to-4 unit properties that are financed. In early 2009, the GSEs raised that limit to ten 1-to-4-unit properties. In order to qualify under Fannie Mae's standards for mortgages on more than four properties, as of early 2009, investors must make a down payment of at least 25 percent for a 1-unit property, and for a 2-unit to 4-unit property, investors must make a down payment of at least 30 percent and must bank six months of reserves for each investment property. Some institutional lenders also limit the number of mortgage loans they make to a foreclosure investor.

As noted above, a foreclosure investor cannot assume a loan guaranteed by the FHA. Only persons who occupy the property as their principal residence can benefit from FHA loans. However, if an investor makes the property his principal residence, the investor can assume the FHA loan. The advantage to making the property the principal residence is that the loan can be assumed by persons whose credit rating is not high enough to support a conventional loan.

C.   "Subject to" versus Assumption

A mortgage or deed of trust has no legal viability by itself. There must be an obligation that is secured by the mortgage or deed of trust. The obligation is almost always a debt. In our case, it is a debt from the borrower to the lender. The debt is evidenced by a promissory note that the borrower signs and delivers to the lender. The promissory note contains the payment terms, such as the interest rate, the due date and the amount of the monthly payment. The repayment of the debt is secured by the mortgaged property. If the borrower fails to pay the debt in accordance with its terms, the lender can foreclose and sell the property and apply the proceeds of the sale to payment of the debt. Because the promissory note represents the debt and contains the borrower's promise to repay the debt, the note can be assigned to third parties. A lender can hold the note and collect the monthly payments or can sell the note, and the note purchaser then collects the monthly payments. However, if the lender sold the note but held onto the mortgage for the lender's own account, the note would be unsecured, the mortgage would no longer be securing an obligation and the mortgage would have no further force or effect. Naturally, no one sells a mortgage note without including the mortgage in the sale.

When a foreclosure investor purchases a property that is encumbered by a mortgage, the investor has three potential courses to take. The first is to pay off the mortgage. This usually does not require anyone's consent, although, in the commercial and industrial context, the investor may have to pay a prepayment penalty.

The second course is to assume the mortgage. This phrase is short hand for the investor agreeing with the lender to take over the obligations under the promissory note and mortgage and become legally obligated to perform those obligations. The foreclosure investor enters into an agreement with the lender to assume the loan. This can occur if the lender does not insist on exercising the due-on-sale clause in the mortgage. If the interest rate on the loan is higher than the current rate, the lender has an incentive to agree to the assumption. If the interest rate under the loan is less than the current rate, the lender is more inclined to call the loan and make the investor obtain new financing at the current rate of interest. Of course, the threat of foreclosure, under which the property may become REO, can inspire the lender to consent to the assumption without an increase in the interest rate. In any event, if the investor intends to assume the loan, the investor faces the due-on-sale issue.

The borrower should require the lender who consents to an assumption to concurrently release the borrower from the obligations. The reason is that the borrower has agreed with the lender to be legally obligated to perform the obligations under the note and mortgage. Even if the investor assumes the obligations and becomes legally obligated to perform the obligations, the borrower remains secondarily liable for performance. If the investor defaults, the lender can still pursue the borrower for payment of the debt. However, if the lender releases the borrower, then the borrower is no longer liable and is not affected by the investor's default.

175

The third course is to acquire the property subject to the mortgage. This means that when the investor closes the purchase of the property, the mortgage still encumbers the property, the borrower is still primarily liable for payment of the debt and the investor does not obligate himself to the lender to perform the obligations under the loan. Acquiring the property subject to the mortgage triggers the due-on-sale clause. If the lender elects to enforce the clause, the investor is not able to take title subject to the mortgage. If the investor has already closed the purchase of the property, the lender's enforcement of the due-on-sale clause forces the investor to refinance the mortgage. Assuming that the lender does not enforce the due-on-sale clause, the "subject to" method benefits the investor because he can default under the mortgage without becoming liable for payment of the debt. Of course, the investor loses the property in a foreclosure and any funds expended such as the down payment, repairs, improvements and real estate taxes.

Although the "subject to" method leaves the borrower primarily liable, many borrowers are comfortable with this course or structure the transaction to become comfortable. For example, the borrower may have been planning to abandon the property. A sale to the investor has the possibility of bringing the loan current and keeping it current. So long as the investor makes the payments, the borrower's credit rating is not adversely affected in the way it is if the borrower defaults on the loan and goes into foreclosure. On the other hand, a borrower with a mortgage loan outstanding in the borrower's name is unable to get another loan to fund the purchase of a replacement residence. The investor should get the borrower to acknowledge in writing the negative effects of a "subject to" deal or expect at some point in the future to be contacted, and maybe sued, by the borrower to force the investor to pay off the loan and free up the borrower's credit. As an example of structuring a deal, if the investor makes a substantial down payment, the investor is unlikely to default and walk away from the property.

One trap for the investor in a "subject to" deal is the borrower's bankruptcy. The borrower remains liable on the promissory note. If the borrower files for bankruptcy, the lender is named as a party to the proceeding. At that point, the lender joins in the bankruptcy proceeding to protect the mortgage lien, and the investor as the owner of the property is drawn into the proceeding. If the investor took title without getting the lender's consent, the bankruptcy informs the lender of the sale, which can impact the lender's dealings with the investor, including the exercise of the due-on-sale clause.

Regardless of the course the foreclosure investor elects to follow, the investor purchases the property and becomes the owner with all the rights (to occupy the property, to lease the property and to collect the rents and profits, etc.) and all the obligations (to perform the covenants in the mortgage, to pay real estate taxes, to maintain and repair the property, liability for injuries on the property, etc.) associated with ownership.

If the borrower, investor and lender are unable to reach an agreement on financing through the investor assuming or taking subject to the existing mortgage, the investor must finance the entire purchase price and closing costs. For this financing, the investor can turn to debt financing, which is discussed in Subchapter V-3.E. If, on the other hand, the borrower, investor and lender agree to an arrangement whereby the investor assumes or takes subject to the existing mortgage, the investor is financing only the down payment and closing costs. This is a relatively small amount that can be financed by various forms of credit lines, such as credit cards or home equity loans.

D. Lines of Credit

If the deal the investor negotiated calls for the investor to produce a relatively small amount of capital, the investor can consider tapping into lines of credit. The typical foreclosure investor does not have access to the lines of credit that major corporate borrowers utilize, but the investor probably has access to smaller lines of credit that can be tapped to pay the down payment and closing costs. One source of funds is credit cards.

Some credit cards have low interest rates, and some charge high interest rates. The investor with a good credit rating should be able to find credit card companies that will issue him a credit card bearing a low interest rate. The investor should not use credit cards with high rates of interest. The investor draws on the line of credit that the card provides and uses that cash to pay the down payment and closing costs. Some investors use several cards to generate the necessary funds. The credit card debt is repaid by rents from the property or proceeds from a sale of the property (although in the case of a sale, there will be a period of time when no income has been earned and the investor is making monthly payments out of pocket).

Another source of funds is a home equity loan or secured line of credit. The investor arranges with a lender, typically a bank, for a home equity line of credit. The investor gives the lender a second mortgage on a property owned by the investor, often the investor's home, to secure a line of credit. The investor has the right to draw funds on the line of credit up to the maximum amount. The investor pays down the line whenever the investor chooses, and the amount paid down becomes available for borrowing in the future. If the investor never uses the line of credit, there is no charge for having it.

A third source of funds is a life insurance policy held by the investor. Policy holders who have built up the policy's cash value can borrow those funds. Under most policies, the loan will bear interest, and if the loan is not repaid, the death benefit is reduced by the amount of the loan and interest.

E.   Debt Financing with Institutional Lenders

There are several sources of debt financing, beginning with institutional lenders. Institutional lenders include banks, credit unions and mortgage companies. Institutional lenders make conventional loans, FHA loans, VA loans and commercial or industrial loans that are often structured to make them eligible for securitization.

A foreclosure investor can go directly to an institutional lender and apply for a loan or he can utilize a mortgage broker to find a lender. A residential mortgage broker is licensed by the state and is in the business of accepting the investor's loan application and arranging the loan between investor and a lender. The investor pays the mortgage broker a fee for his services, which is usually around one point. A competent mortgage broker has contacts with several lenders and knows which lenders are willing to finance the type of deal the investor is proposing and knows which lender has the best rates at any time. The Federal Reserve Board, on its website, offers the following caution regarding mortgage brokers: "Brokers generally take your application and contact several lenders, but keep in mind that brokers are not required to find the best deal for you unless they have contracted with you to act as your agent."

The foreclosure investor is negotiating with the lender in most foreclosure situations. The lender can be a source of financing for the investor. The lender is familiar with the property, the nature of the default and can be in a position to extend a loan to the investor.

There are several types of conventional loans that an investor can seek. They include fixed rate loans for differing numbers of years, such as a 30-year term, a 20-year term or a 15-year term. The interest rate varies with the length of the term. One advantage of a conventional loan is that the investor can obtain a loan with a 30-year term. The longer term provides for a smaller monthly payment which can help the investor's cash flow. Also, an institutional lender may be willing to include the closing costs as a part of the loan, reducing the amount of cash the investor must produce in order to close the acquisition.

An investor can also apply for an adjustable rate mortgage, referred to as an "ARM." Under an ARM, the rate of interest and monthly payment adjust upward and downward at set intervals. The length of time between adjustments is called the "adjustment period." An adjustment period can be one month, one quarter, six months, one year, three years or some other interval. ARMs are described by the term of adjustment period. For example, an ARM with the rate adjusting every three years would be called a 3–year ARM, and the interest rate and monthly payment is adjusted once every three years. An ARM with a 1-year adjustment period is called a 1-year ARM, and the interest rate and payment may adjust once every year.

The interest rate charged to the investor is based on an index and the lender's margin. The index measures rates generally, and the margin represents the lender's profit margin. Examples of indexes include the

London Interbank Offered Rate, referred to as "LIBOR," the one-year constant-maturity Treasury ("CMT") securities, the Cost of Funds Index ("COFI") or the lender's own personal cost of funds. These indexes can be found on the Internet. The margin is set by the lender. Some lenders will give a lower margin to an investor with a better credit rating. Assume that the lender uses LIBOR as the index and charges a margin of two percent. If LIBOR were 3% and the margin is 2%, the rate charged is 5%. A rate in which the index has not been discounted is called a "fully indexed rate." A lender who discounts the amount of the index is said to be offering a "discounted indexed rate."

If the index has increased when the adjustment period expires, and it is time to set the new rate, then the monthly installment increases. However, there are limits on the amount by which the interest can increase. These limits are referred to as "interest rate caps." Investors encounter at least two kinds of interest rate caps.

One kind of interest rate cap is a periodic adjustment cap. Not all lenders offer this cap. Under this kind of interest rate cap, the amount by which the interest rate can be moved up or down during the adjustment period is capped. For example, assume that the interest rate is 4% and the periodic cap is 2%. At the adjustment period, the index has increased from 3% to 6%, a 3% increase. Assume that the monthly payment before adjustment was $1,800, the monthly payment using a 3% increase would be $2,200 and the monthly payment using a 2% increase would be $2,000. The difference in the monthly installment between an uncapped rate and the capped rate is $200. During the ensuing adjustment period, the investor pays $2,000 per month, a savings of $200 per month or $2,400 per year. The interest rate without the cap would have been 7% but it was capped at 6%. The difference is called the "carryover." Some ARMs provide that if there is a carryover, and if the index stays the same or has decreased at the next adjustment, the rate is increased by the amount of the carryover. In that case, the monthly payment increases even though there has been no increase in the index.

The second kind of interest rate cap is the "lifetime cap." The lifetime cap sets a limit on the amount by which the interest rate can increase over the life of the loan. Federal law requires that virtually all ARMs have a lifetime cap. For an example of a lifetime cap, assume that the interest rate at the commencement of the ARM is 5% and there is a lifetime cap of 7%. Assume further that for the next 10 years, the index increases by 1% every year, so that the cumulative increase over 10 years goes from 5% to 15%. However, the ARMs lifetime cap is 7% which, when added to the initial rate, produces a maximum rate of 12%. The interest rate cannot exceed 12% during the term of the ARM.

Interest rate caps are not the only kind of cap that an ARM may carry. Some ARMs cap the amount by which the monthly payment may be increased at each adjustment. Assume that the ARM's payment cap is 6.25%. The monthly payment cannot increase by more than 6.25% even if the index has increased by a greater rate. For example, if the amount of the monthly payment is currently $1,200, the maximum amount to which it can increase is $1,275 (6.25% of $1,200 equals an additional $75). Although the amount of the monthly payment is limited, the amount ultimately due to the lender is not capped. Any interest that is not paid due to the payment cap is added to the ARM's balance. This results in negative amortization. Under negative amortization, the lender adds any unpaid interest to the principal balance of the loan. The unpaid balance of the loan increases, and interest is compounded because interest is charged on the interest that has now become part of the loan balance. Negative amortization is discussed in more detail below.

There are a variety of ARMs in addition to standard ARMs. One type is the hybrid ARM. A hybrid ARM is an ARM in which the rate of interest and monthly payment are fixed at the commencement of the mortgage for a period of time. This period can run from as little as one month to a number of years. After the expiration of the initial period, the interest rate and the monthly payment adjust upward and downward at set intervals. Hybrid ARMs are described by the number of fixed years followed by the term of adjustment period. For example, in a 3/1ARM, the interest rate is fixed for three years and then each year thereafter, there is an adjustment period during the year.

Another type of ARM is the interest-only ARM. Under this kind of ARM, the investor pays only interest for a specified period of years, typically from three to ten years. The advantage to the investor is that, at the outset, the monthly payments are smaller. After the interest-only period expires, the amount of the monthly payment increases because principal has been added to the interest. If the investor's strategy is to dispose of the property before the interest-only period expires, the interest-only ARM can be a good option. However, the investor must be assured that the property can be sold at an acceptable price in that time frame. If not, the investor's cash flow can be impacted.

Another type of ARM is the payment-option ARM. The payment-option ARM contains a variety of different methods – or options – for making monthly payments. A payment-option ARM typically includes the following options: (i) a fixed term option, such as a 15-, 30-, or 40-year payment schedule, for the payment of principal and interest. These payments reduce the unpaid balance due under the mortgage; (ii)
an interest-only option, under which the investor pays only interest. The principal balance of the loan is not reduced; (iii) a minimum payment option that, under certain circumstances, can be less than the amount of interest payable for a given month. If that is the case, these payments do not reduce the principal balance due under the mortgage, and all unpaid interest is added to the principal balance of the loan, thus compounding the interest. Under this option, there may be a balloon payment due at the end of the loan. Advantages of the payment-option ARM include a low interest rate at the beginning of the loan, so, if the investor can sell the property quickly, the cost is less. However, the interest rate soon increases to approximate market rates. A disadvantage arises if the investor makes only the minimum monthly payments and interest is added to principal. The loan will then experience negative amortization.

Periodically, usually at five year intervals, a payment-option ARM is recast. This means that the lender recalculates the amount of the monthly payment so that the loan amortizes within the remaining term of the loan. For example, if the ARM secures a 30-year loan, and the loan is recast at year 5, there are 25 years remaining and the monthly payment is reset to amortize in 25 years. One risk is that the amount of the monthly payment increases if the investor has takes the minimum payments option, or the increase in interest rates has exceeded the payments made by the investor. A payment cap will not apply, and there can be a material increase in the amount of the monthly payment whenever the loan is recast.

Various versions of ARMs can result in negative amortization. Negative amortization is the opposite of amortization. Amortization under a mortgage is the reduction and eventual elimination of the debt by installment payments at regular intervals over a specified period of time; each installment is applied first to the payment of interest currently due and the balance of the installment applied to principal. For example, assume a debt of $100,00bearing interest at the rate of 10% per annum and amortized over 30 years. A borrower pays the lender equal monthly installments of $877.57. In the first month, the borrower will have paid $833.33 in interest and $44.24 in principal. In the second month, the borrower will have paid $832.96 in interest and $44.61 in principal. In the last month, the borrower will have paid $7.25 in interest and $870.32 in principal, and the loan will have been paid in full. However, under negative amortization, if the borrower had only paid $50.00 in the first month, the interest payment would be $33.33 short. That amount would be added to the principal and bear interest in the second and subsequent months until paid.

A payment cap can cause negative amortization because only the amount by which the monthly payment can increase is capped. Increases in the interest rate are not capped. As a consequence, monthly payments may not fully pay the interest due from month to month. The lender adds the unpaid interest to the principal. Because interest is charged on the outstanding principal, the borrower winds up paying interest on interest, which compounds the interest. The end result can be a loan at the end of the term that is greater than the loan at the commencement.

ARMs that can result in negative amortization often contain an increased principal-to-original principal ratio clause. This is, in effect, a cap on negative amortization. The increased principal ratio is usually set at a limit of 110 percent to 125 percent of the original loan amount. For example, if the original ARM is a loan of $500,000 on a property worth $525,000, and if the ratio were 125 percent, if the loan negatively amortizes to a principal amount of $625,000, the ARM becomes fully amortizing and all principal and interest is payable in equal installments within the remaining term of the loan. Any payment cap would not apply. If the negative amortization sets in early and the investor wants to refinance, there may be a penalty.

Investors may find that the ARMs they are considering, including interest only and payment-option ARMs, contain prepayment penalties. Prepayment penalties require the investor to pay a fee or penalty if the investor pays off or refinances the ARM prior to its maturity or other allowable periods. There are two kinds of prepayments penalties. A "hard prepayment penalty" requires the investor to pay the fee if the pay-off occurs for any reason during the penalty period, including a sale of the property or refinance of the ARM. The other kind of prepayment penalty is referred to as a "soft prepayment penalty." Under a soft prepayment penalty, the investor must pay the fee upon a refinance of the ARM, but not upon a sale of the property. Further, some ARMs secure loans containing prepayment penalties that are triggered upon a partial prepayment.

A foreclosure investor may structure a deal using a hybrid ARM to pay the initial low interest rate with the intent to refinance at the time of adjustment. An investor with this strategy must determine whether there is a prepayment penalty. If the interest rate adjusts at the end of the second year, but the prepayment penalty runs for five years, the investor is required to pay the penalty in order to implement the strategy. The penalty can be a considerable amount.

ARMs present advantages and disadvantages to the foreclosure investor. First, as noted above, the investor can get the benefit of a reduced interest rate and reduced monthly payment in the early stages of an ARM. Under the payment-option ARMs, the investor can adjust payments to fit the current circumstances. The reduced rate may enable the investor to generate cash flow from rental property. The cash flow can be applied to the acquisition of other foreclosure properties. Appreciation is another possible benefit. In a hot market, where a property receives ten offers within a week of being listed for sale, the investor who has allowed unpaid interest to accumulate may be able to sell the property for at a price that exceeds the accumulated interest. Of course, in a declining market, this strategy results in dilemma for the investor.

Although an ARM can be used to manage an investor's finances, the investor must comprehend the best way to implement that management. Additionally, the investor must be prepared to manage the risks of an ARM. Under an ARM, interest rates can increase. Moreover, the amount of the monthly payment can increase even if interest rates remain steady. The investor should review the annual percentage rate ("APR"). An APR that is considerably higher than the initial rate means that there will be substantial increases during the loan term. Another risk of an ARM is the effect on second mortgages. When the investor has an ARM with a negative amortization feature, no one except the investor knows if the principal amount of the loan is allowed to increase. If the investor wants to obtain additional funds by tapping the equity in the property by getting a second mortgage, the investor will find that lenders are reluctant to take a second position because they do not know how large the first mortgage can increase, and thereby affect the investor's ability to repay the first mortgage ARM. The second mortgage lender underwrites the loan by assuming that the investor has negatively amortized the ARM loan to the fullest extent, and that calculation could eat up the equity.

There are other loans that were popular in the mid 2000's, such as no documentation (or low documentation) loans and non-verification of income loans (or stated income loan). After the credit meltdown, these types of loans will be difficult to obtain.

F.   Debt Financing with Private Money Lenders

In addition to institutional lenders, the foreclosure investor can seek financing from "private money lenders." Private money lenders are also referred to as "hard money lenders." Hard money lenders are individuals or private companies that are not regulated lending institutions but provide loans secured by real property. Hard money lenders may operate independently, or may be informally affiliated with a group or network of other lenders, such as through a real estate brokerage firm or a mortgage broker. Persons desirous of becoming hard money lenders can find opportunities on the Internet.

185

When searching for a hard money lender, the foreclosure investor can tap the same sources of information on the Internet that persons seeking to make loans utilize. Additionally, investors should not overlook potential hard money lenders such as family members, friends and colleagues and other real property investors. The investor who attends real estate programs and seminars can use these opportunities for networking. The investor does need to understand the reasons why a person would consider becoming a hard money lender.

Hard money lenders make hard money loans because they find that the return on their investments exceeds returns on alternative investments with comparable risk. Consequently, hard money loans bear interest at a higher rate than loans from institutional lenders. Larger hard money lenders may borrow the funds from lines of credit they maintain and then re-loan those funds to investors at a higher rate of interest. Hard money lenders may have taken a beating in the stock market and are now looking for a more stable income stream. Hard money lenders typically prefer short terms loans so that they can realize their return and have funds available to do the next deal. Hard money lenders customarily do not scrutinize an investor's financial condition as sharply as an institutional lender because a hard money loan is more focused on the value of the collateral. Therefore, investors with a lower credit rating, or who are unable to verify income, or who are seeking to acquire unusual properties, or who need to act quickly and cannot get a loan from an institutional lender may be able to procure financing from a hard money lender. The hard money lender is concerned with the investor's track record of making monthly payments. If the lender believes that this project enables the investor to make those payments, the lender gives the proposal serious consideration. The investor may have to document the investor's ability by providing financial statements, income tax returns, credit reports, analyses of the property data on comparable sales, estimated rehab costs, lease abstracts, confirmation that the investor has the funds needed to make the down payment and similar information.

Hard money lenders are more flexible than institutional lenders and can structure deals to accommodate the investor. They can also be creative in deciding the terms of the loan. Since hard money lenders are able to accommodate riskier investors, or riskier deals, they expect a return comparable to the risk. In order to minimize the risk, hard money lenders require a substantial loan to value ratio. They may require that the investor's equity in the property, after rehabilitation, be as much as 25 to 50 percent. Depending on the deal, this may permit financing of 100 percent of the purchase price. For example, if the investor is paying $100,000 for a property that needs $50,000 in repairs and will have a market value upon completion of $200,000, the ratio of purchase price to finished value would be 1 to 2, or 50 percent ($100,000/$200,000). There are hard money lenders who specialize in funding rehabilitation projects and could help in this hypothetical. However, it is not unusual for a rehab lender to make the loan only after the work is completed and has passed an inspection, so the investor needs either to have the cash available to pay the contractors, or to make arrangements with the contractors for a single payment at the completion of the work. In a market where no construction work is being performed, it may be possible to get a contractor to agree to such an arrangement, but in a vital market, such an arrangement is difficult to negotiate.

To compensate hard money lenders for the risks they are taking, they charge an interest rate that is higher than the rates available from institutional lenders. The spread between hard money rates and institutional rates can range from six to twelve percent or more. Another source of compensation is points. A hard money lender might charge from four to eight points to make a loan. A point is equal to one percent of the principal amount. Although hard money loans are more expensive than institutional loans, they may be the only source available to an investor. The investor simply has to analyze the costs and expected return, and if the hard money loan makes economic sense, the investor should proceed.

G.   Equity Financing

Debt financing is the financing of the acquisition through a loan – in other words, by using debt. Equity financing is the financing of the acquisition through equity in the property. The term "equity financing" does not refer to the equity in the property, *i.e.,* the difference between the property's market value and the amount of the loan. Instead, it refers to an ownership interest. The equity financier is not a lender. The equity financier holds an interest in the ownership of the property. This can be as a partner of the partnership that purchases the property, or as a member of a limited liability company that purchases the property, or as a tenant in common in the property, or as a principal in a joint venture that purchases the property.

The advantage of using a partnership, or joint venture, or limited liability company ("LLC"), is that these entities employ pass-through taxation. This is in contrast to a typical "C" corporation. An "S" corporation is an exception to the rule and does allow pass-through taxation. To explain, a corporation is a separate legal entity for tax purposes, and the corporation pays tax on its income. Then, the income is distributed to the shareholders as dividends, and the shareholders pay tax on the dividend income, so corporate income is said to be subject to double taxation. In a partnership or LLC, the entity is not a separate legal entity for tax purposes, and the income is not taxed at the entity level. The entity's untaxed income is passed through to its partners or members, and those partners or members are taxed individually. The partners and members also receive deductibles such as operating expenses and depreciation. Because real estate has a number of tax benefits, if title is to be held in an entity, it is usually held as a partnership or LLC so that the partners and members can use those benefits.

The advantage of using an LLC instead of a partnership is that an LLC has limited liability similar to a corporation. Members are not personally liable for the LLC's obligations. The investor should discuss the choice of entities with his attorney for each particular investment. .

In a typical real estate partnership, one partner does the basic work putting the deal together by finding the property, doing the due diligence and documenting the deal. The other partner puts up the money. The partners can strike any kind of deal they want, but it probably has a greater chance of success if the terms are fairly negotiated. For example, the hands-on partner can be reimbursed for out-of-pocket expenses and compensated for time spent. The money partner can receive a negotiated return, and then both partners can share any additional revenue. Some partnerships include several money partners. Partnerships that have limited partners who provide the money are often referred to as "real estate syndications." However, investors can market their project to only a limited number of potential partners before that marketing becomes subject to the securities laws of the state and Federal Government. An investor who is planning to bring in several money partners must review the project with a securities attorney before proceeding.

The terms of a partnership should be set down in a written agreement. If the parties desire to use a limited liability company ("LLC"), they must prepare an agreement and register the company in accordance with the laws of the state in which the LLC is formed. The investor should retain an attorney to prepare the LLC agreement, and register it in order to ensure that liability is in fact limited.

A partner can also act as a debt financier. The partner makes a contribution to the deal in the form of a loan, and the partner's return is in the form of loan repayments. Some no-money-down deals can be structured in a partnership form, as discussed above in Subchapter V1.N.

H.   Lease with Option to Purchase as Landlord

Under this method, the investor acquires a property and promptly leases the property to a tenant who intends to purchase the property but is not currently in a position to complete the purchase. The tenant enters into a lease with an option to purchase the property. The tenant makes a non-refundable payment to the investor upon executing the lease and occupying the property. This is an option payment. Part of the monthly rent is credited to the purchase price if the tenant exercises the option. If the tenant does not exercise the option, the investor retains the option payment. The option payment can be used to pay the investor's down payment, and the rent can be applied to monthly payments under the mortgage.

The lease with option to purchase entered into by the foreclosure investor as tenant can be combined with the lease with option to purchase entered into by the foreclosure investor as landlord to finance an acquisition. The investor leases a property from a borrower with the option to purchase, and then subleases the property to a third party under a sublease with the tenant's option to purchase. This pairing of a lease and sublease is sometimes referred to as a "sandwich lease option." This arrangement can work in cases where the borrower is willing to accept installment payments. However, there is no guarantee to the borrower that either the investor or the subtenant will ever exercise their respective options. If the investor intends to dispose of the property, then the investor needs to find a subtenant who is able to qualify for a loan to finance the purchase of the property upon exercise of the option. The subtenant's purchase price is used to pay off the mortgage on the property.

When structuring a sandwich lease option deal, the investor must be sure that the term of his lease is longer than the term of the sublease. Otherwise, the investor will be in default when the lease expires, and the subtenant is evicted by the owner. A foreclosure investor concerned about entering into a long term lease could set up a lease with a shorter term with one or more options to extend the term. The investor must also address the issues affecting a lease option described in Subchapter V-1.H.

I.   Equity Sharing

Equity sharing is a possible technique when the property is not underwater and the borrower and foreclosure investor have time to build up equity that can be shared by the parties. . Under this technique, the borrower's debt will approximate the market value of the property. The investor takes title to the property subject to the mortgage or assumes the mortgage. The investor gets the tax advantages of ownership and the borrower is relieved from making the mortgage without suffering the damage to the credit report caused by a short sale or foreclosure. After a few years, perhaps three to five years, the investor sells the property for a profit. The investor and the borrower share the amount of equity that has been built up. The exact amount each party receives is negotiated at the outset. The investor and borrower must provide early exit clauses in their agreement,

providing for cash penalties or other consideration if one party cancels
s the deal before the term has run.

This approach costs more than a lease, but the tax benefits and the
accumulation of equity may make it worthwhile. Also, this is a
technique that allows the investor to acquire ownership of the property
on a no-money-down basis without making a down payment and
without having to qualify for a bank loan. The advantage to the
investor is earning a share of the property's appreciation without
having to pay any of the expenses.

A variation of this technique is the investor identifying the property
and then finding a third party who wants to acquire the property but
cannot afford the down payment. The third party obtains a loan to pay
off the mortgage and the investor provides the down payment. The
third party occupies the property and makes the payments on the
mortgage. At the end of the term of the agreement, the third party
either buys out the investor at an agreed amount, or the property is
sold, the down payment and loan are repaid, the third party is
reimbursed for cash invested in refurbishing the property, and the two
parties share any appreciated equity. Also, it is possible for the
third party to refinance the property if he wishes to retain title. The
risk to the investor is that the value of the property may decline and the
third party will not be able to repay the down payment. Another risk
to the investor is that the third party may default under the mortgage,
the lender forecloses, and the investor loses the entire investment.

The foreclosure investor must pay careful attention to tax
considerations. The arrangement must be structured and the
agreement must be drafted so that the investor is not characterized by
the Internal Revenue Service ("IRS") as a lender, and the other party is
not characterized by the IRS as a tenant under the tax laws.

CHAPTER V-4   CREDIT RATING

It is always advisable for the investor to qualify for financing before
finalizing a transaction. The ability of the foreclosure investor to
borrow from institutional lenders and hard money lenders is impacted

by the investor's credit reports and credit score. The investor must understand how credit reports are prepared, how credit ratings operate, and credit scores are determined.

A.   Credit Reports

Lenders review the credit report of the foreclosure investor. Credit reports are prepared by three major credit reporting agencies. These credit bureaus are Equifax, Experian and TransUnion. The credit agencies prepare credit reports by compiling information on investors' credit history. They review bank loans, mortgages, credit cards, automobile loans, student loans, and various other forms of credit extended to the investor in the preceding seven years.   For each account addressed, the report shows the date the investor created or opened the account, the amount currently due, the high credit limit, the highest balance attained in the account, the terms of the credit, the amount of any fixed monthly payments, the amount of any minimum monthly payment and the current status of the account such as whether it is open, closed, paid in full, inactive or delinquent.

A negative credit fact continues to be reported for seven years. The credit report also covers public records, such as judgments filed against the investor, foreclosures, any bankruptcy filing and any tax liens. A bankruptcy proceeding continues to be reported for ten years. An unpaid judgment against the investor is reported for the longer of seven years or until expiration of the statute of limitations. Positive credit facts remain a part of the record for the life of the investor. Credit history covers the number of times an account was timely paid the number of times an account was paid late, and how late the payment was, such as 30 days, 60 days or more than 90 days. A credit report also lists any companies that reviewed the investor's credit report in connection with an application for credit within the preceding two years. This alerts lenders to investors that are overextending themselves. Further, if an investor has applied to several lenders in a short period of time, that fact may indicate that the investor has trouble obtaining financing, which might suggest that other lenders consider him to be a credit risk. On the other hand, the FICO model omits inquiries made within 30 days of an application for a mortgage or car loan. Additionally, the number of inquiries is typically not given great weight in the evaluation process.

Credit reports issued by one credit bureau may differ from the credit reports issued on the same investor by another credit bureau. The reason is that creditors and lenders report credit incidents to one, two or all three of the credit bureaus. If the incident is not reported to one of the agencies, that agency is working with different data than the others which results in a different report. Another reason for a different report is that each of three national credit bureaus reports its own data independently.

B.   Credit Scores

The need of lenders to evaluate borrower's credit worthiness led to the development of credit scores. A credit score is a number. Credit bureaus derive the number from various factors contained in the borrower's credit report, such as credit history, the length of time that a prospective borrower has secured credit, and the kinds of credit the borrower maintains. Credit scores are produced by mathematical formulae that should describe a prospective borrower's ability to repay a loan. Credit scores are a standardized way for lenders to assess the risk of default by a particular borrower. One advantage of credit scores is that subjective facts are eliminated from the process of evaluating credit worthiness, making the process objective and based on factors affecting credit risk.

Credit scores are also called "FICO" scores. The term "FICO" was developed by Fair Isaac Corporation, Inc., a corporation founded in 1956 by Bill Fair and Earl Isaac. FICO is a credit-scoring formula designed to measure the risk that a borrower may default in repayment of a loan. Lenders began using FICO scores extensively after Fannie Mae and Freddie Mac recommended their use. FICO scores range for 300 to 850. The higher credit scores reflect a higher probability of timely repayment. Scores below a certain point make an individual a subprime credit borrower. According to a pamphlet posted by the Fair Isaac Corporation at its web site, over half of the persons with credit reports in the United States have credit scores between 650 and 800+. Each of the credit bureaus uses its own formula for generating a credit score, but all of these formulae were developed by the Fair Isaac Corporation.

A number of factors go into calculating a credit score. About 35 percent is allocated to credit history. Other factors are weighted as follows: amounts owed – 30 percent; length of credit history – 15 percent; inquiries for new credit – 10 percent; and types of credit in use – 10 percent.

Credit scores are not the only factor that lenders consider in deciding whether to extend credit. Other factors that a lender may take into account include the amount of the investor's income, employment status and credit history.

C.   Effect of Credit Score on Financing Terms

Credit scores affect the terms of financing that a foreclosure investor can obtain. For example, a web site maintained by MyFICO, a division of Fair Isaac, displays this table showing how interest rates and monthly payments for a $300,000 mortgage loan with a 30-year term vary with the credit score:

FICO® score	APR *	Monthly payment
760-850	4.658%	$1,548
700-759	4.880%	$1,589
680-699	5.057%	$1,621
660-679	5.271%	$1,661
640-659	5.701%	$1,741
620-639	6.247%	$1,847

*For scores above 620, these APRs assume a mortgage with 1.0 points and 80% Loan-to-Value Ratio for a single family, owner-occupied property.

It is generally believed that investors with scores below 620 may find it very difficult to obtain financing from institutional lenders, and possibly even hard money lenders. The investor should obtain copies of the his credit reports and credit scores from the three credit rating agencies so that he knows whether conventional loans are available.

There are many paths in addition to conventional loans that a foreclosure investor can follow to finance the purchase of a property. Once the investor has settled on the financing method, it is time to close the purchase.

CHAPTER V-5   CLOSING THE PURCHASE

We have discussed various methods of financing or otherwise paying for the acquisition of real property.   Now it is time to close the purchase.

The customs and practices governing the purchase and sale of real property vary from state to state.   In New York and New England, attorneys handle closings of residential properties.   In California, escrow companies and real estate brokers handle closings of residential properties.   This subchapter does not address all of the varieties of closings, but concentrates on the matters that are important to the acquisition of property in one of the stages of foreclosure.

A.   Moving Quickly

In the foreclosure arena, the advantage goes to the investor who can close the deal the fastest. Depending on the deal, there may be a few or there may be many players. These players can include the borrower, the foreclosure investor, the original lender, a new lender or lenders, a mortgage broker, one or two real estate brokers, the title insurance company, the escrow agent or settlement agent and the attorneys for one or more parties. The investor cannot control how quickly these individuals move, but the investor can influence their speed. First, the investor should inform all parties of the need for a quick closing. Second, the investor can draw up a closing memorandum listing the parties, the documents to which they relate, the costs, disbursements and prorations of the transaction. This memo should be circulated to the parties to be sure they know what is expected of them. Third, the investor can arrange to prepare, or help to prepare, documents so that they are completed promptly. Fourth, the investor can verify that he has completed all of his responsibilities in a timely manner.

In the pre-foreclosure stage, there are probably not any real estate brokers present at the closing to assist the parties. If the foreclosure investor is inexperienced at closings, and there are no brokers, the investor should retain a real estate attorney to advise the investor.

In the default and auction stage, the borrower may have waited until the last minute to decide to sell the property. If there is not enough time left to close before the auction, the investor can enter into an agreement with the borrower, subject to the lender's approval to postpone the auction, and then request that the lender postpone the auction based on the investor's deal with the borrower. If the lender agrees, the investor should take all steps needed to close as soon as possible.

B.   Do Not Release Funds Until Certain Events Occur

When closing the purchase, the foreclosure investor must be certain that everything in the agreement has occurred before releasing any funds. For example, if the borrower is required to vacate the property before the closing, the investor must inspect the property to confirm that the borrower has vacated and to determine if the borrower has damaged the property intentionally by trashing it or unintentionally through careless movers. If the investor is reinstating a loan in default, the investor should not pay the lender until the investor has recorded the deed and the title insurance company has issued (or confirmed that it will issue) the title insurance policy. The investor should not pay any junior liens, tax liens or judgment liens before title has closed.

C.   Closing Documentation

At the closing, the escrow agent or title company representative prepares a closing statement setting forth all funds deposited in the closing, and the party who deposited the funds, the funds disbursed from the closing proceeds, and to whom the funds were disbursed. The statement lists all costs paid out of the closing, such as real estate taxes, mortgages being paid off, judgment liens, title insurance premiums and other costs. This statement has been prescribed by the Department of Housing and Urban Development ("HUD") and is known as the HUD 1 Settlement Statement. The form of the HUD 1

Settlement Statement can be found on HUD's web site at http://www.hud.gov/offices/adm/hudclips/forms/files/1.pdf . The form is derived from HUD's responsibility under the Real Estate Settlement Procedures Act ("RESPA") to prescribe a standard real estate settlement form to be used for all transactions involving federally related mortgage loans. The form is now widely used in all kinds of residential real property closings. The foreclosure investor must review the form carefully to be sure it is complete and correct. Closing costs can include some or all of the following: the real estate broker's commission; the loan origination fee or points to cover the lender's costs in making loan; the loan discount fee or "points" charged to reduce the interest rate payable under the loan; mortgage insurance application fee covering an application for mortgage insurance; the loan assumption fee charged by the lender when the investor assumes the existing mortgage loan; the mortgage broker's fee; interest on the loan accruing from the closing to the first monthly payment; the mortgage insurance premium; the casualty insurance premium; any flood insurance premium; the title company's charges; the settlement or closing fee paid to the settlement agent or escrow agent; fees for the preliminary title report or title insurance commitment; document preparation fee charged by some title companies or lenders for preparation of final legal papers; notary fee charged by the person who notarizes the closing papers; the lender's attorney's fees; title insurance premiums for the owner's and lender's title insurance policies; recording fees; transfer taxes; survey charges; pest and other infestation inspection fees; and lead-based paint inspection fee. If the investor after reviewing the settlement statement finds an erroneous entry, the investor should point the error out to the closing agent or lender's representative.

RESPA is a federal statute regulating real property closings involving loans secured with by a mortgage or deed of trust on a one-to-four family residential property. These loans include refinancings, assumptions of the loan and home equity lines of credit. RESPA is enforced by HUD. According to HUD's web site, "RESPA is about closing costs and settlement procedures. RESPA requires that consumers receive disclosures at various times in the transaction and outlaws kickbacks that increase the cost of settlement services." RESPA requires lenders and mortgage brokers to deliver to the

197

investor, at the time the investor applies for a mortgage loan, a Good Faith Estimate ("GFE") of the settlement costs. This statement lists the charges the investor will probably have to pay at the closing. Because the statement is only an estimate, the actual charges at the closing may differ. RESPA, by its terms, does not apply to commercial and industrial properties, and the investor may not find its forms in a closing involving those types of properties. If RESPA forms are not utilized, the investor's real estate attorney or real estate broker prepares a closing statement listing all of the costs and disbursements that need to be accounted for.

The investor should carefully review the real estate tax prorations to be sure they have been accurately calculated. Real estate taxes become liens before they become payable, and then they are paid in quarterly or semi-annual installments. Accordingly, either the borrower will have paid taxes for a period that extends after the closing, or the property will be subject to taxes for a period prior to the closing. The parties will prorate the taxes so that the borrower pays taxes until the closing, and the investor will pay taxes after the closing. Taxes can be prorated using a 365-day year or a 360-day year. The investor should insist on a 365-day year (except in Leap Year) so that the taxes are equitably shared by the borrower and the investor. If the investor is assuming or taking subject to the existing mortgage, interest and other charges under the mortgage will need to be prorated. In a commercial or industrial property occupied by tenants, rents need to be prorated. Other charges, such as utility bills in a commercial property, and fuel oil in any property, should also be prorated. The utility meters should be read the day before the closing.

The foreclosure investor is entitled to receive a HUD 1 Settlement Statement a day before the closing, but many real estate charges are not determined until the date of the closing. The investor should be certain to have arranged for sufficient funds to pay the costs shown in the settlement statement or closing statement, and enough funds to cover any costs not yet finalized, and enough funds to cover any unexpected contingencies. Often, closings generate surprises, and the investor needs to be prepared to resolve them.

D.   Post-Closing Matters

The foreclosure investor must arrange before the closing for certain matters that apply following the closing. For example, there should be casualty and liability insurance in place at the moment of the closing to protect the investor. Utilities need to be told that the property will be under new ownership on the day of the closing so that the investor is not charged for utilities enjoyed by the borrower. The investor should employ a management company if the investor will not manage the property directly. If the investor intends to hold the property, and it is vacant, the investor should retain a real estate broker to market the rental space. If the property is a fixer upper, the investor should seek a contractor to perform the work (unless the investor is a do-it-yourselfer). If the property has suffered damage, such as broken windows, the damage needs to be repaired quickly to prevent any storms from further damaging the property. In a commercial or industrial building, the investor should send letters to all the tenants informing them of the sale, giving them a contact number for the investor or his agent, and instructing them on where and to whom rent checks should be sent.

PART VI – CONCLUSION

In the last one hundred years, real property investors have experienced euphoric appreciation and depressing devaluation. Interest rates have ranged from a few percentage points to the mid-teens and more. Prices have skyrocketed in some areas and declined in others, both movements occurring at the same time.

Economic conditions change over time. Economic conditions in one part of the country can vary greatly from conditions in another area. During the oil boom, real property values soared in Dallas and Houston. Shortly thereafter, values collapsed and stagnated for several years. In the early 80's, property values fell in Los Angeles. Later they climbed. During the Savings & Loan crisis, fortunes were made in foreclosed properties. In short, the conditions that prevail today will change tomorrow or the next day.

As conditions change, foreclosure investors adapt to the environment and use different approaches to accomplish their goals. The principles, methods and techniques profiled in this book have been employed in various economic conditions and have stood the test of time. Regardless of the economy, the foreclosure investor can rely on the information in this book to find a method that will lead to success in foreclosure investing. Using these strategies, the foreclosure investor can flourish in any market.

CHAPTER VI-1   INVESTING IN A RECESSIONARY ECONOMY

Foreclosure investments involve risk. However, all investments involve risk. The recession of 2008 showed the world what can happen if investors ignore risk. That is one reason why it is important to identify and reduce risks. This chapter gives the foreclosure investor tools to make successful investments while minimizing the risks inherent in a recessionary economy.

The first step to successful investing in a recession is to realize that neither the foreclosure investor nor anyone else can predict with certainty in which direction the economy will head. Economists can establish when a recession has reached the bottom only after the recovery is well underway. Commercial properties can be subject to the vagaries of the market. If consumers become too wary to spend, retail and shopping center tenants will not be able to pay their rents. If the economy continues in the doldrums and office tenants continue to lay off employees, the inventory of available space will continue to grow, and office rents will not recover, and may drop even further.

Therefore, commercial properties carry considerable risk. However, there is another class of properties with less risk if purchased in the right manner. That is the single family residence.

The key is to acquire the single family residence for its cash flow and not for speculation. In a recessionary economy, there are two factors that the investor must take into account when analyzing the cash flow. The first is the amount of operating costs, taxes and mortgage payments that the rental stream will be able to cover each month. The second is the dependability of the rental stream.

The amount of operating costs, taxes and mortgage payments depends in large part on the purchase price that the foreclosure investor pays for the property. To determine a correct purchase price, the foreclosure investor must determine the rental value of the residence and then finance the purchase of the property at a price that will be covered by the rental stream. For example, if the investor determines that he should be able to rent the property for $450.00 a month, the mortgage payments, operating costs and taxes must be less than $450.00 per month. The investor will then make an offer that can be financed with a mortgage loan that can be paid in full by the rents.

The second factor is the dependability of the rents. One excellent way to improve dependability is to obtain government backing of the tenant's rent payments. The Section 8 program, or Housing Choice Voucher Program, provides government backing of rents. The investor can acquire a single family residence that qualifies for the Section 8 voucher program and rent it to an eligible family.

Section 8, also known as the Housing Choice Voucher Program, is administered by the Department of Housing and Urban Development ("HUD"). Section 8 is a federal program that provides rental subsidies to low-income renters. Persons who qualify for the rental subsidy are persons whose income is below fifty percent of the median income for the area. Local public housing authorities administer the program at the local level. Landlords must have their rental properties inspected by the local public housing authorities to confirm that the property meets federal standards. A landlord who leases to a Section 8 tenant will receive a rent subsidy check monthly from the government.

This Section 8 strategy provides the investor with more assurance of success than alternative real estate investments. Under this strategy, if the economy goes down, there will be more people who qualify for Section 8 housing and more prospective renters. If the economy improves, the Section 8 lease is only for one year, and when the lease expires, the investor can sell the property. This makes the Section 8 strategy recession proof.

Another key is to make your profit at the closing of the purchase. Never pay the full market value for the property. Always make an offer that is well below the market price. How does the foreclosure investor know what a good price would be? The investor must identify an area or neighborhood where there are prospective Section 8 properties. This would be an area where lower income persons live and where many properties are being or have been foreclosed. Find several real estate brokers who have listings in the area. Then spend a day with each broker traveling through the area looking at available properties. After about a week spent touring an area, the investor should have a good idea of the market for that area, both as to prices and rents.

Consult with the brokers who have the listings for the properties. If an offer is made through the listing broker without the involvement of another broker, the listing broker is entitled to the full commission. This will give a listing broker a strong incentive to close a sale.

Once the investor has become familiar with an area and has identified prospective purchases, the investor should make offers that are well below the market prices. For example, if a single family residence is listed for $175,000, make an offer for $125,000. If the market later goes up, the investor's profit will be even greater. If the market declines, the profit will be less, but there is sufficient cushion built into the price to protect the investor against a loss.

Because the investor will be making offers at prices well below the market, there will not be very many acceptances. Accordingly, the investor should make two or three hundred offers. If the investor makes hundreds of offers, at least a couple should be accepted.

Here then are the tools for successful foreclosure investing in a recession:

- When seeking advice, listen only to investors who have actually completed foreclosure purchases. Many people are willing to give advice and share their opinions, but they often do not understand the process. Listen only to persons experienced in the field.
- Close your eyes and ears to the media. The media specializes in the gloomy side of life. Although the media purports to give expert advice, they do not any better at predicting the future than a gypsy with a crystal ball.
- Take speculation completely out of the equation. Make your profit on the day you close the purchase, not in future speculation.
- Become thoroughly familiar with the Section 8 requirements and be certain that every property you are considering qualifies for Section 8 rent subsidies. The Section 8 regulations prescribe the number of bedrooms and the size of the rooms for the level of rent support. Not every house will qualify for

Section 8. Consult with the local public housing authority and be certain that the house you purchase will qualify.

- If you are new to this strategy, start with a single family house. In the lease, assign the obligations of cutting the lawn and keeping the house in good condition and repair to the tenant. That way, the investor does not have the weekly burden of cutting the lawn or raking the leaves, and if something goes wrong, the tenant will take care of it instead of calling you in the middle of the night. After acquiring some experience, you can consider moving up to a two-family residence. However, multi-family residences are more complicated to administer. For example, which tenant will be responsible for mowing the lawn? How do you resolve a dispute when the upstairs tenant makes too much noise? What happens if the tenant responsible for shoveling snow off the sidewalk fails to do the work? With more experience will come the ability to deal effectively with these kinds of problems. However, for the investor who is just starting out, minimize the complications by purchasing a single family residence.
- The best way to perform your due diligence is to consult with several different real estate brokers. Different brokers will have different listings, different information and different insights into the area and the market. Spend at least a day with each broker and spend at least a week investigating the market. The investor will gain tremendous knowledge about the area, the schools, prices and other useful facts.
- Retain several different attorneys to represent you in different deals. This way, you learn a great deal about real property law and practices.
- If the investor does not have his own money, the best source of funding is a partner. The investor should find a money partner who will put up the down payment. If the investor can find a single family residence listed for $200,000 and makes an offer of $100,000 that is accepted, the investor makes $50,000 and the partner makes $50,000 and the investor acquires a property without having to put any of the investor's own money down.
- Some investors are afraid of low income neighborhoods, but those neighborhoods are the places where investors will find the best deals. They are where the money is. The tenant's rent

is paid by the government so the landlord does not have to pursue the tenant for the rent. Tenants tend to respect landlords who treat them with dignity and respect and expect them to live up to their obligations. For example, the tenants will be required to keep the property in good condition. To establish the property's condition, the investor should take photographs of the property and have the tenants sign the photographs.

CHAPTER VI-2 SIGNIFICANCE OF $101

Self-discipline, confidence and positivity are the building blocks of a successful foreclosure investor. Your self-discipline, confidence and positivity will help you press on when others quit because they give you an edge that most ordinary people do not have. This edge will prepare you for challenges and allow you to ease into situations where you were previously too nervous and unsure of yourself. While all three traits are distinct, they work in concert to complement and strengthen each other.

The major difference between a very successful person and a person who is not so successful is the lack of self-discipline. Self-discipline enhances your confidence. In the usual course of your finding properties, you will come across some properties that you believe can be good investments but you begin to doubt your judgment for any number of reasons. For example, a property may have been on the market for a long time but has not sold and you may view that as a major drawback. In the alternative, you may find a property in which you become enamored at sight, but through your analysis, it does not make economic sense to purchase. Self-discipline will keep you on track to make informed decisions. It affords you the confidence to know that your evaluation of each deal is sound.

To become successful in the real estate business, you must truly believe in your success and act on your belief that you can succeed. The power to activate your mind through positivity sets you forward on the path to build your success. The more positive your thinking, the more confident you will become. Your high level of confidence will not only allow you to play the game, but play the game to win. Your confidence is essential when it comes to making decisions, speaking to other people, and asserting your success potential. Your desire to succeed will propel you to see your goals through to fruition.

Your self-discipline, confidence and positivity will be tested by external and internal forces. Your strategy, methods, approach or positive manner may be criticized by others that purport themselves as experts in real estate. In addition, a lack of confidence in your ability to analyze a property or communicate with others can make it difficult for you to move forward. Further, if you lack self-confidence, you may be governed by fear which may make you walk out on some great opportunities. In moments of trepidation, you should seek an inner strength that we each possess.

People find their inner strength in different ways. In certain difficult situations, I try to gain strength by connecting my soul to the source where it originated from -- Almighty God. I always tend to feel a strong connection between spiritual and financial strength. The strong belief in this connection is the one that made me write the book, "*26 Steps To Spiritual & Financial Riches- How Spirituality Led To a $7 Million Gain.*" This book will help lead you towards that self-discipline which is needed to gain long term success in life. If you would like a free copy of this book, you can either write us or send an e mail through our website at www.BillionaireBestSellers.com.

While the manner in which one finds that strength may differ, the concept remains unfettered – if doubt or fear is caused by external or internal forces, seek that strength to support your self-discipline, confidence and positivity. In order to fully benefit from the knowledge contained in this book, I want you to be very self-confident and fearless. The concept of putting down $101for many properties applies on different levels but it is derived from my source of strength.

There is no major secret in my putting down $101 for many properties. I think I am "0" without "1" on both sides of me. That "1" is the one who is prevalent in all and is in control of all of us.

The following incident made my faith strong in this belief.

A broker by the name of Dean Tassis took me to see a property at 100 Lattingtown Road, Glen Cove, New York,. It was a newly constructed building on 15 acres and had a bank lien of $8.2 million. At the time, I had $1.2 million in cash, asked the bank to accept it as an offer, and was laughed at. I requested him to take $101 from me and hold it for just for one day. I requested him that if, after holding the $101 for one day, he changed his mind and decided to sell me the property for $1.2 million, he should let me know. Otherwise, he should simply return the $101 to me. I knew that this $101 was not just ordinary money, as it had an ingredient of my prayer associated with it. Initially, he was hesitant to accept $101 but, on the broker's insistence, he agreed to do so. The next day bank officials agreed to accept my $1.2 million for the property.

I am happy that I was not lured by the temptation of selling the contract of sale for $4.5 millions and pocket as profit of $3.3 million to myself. I later transferred the contract of sale to the temple for $1.2 million as I had originally planned. Today after 11 years, the same property should appraise at around $15 million, making the community richer by about $14 million. I am happy to see the miracle of $101.

Some other properties that I acquired include 350 West 145th Street, Bronx, New York and 911 Simpson Street, Bronx, New York. Both of these properties are multi-family buildings. I purchased 4649 Memorial Drive, Decatur, Georgia which is a 172 room motel. All I had to do was take over a non-recourse mortgage and, as a result, I received income from it month after month for the last 3 years. It was taken care of with my investment of $101.

As I have come to the end of my book, I don't have the room to prolong my list. I wanted to make a point by giving you some specific examples of the properties that I purchased with $101 down. Such successes explain why I wrote so many books on the power of prayer and world religions, and why I want to share these experiences with you. Remember the significance of $101.

GLOSSARY

Acceleration clause - A provision in a promissory note or mortgage that allows the lender to declare the entire amount of the loan due and payable in the event of a default, including the borrower's insolvency or bankruptcy.

Actual notice - Actual notice is anything that the person in question actually knew about. See constructive notice.

ADA - Americans With Disabilities Act.

Adjustable rate mortgage – A mortgage securing a loan where the rate of interest and the amount of the monthly payment adjust upward and downward at set intervals according to corresponding changes in an index. All adjustable rate mortgages are referenced to indexes. Examples of indexes include the London Interbank Offered Rate ("LIBOR"), the one-year constant-maturity Treasury ("CMT") securities, the Cost of Funds Index ("COFI") or the lender's own personal cost of funds.

Adjustment period - Under an ARM, the length of time between adjustments. An adjustment period can be one month, one quarter, six months, one year, three years or some other interval.

AEA - American Escrow Association.

AIR - American Industrial Real Estate Association.

ALTA - American Land Title Association.

Amortization - The reduction and eventual elimination of the debt by installment payments at regular intervals over a specified period of time; each installment is applied first to the payment of all interest currently due with the balance of the installment applied to principal.

APR - Annual percentage rate.

ARM - Adjustable rate mortgage.

Assignment of rents – A security instrument executed by a borrower for the benefit of a lender to secure a debt or obligation by giving to the lender the right to collect the rents during a default by the borrower. A mortgage or deed of trust will contain an assignment of rents, but assignments of rents can also be separate documents.

Balloon mortgage loan - A mortgage loan that does not fully amortize by the maturity date and therefore the final payment is larger than the monthly installments. For example, the monthly payments could be calculated based on a 30-year amortization schedule, but the final payment could be due at the end of the tenth year when the entire remaining unpaid balance will be due and payable.

Balloon payment - The final lump sum payment due at the maturity date of a balloon mortgage loan.

Beneficiary - One of three parties to a deed of trust. The beneficiary is the party for whose benefit the deed of trust was made to secure a debt or other obligation owed to the beneficiary. In the typical foreclosure context, the beneficiary is the lender who made a loan, and repayment of the loan is secured by the real property.

Big box retailers – Retail stores that occupy the entirety of a large, stand-alone building which is usually situated either on its own lot or in a strip mall or shopping center. These are customarily referred to as "big box" retailers because their stores resemble big boxes with a single occupant.

BLS - Bureau of Labor Statistics.

Bond lease - A lease under which the tenant pays virtually all of the costs of both operating and owning the property. It is called a bond lease because the landlord receives the rent without any deductions, just as if it were the payment of principal and interest under a bond. It is like a bond because the risk assumed by the landlord is the financial stability of the tenant.

Borrower – A person or entity that receives a loan of funds that the person or entity is obligated to repay, usually with interest.

BPO - Broker's price opinion.

Cap rate – The capitalization rate, which is the investor's return on his or her investment.

Caps – See interest rate caps.

Carryover – Under an ARM, the difference between in the monthly installment between an uncapped rate and the capped rate.

CC&R's - Covenants, conditions and restrictions. CC&R's are typically recorded against real property to regulate how the real property can be developed and used.

Certificate of occupancy – A certificate issued by the municipal authority in which the real property is located prescribing the lawful uses of the property. A building can be used only for the uses specified in the certificate of occupancy for the building.

Closing – The consummation of a real property transaction, such as a sale or financing, where documents and funds are exchanged. The documents to be recorded, such as the deed and mortgage or deed of trust, are delivered to the county recorder for recording. In some states, a closing is handled by a title company or escrow company while in other states, a closing is handled by an attorney.

CMT - The one-year constant-maturity Treasury securities.

COFI - Cost of Funds Index.

C of O - Certificate of Occupancy.

Common elements - The physical parts of a multi-tenant building or other multi-occupant real property that are owned and used in common by all unit occupants.

Comparable properties – Properties in the neighborhood comparable to the property being valued that are similarly situated and that have recently sold.

Comparable sales method - A method of valuing a property by comparing it to comparable properties similarly situated in the neighborhood that have recently sold.

Comps – Comparable properties.

Condominium – A condominium is usually a multi-family residential structure in which each resident occupies a unit or an apartment although there are commercial and industrial condominiums as well. Under a condominium scheme, the unit consists of air space plus an undivided interest in the common elements, and the unit owner also owns shares in the condominium association. The physical parts of the building, the utilities that serve more than one unit and the land underlying the structure are owned and operated by the condominium association.

Conforming loan - A loan that conforms to the standards prescribed by Fannie Mae and Freddie Mac for the purchase of residential mortgages.

Constructive notice - Constructive notice is notice of (1) anything that an inspection of the property and inquiry regarding the things found would have revealed, such as the presence of tenants or the existence of oil wells on the land or roads running across the land, and (2) anything that has been recorded in the appropriate land records.

Cooperative - A cooperative is usually a multi-family residential structure in which each resident occupies a unit or an apartment although there are commercial and industrial cooperatives as well. Under a cooperative scheme, the owner owns shares in the cooperative corporation or limited liability company and leases the unit from the cooperative. The cooperative owns the building. The borrower's interest is that of a tenant in the building and a shareholder in the cooperative.

Credit bureaus - Equifax, Inc., Experian and TransUnion LLC. The credit bureaus prepare credit reports by compiling information on borrowers' credit history, including bank loans, credit cards, automobile loans, student loans and other credit covering the preceding seven years.

Credit history – The historic record of an individual's repayment of debt. Lenders review a borrower's credit history when deciding whether to advance credit to a borrower.

Credit report - A report of a borrower's credit history prepared by a credit bureau. Lenders review a borrower's credit history when deciding whether to advance credit to a borrower.

Credit score - A credit score is a number that the credit bureaus derive from various factors contained in the prospective borrower's credit report, such as credit history, the length of time a prospective borrower has had credit and the kinds of credit. Credit scores are produced by mathematical formulae and should describe a prospective borrower's ability to repay a loan. Credit scores are also called "FICO" scores. See FICO scores.

Debt service - Payments of principal and interest on a loan.

Debt service coverage ratio – The ratio produced by dividing the annual net operating income by the annual payments of principal and interest on the loan.

Deed in lieu of foreclosure - A deed to mortgaged property given by a borrower who is in default under the mortgage to the lender, typically in exchange for a release from all obligations under the mortgage. Also referred to as a "deed in lieu."

Deed of trust – 1. A security instrument by which the owner of an interest in real property (*i.e.,* the trustor) conveys title to the real property interest to a trustee for the benefit another person or entity (*i.e.,* the beneficiary) to secure payment of a debt or repayment of a loan or performance of an obligation. 2. An instrument by which a borrower grants title to real property to a trustee to secure the borrower's obligations to the lender. Although the deed of trust takes the form of a transfer of title, the borrower continues to own the real property. The trustee becomes involved only if there is a default. 3. See mortgage.

Deficiency - The unpaid balance of a loan remaining after completion of a foreclosure sale and application of the sale proceeds to reduction of the debt.

Deficiency judgment - A judgment obtained by a lender requiring the borrower to pay the deficiency.

Discounted indexed rate - An interest rate under an ARM that has been discounted.

Due diligence - The process of investigating factual matters affecting real property.

Due on sale clause – A clause contained in a mortgage or deed of trust that gives the lender the right to declare a default and accelerate the debt upon the happening of any of these events without the lender's prior written consent: a transfer by the borrower of title to all the real property collateral or any part of the collateral; a transfer of any interest in the real property; or a direct or indirect transfer of any interest in the borrower.

Duplex – A multi-tenant residence with two residential units, such as two townhouses connected together.

Encumbrance – A claim or liability that affects real property and impairs its value or utility. Encumbrances include leases, liens, mortgages, easements, rights-of-way, encroachments and CC&R's.

Equity - The market value of the property less all liens (except non-delinquent tax liens and assessments) encumbering the property, including the foreclosure costs that the property owner will have to pay to reinstate the loan and the amount due under the mortgage and any junior mortgages and delinquent tax liens.

Escrow - The process of depositing documents and funds in the possession of a neutral third party, called an escrow agent, to hold until performance or occurrence of conditions, as set forth in written escrow instructions between the parties to a transaction. Upon the performance or occurrence of conditions, the escrow agent distributes the documents and disburses the funds to the parties that are to receive them in accordance with the escrow instructions.

Escrow agent – The neutral third party who holds the funds and documents in an escrow.

Estopped – A legal concept which means that the person making a statement or representation cannot later be allowed to deny that statement or representation.

Estoppel certificate – A written document signed by a tenant in which the tenant confirms that the lease is currently in effect, that the lease has not been amended (or describing the amendments), that the landlord is not in default under the lease (or describing the defaults), that the tenant has not prepaid the rent (or describing the prepayments) and describing any options held by the tenant to purchase the property or lease additional space or extend or terminate the lease.

Fannie Mae - Federal National Mortgage Association

Fee simple – Absolute title to real property in which the owner has any and all ownership rights and interests. The most complete and absolute form of ownership of real property. Fee simple means that any and all ownership rights and interests in or associated with the real property are owned by the owner. Fee simple title is frequently referred to as "fee simple absolute."

FHA - Federal Housing Administration.

FHFA - Federal Housing Finance Agency.

FICO - Fair Isaac Corporation, Inc.

FICO scores - A credit-scoring formula developed by Fair Isaac Corporation, Inc. to measure the risk that a borrower may default in repayment of a loan.

Fixtures - Things that were moveable at one time but are now attached to and have become an integral part of real property, such as chandeliers and other light fixtures, furnaces, heating and air-conditioning ducts, fences, septic tanks, elevators and garage doors.

Flipping - The practice where an investor purchases a property and quickly sells it, sometimes immediately following the purchase.

Foreclosure – The process whereby a lender arranges for the sale of real property securing a loan that is in default and applies the proceeds of the sale to reduce the loan. Foreclosure can be a "judicial foreclosure" which is a sale conducted by a court as part of a lawsuit brought by the lender against the borrower or a "non-judicial foreclosure" which is a sale conducted by the trustee under a deed of trust or "strict foreclosure" where the lender sues the borrower and secures a court order declaring the borrower in default and setting the time within which the borrower may redeem the property or title to the property vests in the lender without a sale.

Foreclosure sale - A sale by auction at which the mortgaged property is sold to satisfy the secured debt or obligation. The auction can be conducted by an officer of the court under a mortgage or the trustee under a deed of trust. At the auction, the lender has the right to submit a credit bid in an amount up to the amount owed to the lender, including the accelerated principal amount, the accrued interest, late fees and charges, penalties, attorney's fees, the costs of a title search and appraisal, courts costs and the costs of sale such as marshal's fees, advertising and trustee's or auctioneer's fees.

Freddie Mac - Federal Home Loan Mortgage Corporation

Front foot – The footage of a first floor retail store along a street.

Fully indexed rate – An interest rate payable under an ARM in which the index has not been discounted.

General partners - Members of a general partnership or those members of a limited partnership who have management responsibility for the partnership and who, in either case, have unlimited personal liability for the obligations of the partnership.

General partnership - An association of two or more people or entities conducting business together for profit as co-owners and sharing in the profits and losses.

GFE - Good faith estimate.

Good faith estimate - An estimate that RESPA requires lenders and mortgage brokers to deliver to a borrower at the time the borrower applies for a mortgage loan of the charges the borrower will probably have to pay at the closing of the loan.

Grantor – A term sometimes used to refer to the trustor under a deed of trust.

Gross lease - Under a gross lease, the tenant pays rent, and the landlord pays the costs of operating the property.

GSE's - Government sponsored enterprises.

Hard money lenders - Private or non-institutional lenders.

Hard prepayment penalty - Under an ARM, a prepayment penalty that is payable if a pay-off of the principal balance of the loan occurs for any reason during the penalty period, such as a sale of the property or refinance of the ARM.

Home equity line of credit – A revolving loan secured by a mortgage on the borrower's home whereby the borrower draws down cash against the equity in the home, subject to a maximum amount. The mortgage is usually in second position.

HUD - Department of Housing and Urban Development

HUD-1 Settlement Statement – A closing statement prescribed by the Department of Housing and Urban Development ("HUD") setting forth all funds deposited in the closing and who deposited the funds and showing all funds disbursed out of the closing and to whom the funds were disbursed. The statement will list all costs paid out of the closing, such as real estate taxes, mortgages being paid off, judgment liens, title insurance premiums and other costs. The form of the HUD-1 Settlement Statement can be found on HUD's web site. The HUD-1 Settlement Statement is also known as the "closing statement."

HVAC - Heating, ventilating and air-conditioning.

Improvements - Things that are constructed on land, such as buildings, roadways, bridges, tunnels, telephone poles, wells and towers.

Income method - A method of valuing a property by capitalizing the income from the property.

Interest rate caps – Under an ARM, limits on the amount by which interest can increase. See caps.

IRS - Internal Revenue Service.

Jumbo loan - A residential loan that exceeds the maximum amount specified for a conforming loan. These loans are not purchased by Freddie Mac or Fannie Mae but are purchased and securitized in the secondary market.

Junior lien or mortgage – A lien or mortgage that is lower in priority than another lien or mortgage encumbering a property. A mortgage securing a home equity loan is junior to a mortgage securing the loan used to finance the purchase of a property.

Landlord – The party to a lease who is the owner of an interest in real property who conveys to a tenant the right of the tenant to use and occupy that interest. In the typical foreclosure context, the landlord owns the real property and leases part or all of the real property to the tenant.

Lease - An agreement between a landlord and a tenant whereby the landlord conveys to the tenant the right of occupancy and possession of real property for a specified period of time in return for the tenant's payment of rent and performance of the tenant's covenants under the lease.

Lender - A person or entity that loans funds to a borrower that the borrower is obligated to repay, usually with interest.

LIBOR - London Interbank Offered Rate.

Lien – An encumbrance on property that secures an obligation and gives the lien holder the right to sell the property if the obligation is not paid or performed.

Lien theory states – States that use judicial foreclosures are referred to as lien theory states because the mortgage is deemed to create a lien on the real property.

Lifetime cap – Under an ARM, an interest rate cap under which the amount by which the interest rate can increase over the life of the loan is limited. Federal law requires that virtually all ARMs have a lifetime cap.

Limited liability company – An entity that has some characteristics of a corporation, such as limited liability for its members, and some characteristics of a partnership, such as being able to elect to be treated as a pass-through entity for income tax purposes and having a less formal management structure.

Limited partners – Members of a limited partnership who are named as limited partners and who do not participate in the management of the limited partnership. The liability of a limited partner for the obligations of the limited partnership is limited to the amount of capital already contributed to the partnership plus the amount of capital the limited partner has agreed to contribute to the partnership in the future.

Limited partnership - A partnership formed in accordance with the law of a particular state having at least one general partner who has unlimited liability and at least one limited partner.

Lis pendens - *Lis pendens* means "suit pending." A *lis pendens* is a notice recorded in the public land record that a lawsuit has been filed against the real property.

LLC – A limited liability company.

Loan servicer – The organization that manages a loan on behalf of a lender or group of loan purchasers after a lender has made the loan. The servicer records payments, sends out loan statements, endeavors to collect delinquent loans and provides other services as required by the lender.

Loan to value ratio - The ratio of the amount of the first mortgage loan to the value of the property.

Loss mitigation department – The lender's department responsible for dealing with delinquent loans.

Loss mitigators – The lender's employees charged with dealing with delinquent loans.

Margin - The profit to a lender on an ARM constituting the difference between the interest rate under the ARM and the index on the ARM. The margin is fixed while the index increases and decreases.

Maturity date – The date that the final payment under a promissory note becomes due and payable.

MBA - Mortgage Bankers Association of America.

MBS - Mortgage-backed securities.

Mixed-use properties – Properties that are used for both residential and commercial purposes.

MLS - Multiple Listing Service.

Mortgage – 1. A security instrument by which the owner of an interest in real property (*i.e.,* the mortgagor) grants a lien on that interest in favor of another person or entity (*i.e.,* the mortgagee) to secure payment of a debt or repayment of a loan or performance of an obligation. 2. An instrument given by a borrower to a lender to secure the borrower's obligations to the lender. Originally, the mortgage took the form of a conveyance of title to the mortgaged property, but eventually it was transformed into an instrument that created a lien on the real property. 3. Some investors use the term mortgage to include the loan secured by the mortgage. 4. See deed of trust.

Mortgage Debt Relief Act of 2007 – A federal law that provides tax relief for forgiveness of indebtedness up to $2,000,000 or $1,000,000 for married couples filing separate tax returns. It is in effect for the calendar years 2007 through 2012.

Mortgagee – One of two parties to a mortgage. The mortgagee is the party to whom the mortgage is delivered to secure a debt or loan or other obligation owed to the mortgagee. In the typical foreclosure context, the mortgagee is the lender who made a loan, and repayment of the loan is secured by the real property.

Mortgagor – One of two parties to a mortgage. The mortgagor is the party who executed the mortgage and delivered the mortgage to the other party to the mortgage to secure a debt or other obligation owed to the other party. In the typical foreclosure context, the mortgagor is the borrower who borrowed funds secured by the real property.

Multi-purpose properties – See mixed-use properties.

Negative amortization – A loan under which the monthly installments are not large enough to pay all of the interest due that month and the unpaid interest is added to the principal and bears interest until paid.

NOI - Net operating income which is calculated by adding up all of the operating expenses, such as the costs of maintenance and repairs, real property taxes, insurance premiums, building utilities, management fees and a vacancy factor, and subtracts them from the total rents. The operating expenses do not include debt service.

Nonrecourse loan - A loan for which the borrower has no personal liability and, if the borrower defaults, is repaid by a sale of the collateral.

Note – Another term for a promissory note.

Notice of default – A notice sent by a lender to a borrower whose loan is in default declaring a default. The notice of default is the first step in the lender's enforcement of its mortgage or deed of trust. The timing of the notice of default, the contents of the notice of default and the means by which it is delivered (say by registered or certified mail) are controlled by state law and therefore will differ from state to state. The notice of default must precisely describe the nature of the default.

Partner – A general partner or a limited partner.

Periodic adjustment cap – Under an ARM, an interest rate cap under which the amount by which the interest rate can be adjusted up or down each time the rate is adjusted is capped.

Planned unit development – A development in which each individual owner owns that owner's building or unit, but all of the owners in the development jointly own the common areas. A planned unit development can be structured differently from a condominium, where each individual owner owns the unit's airspace, but all of the owners in the condominium jointly own the buildings as well as the common areas.

PMI - Private mortgage insurance.

Point – An amount equal to one percent of the amount of the loan.

Power of sale - A provision contained in a deed of trust granting to the trustee the power to sell the real property in the event of a default.

Preliminary title report – A written report made by a title insurance company and given to a prospective purchaser or lender showing the legal description of real property, the owner of the property and the liens and encumbrances affecting title to the real property. A preliminary title report serves basically the same purpose as a title commitment.

Prepayment penalty – A penalty or fee that the borrower must pay to the lender if a loan is paid before the maturity date.

Private mortgage insurance – According to the Federal Reserve Bank of San Francisco, private mortgage insurance or PMI is insurance that lenders require from home purchasers on loans that exceed 80 percent of the home's value. PMI insures the lender against loss in the event of a default.

Pro forma financial statements - One or more financial statements that contain assumptions or are based on conditions.

Promissory note – A written instrument given by one party (the maker) to another party (the payee) containing the promise by the maker of the promissory note to pay a sum of money to the payee. The promissory note will detail the terms of repayment such as the amount of the monthly payments, the interest rate, the date any unpaid balance is due, late charges and prepayment penalties. The promissory note may reflect an obligation arising from the repayment of a loan or from some other kind of debt. In the typical foreclosure context, the maker is the borrower who borrowed funds, and the payee is the lender.

Qualified principal residence indebtedness – Under the Mortgage Debt Relief Act of 2007, debt secured by the borrower's principal residence and used to purchase, construct or substantially improve the borrower's principal residence.

Real estate – See real property. As used in this book, the terms "real property" and "real estate" are used interchangeably.

Real estate owned - Real property that has been foreclosed upon and is now owned by banks and other institutional lenders. See REO.

Real property - (1) land; (2) the things that are constructed on land – referred to as "improvements", such as buildings, roadways, bridges, tunnels, telephone poles, wells and towers; (3) things that were moveable at one time but are now attached to and have become an integral part of improvements – referred to as "fixtures", such as chandeliers and other light fixtures, furnaces, heating and air-conditioning ducts, fences, septic tanks, elevators and garage doors; (4) minerals while they remain in the ground, such as gravel, oil or iron ore; and (5) trees and plants while affixed to the land. As used in this book, the terms "real property" and "real estate" are used interchangeably.

Recorder – The public official responsible for placing copies of relevant documents on the public record and maintaining those records. Sometimes referred to as a prothonotary or registrar of deeds or county clerk.

Recorder's office – The public office where copies of relevant documents are placed on the public record.

Recording – Copying a document into the public records, such as by photocopying or scanning an electronic copy, including certain details of the document such as the names of the grantor and grantee under a deed or the names of the mortgagee and mortgagor under a mortgage, and indexing the document in a way that enables persons searching the records to locate the document.

Redeem – The exercise by a borrower of his or her right of redemption.

Redemption – See right of redemption.

Redemption amount – The full amount owed by a borrower to a lender who has completed a foreclosure sale of the borrower's real property, including the principal of the loan and interest thereon, late charges and penalties and costs of the foreclosure sale.

Reinstatement – The right of a borrower and all persons with interests in the real property, such as holders of junior liens, within a specified period of time after the lender has sent a notice of default to the borrower and to others with interests in the real property to cure the default by paying all amounts due.

Rentable square footage - A method of measuring the square footage in leased premises. The rentable square footage is the useable square footage plus, on a multi-tenant floor, the tenant's share of corridors, elevator lobbies, restrooms and other common spaces. Landlords will charge rent based on the rentable square footage which is measured differently in every building.

Rent roll - A detailed list of tenants occupying space at a property, giving each tenant's name, the commencement date and expiration date of the lease, outlining the square footage and area leased, the amount of the rent, how long each tenant has occupied the premises, and other relevant terms of the lease.

REO – Real estate owned.

REO department – A lender's department responsible for disposing of REO. This department may also be referred to as the "special assets department."

Replacement cost method - A method of valuing a property by determining the cost of replacing the property.

RESPA - Real Estate Settlement Procedures Act

Right of redemption - The right of a borrower who has lost real property under a foreclosure sale to pay the redemption amount to the lender and recover title to the real property.

Sandwich lease option – A pairing of a lease having an option to purchase entered into by the foreclosure investor as tenant with a sublease having an option to purchase entered into by the foreclosure investor as landlord to finance an acquisition.

Secondary market – The market in which promissory notes secured by mortgages are bought and sold, usually as part of a pool of instruments.

Securitization - The process of gathering mortgage loans together into a pool and selling investment instruments such as bonds to investors. The interest and principal on the investment instruments are paid by the income from the underlying mortgages.

Short sale - A sale by the borrower to the foreclosure investor or any other person (other than the lender) of mortgaged real property at a price below the amount due on the loan.

Single family home – A residence that is detached from any other residence or other structure (other than a garage) and situated on a plot of land owned by the owner of the residence.

Soft prepayment penalty – Under an ARM, a prepayment penalty that is payable only upon a refinance of the ARM but not upon a sale of the property.

Stages of foreclosure - The four stages that a foreclosure can go through. The four stages are:

  (1) the pre-foreclosure stage which is the period of time during which the borrower begins to miss payments but the lender has not yet formally declared an event of default.

  (2) the default and auction stage which is the period of time that begins with the lender formally declaring the borrower to be in default and ending with the foreclosure sale.

  (3) the redemption stage which is the period of time that begins after the completion of the foreclosure sale and ends with the expiration of the borrower's redemption period. This stage arises only in the states that grant the borrower a right of redemption and, in those states, arises only if the lender utilized a foreclosure procedure that includes a right of redemption.

(4) the <u>REO stage</u> which is the period time following the expiration of the borrower's redemption period (or following the completion of the foreclosure sale in those situations where there is no right of redemption) during which the lender owns the real property. This stage arises only if the lender was the high bidder at the foreclosure auction or otherwise acquired title to the real property.

Subordinate financing – A loan secured by a mortgage or other lien, the priority of which is lower than the first mortgage.

Subordination, attornment and non-disturbance agreement – An agreement between a mortgagee and a tenant whereby the tenant agrees that the tenant's lease shall be subordinated to the lien of the mortgage and, in the event of a default under the mortgage, the tenant will recognize the mortgagee as the landlord and pay rents to the mortgagee, and the mortgagee agrees that, in the event of a foreclosure of the mortgage, the mortgagee will recognize the lease and will not disturb the quiet enjoyment of the tenant (so long as the tenant is not in default under the lease).

Subprime borrower – A borrower with a troubled credit history.

Subprime mortgage - A mortgage loan given to a subprime borrower.

Tenant - The party to a lease to whom the landlord conveys the right to use and occupy the real property. In the typical foreclosure context, the tenant occupies part or all of the real property and pays rent to the landlord.

Tenant improvements – Improvements made to leased premises, typically commercial or industrial property, to make the premises ready for a new tenant's occupancy or to accommodate a tenant's specific needs.

Title commitment – A written commitment made by a title insurance company and given to a prospective purchaser or lender showing the legal description of real property, the owner of the property and the liens and encumbrances affecting title to the real property and agreeing to issue a title insurance policy subject to the liens and encumbrances identified in the commitment upon the satisfaction of conditions stated in the commitment. A title commitment serves basically the same purpose as a preliminary title report.

Title insurance policy – A policy of insurance pursuant to which the title insurance company will indemnify the insured (usually the owner or the lender) for any losses suffered if the real property is not owned by the person named in a preliminary title report or commitment or if there are encumbrances on the title other than those that are described by the title insurance company in a preliminary title report or if the lender's mortgage does not have the priority specified.

Title theory states – States that use non-judicial foreclosures are referred to as title theory states because the security instrument purports to grant title to the lender or to a third party trustee. However, even though the form transfers title to the lender, the legal title remains in the borrower.

Townhouse - One of a series of residences connected together with party walls between each residence. There can be any number of residences connected together. If there are two units, the structure is called a duplex. If there are three units, the structure is called a triplex. The owner of each unit owns the land underlying the unit.

Triple net lease – Under a triple net lease, the tenant pays taxes, insurance and repair and maintenance and, in some cases, utilities.

Triplex – A multi-tenant residence with three residential units, such as three townhouses connected together.

Trustee - One of three parties to a deed of trust. The trustee is the party to whom the real property is conveyed for the benefit of the beneficiary. In the typical foreclosure context, the trustee is a title company or attorney or other unrelated third party acting for the benefit of the lender who made a loan, and repayment of the loan is secured by the real property.

Trustor - One of three parties to a deed of trust. The trustor is the party who executed the deed of trust and delivered the deed of trust to the trustee to secure a debt or other obligation owed to the beneficiary. In the typical foreclosure context, the trustor is the borrower who borrowed funds secured by the real property. See grantor.

Underwater – The condition where the amount of the debt secured by the property exceeds the market value of the property.

Upside down - Another term for "underwater."

Useable square footage – A method of measuring the square footage in leased premises. The useable square footage is the amount of space that the tenant can actually use for its business in its premises.

VA - Department of Veteran Affairs.

Wholesale flipping - The practice where the investor negotiates and documents the acquisition of real property but, instead of purchasing the property, assigns the investor's right to purchase the property to a different investor, *i.e.,* the assignee.